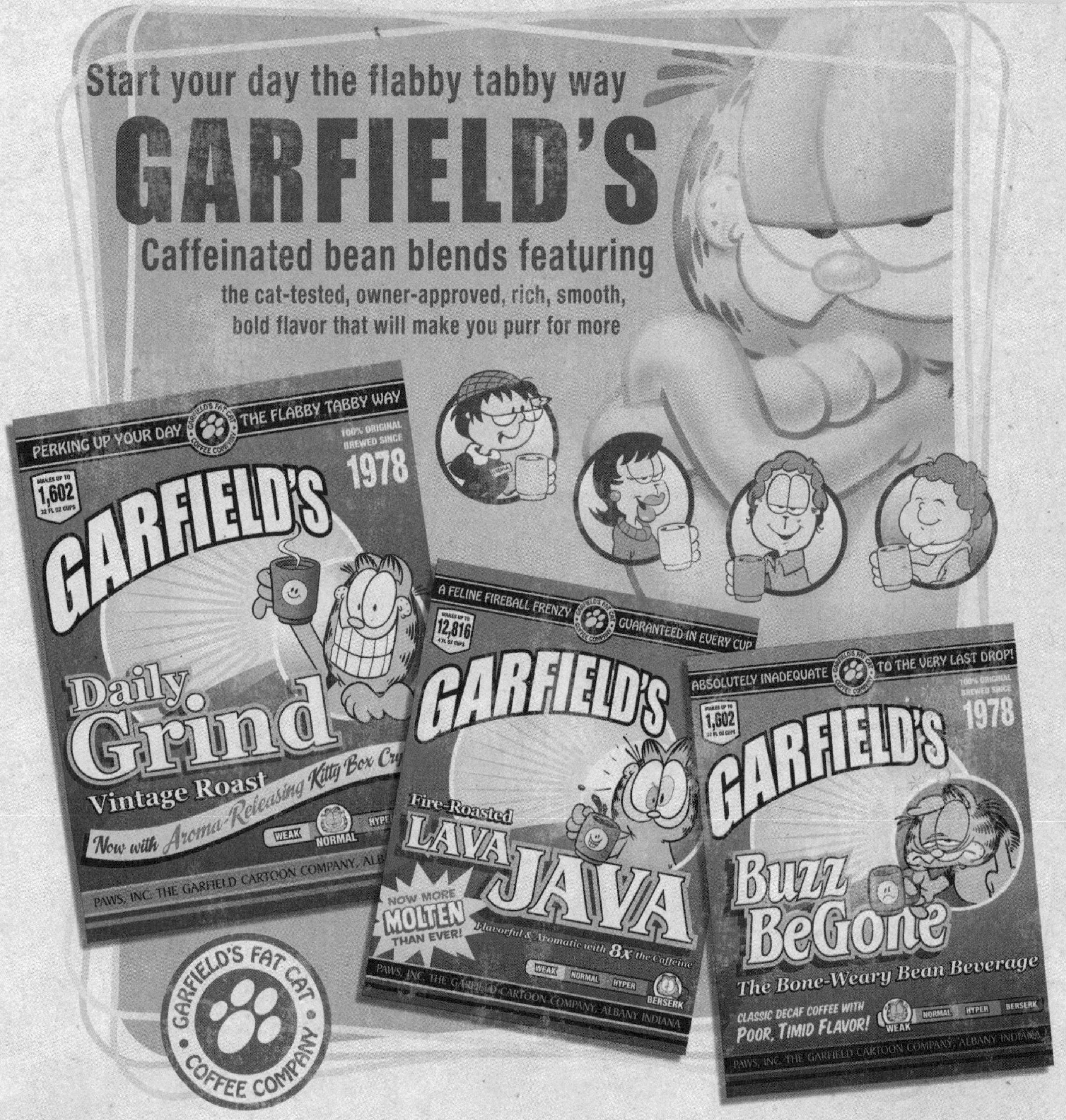
Start your day the flabby tabby way
GARFIELD'S
Caffeinated bean blends featuring
the cat-tested, owner-approved, rich, smooth,
bold flavor that will make you purr for more
PERKING UP YOUR DAY
GARFIELD'S FAT CAT COFFEE COMPANY
THE FLABBY TABBY WAY
100% ORIGINAL BREWED SINCE 1978
MAKES UP TO 1,602 32 FL OZ CUPS
GARFIELD'S
Daily Grind
Vintage Roast
Now with Aroma-Releasing Kitty Box Cry
WEAK
NORMAL
HYPER
PAWS, INC. THE GARFIELD CARTOON COMPANY, ALB
A FELINE FIREBALL FRENZY
GUARANTEED IN EVERY CUP
MAKES UP TO 12,816 4 FL OZ CUPS
GARFIELD'S
Fire-Roasted
LAVA JAVA
NOW MORE MOLTEN THAN EVER!
Flavorful & Aromatic with 8x the Caffeine
WEAK
NORMAL
HYPER
BERSERK
PAWS, INC. THE GARFIELD CARTOON COMPANY, ALBANY INDIANA
ABSOLUTELY INADEQUATE
TO THE VERY LAST DROP!
100% ORIGINAL BREWED SINCE 1978
MAKES UP TO 1,602 32 FL OZ CUPS
GARFIELD'S
Buzz BeGone
The Bone-Weary Bean Beverage
CLASSIC DECAF COFFEE WITH POOR, TIMID FLAVOR!
WEAK
NORMAL
HYPER
BERSERK
PAWS, INC. THE GARFIELD CARTOON COMPANY, ALBANY INDIANA
GARFIELD'S FAT CAT COFFEE COMPANY

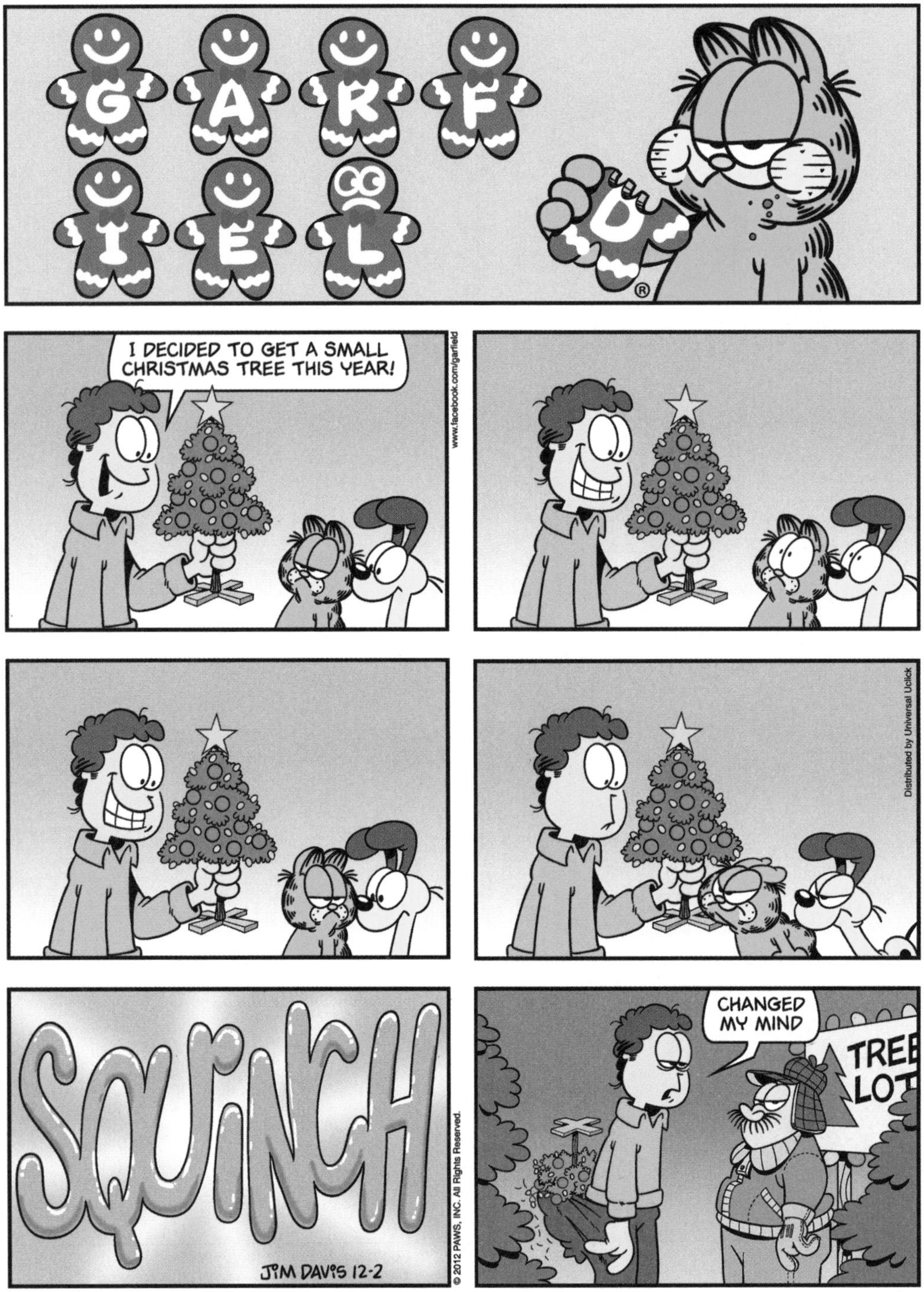
GARF
IEL
D
www.facebook.com/garfield
I DECIDED TO GET A SMALL CHRISTMAS TREE THIS YEAR!
Distributed by Universal Uclick
SQUINCH
JIM DAVIS 12-2
© 2012 PAWS, INC. All Rights Reserved.
CHANGED MY MIND
TREE LOT

Garfield
CLEANS HIS PLATE

BY JIM DAVIS

Ballantine Books • New York

A Ballantine Books Trade Paperback Original

Copyright © 2015 by PAWS, Inc. All Rights Reserved.
"GARFIELD" and the GARFIELD characters are trademarks of PAWS, Inc.

Published in the United States by Ballantine Books, an imprint of Random House,
a division of Penguin Random House LLC, New York.

BALLANTINE and the HOUSE colophon are registered trademarks of Penguin Random House LLC.

ISBN 978-0-345-52608-3
eBook ISBN 978-0-8041-7768-9

Printed in the United States of America on acid-free paper

www.ballantinebooks.com

9 8 7 6 5 4 3 2 1

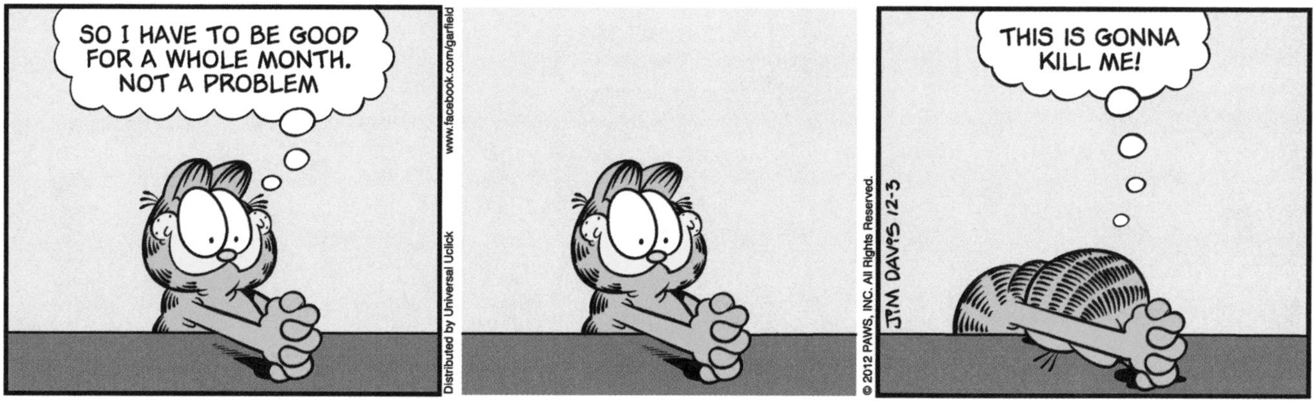
SO I HAVE TO BE GOOD FOR A WHOLE MONTH. NOT A PROBLEM
Distributed by Universal Uclick
www.facebook.com/garfield
© 2012 PAWS, INC. All Rights Reserved.
JIM DAVIS 12-3
THIS IS GONNA KILL ME!

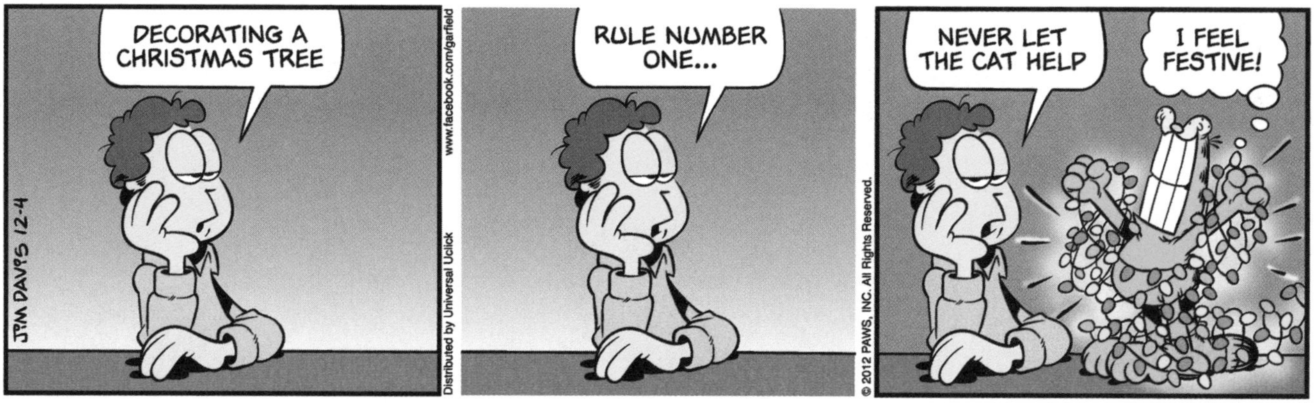
JIM DAVIS 12-4
DECORATING A CHRISTMAS TREE
Distributed by Universal Uclick
www.facebook.com/garfield
RULE NUMBER ONE...
© 2012 PAWS, INC. All Rights Reserved.
NEVER LET THE CAT HELP
I FEEL FESTIVE!

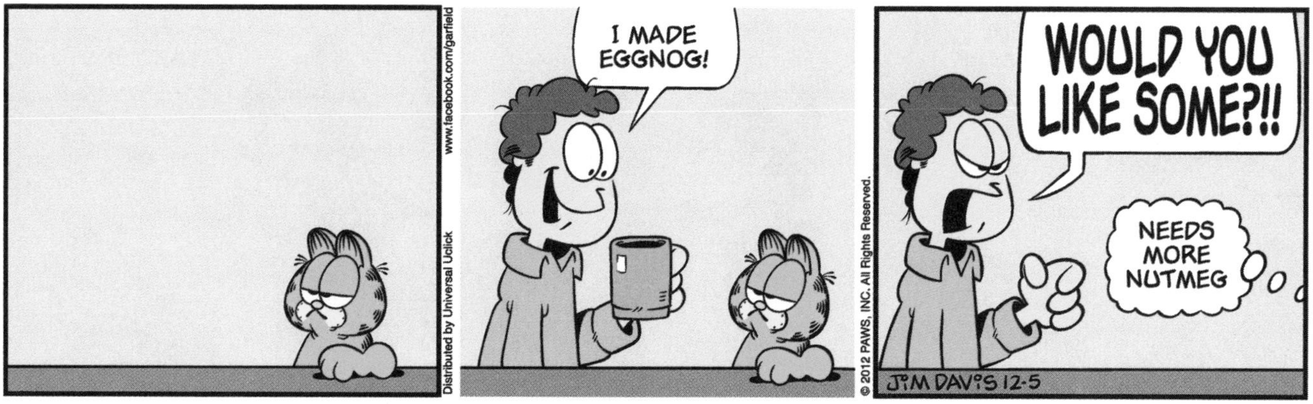
Distributed by Universal Uclick
www.facebook.com/garfield
I MADE EGGNOG!
© 2012 PAWS, INC. All Rights Reserved.
WOULD YOU LIKE SOME?!!
NEEDS MORE NUTMEG
JIM DAVIS 12-5

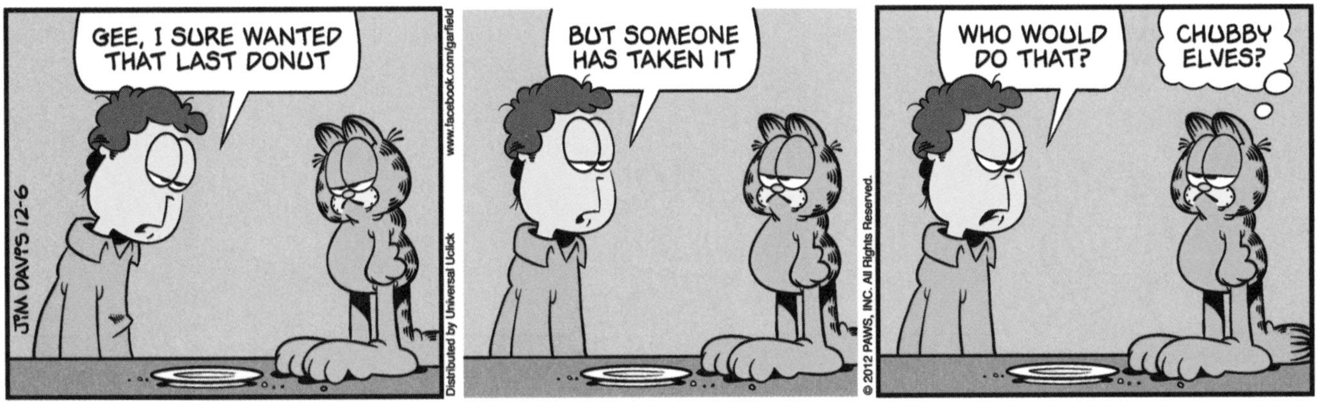
GEE, I SURE WANTED THAT LAST DONUT
JIM DAVIS 12-6
BUT SOMEONE HAS TAKEN IT
WHO WOULD DO THAT?
CHUBBY ELVES?
www.facebook.com/garfield
Distributed by Universal Uclick
© 2012 PAWS, INC. All Rights Reserved.

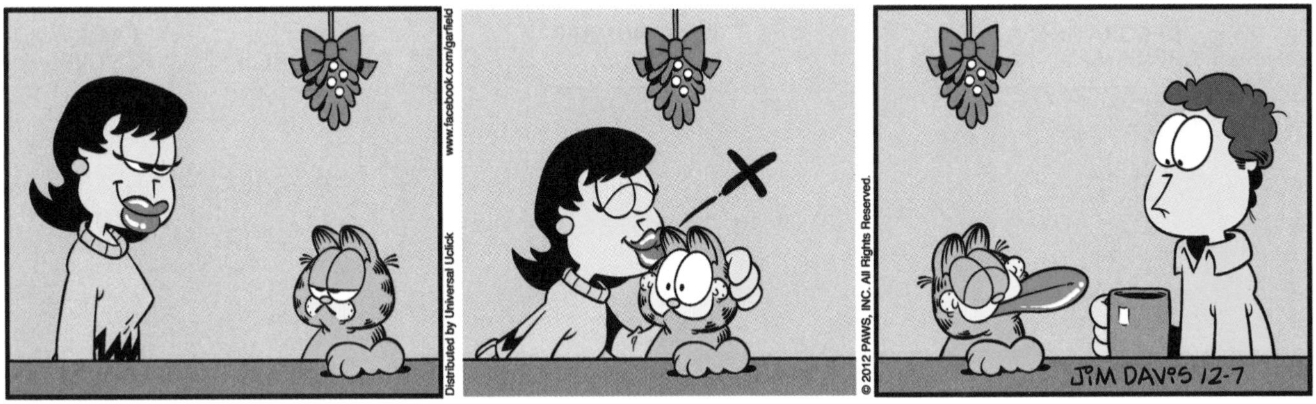
JIM DAVIS 12-7
www.facebook.com/garfield
Distributed by Universal Uclick
© 2012 PAWS, INC. All Rights Reserved.

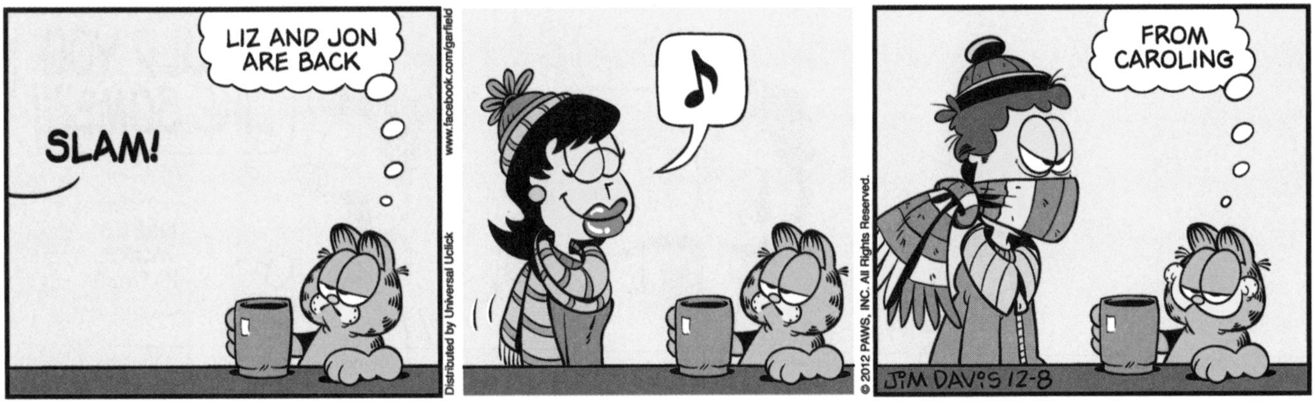
LIZ AND JON ARE BACK
SLAM!
♪
FROM CAROLING
JIM DAVIS 12-8
www.facebook.com/garfield
Distributed by Universal Uclick
© 2012 PAWS, INC. All Rights Reserved.

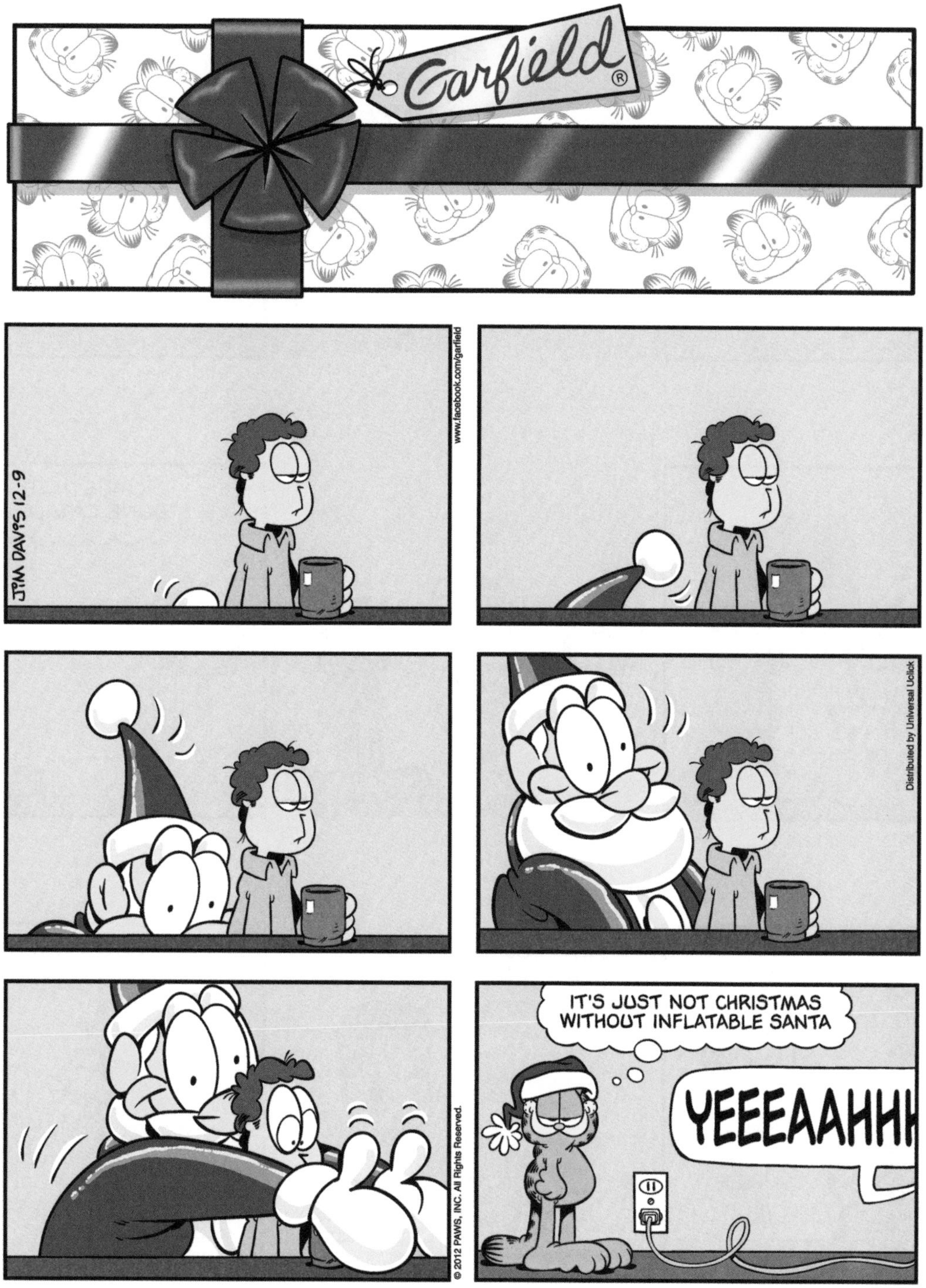
Garfield®
JIM DAVIS 12-9
www.facebook.com/garfield
Distributed by Universal Uclick
© 2012 PAWS, INC. All Rights Reserved.
IT'S JUST NOT CHRISTMAS WITHOUT INFLATABLE SANTA
YEEEAAHHH

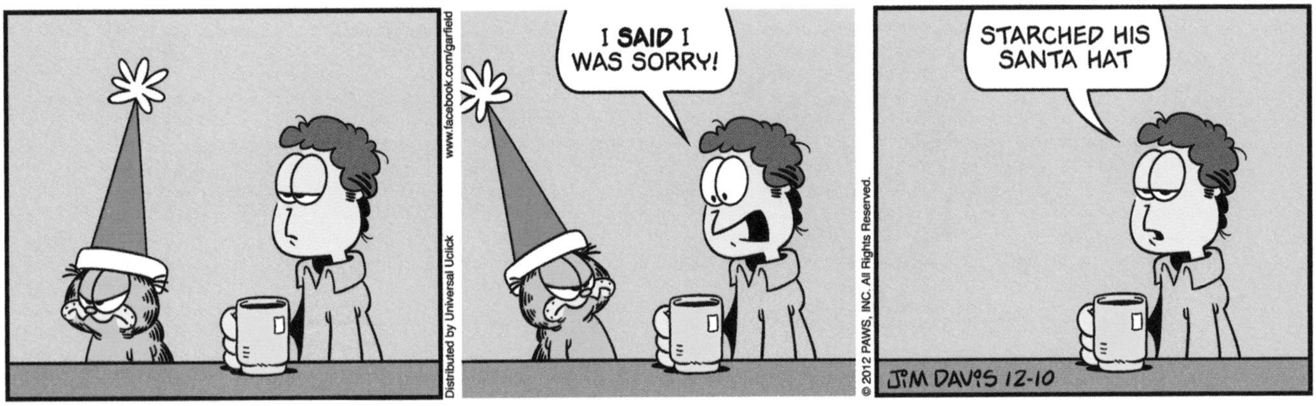
I **SAID** I WAS SORRY!
STARCHED HIS SANTA HAT
Distributed by Universal Uclick www.facebook.com/garfield
© 2012 PAWS, INC. All Rights Reserved.
JIM DAVIS 12-10

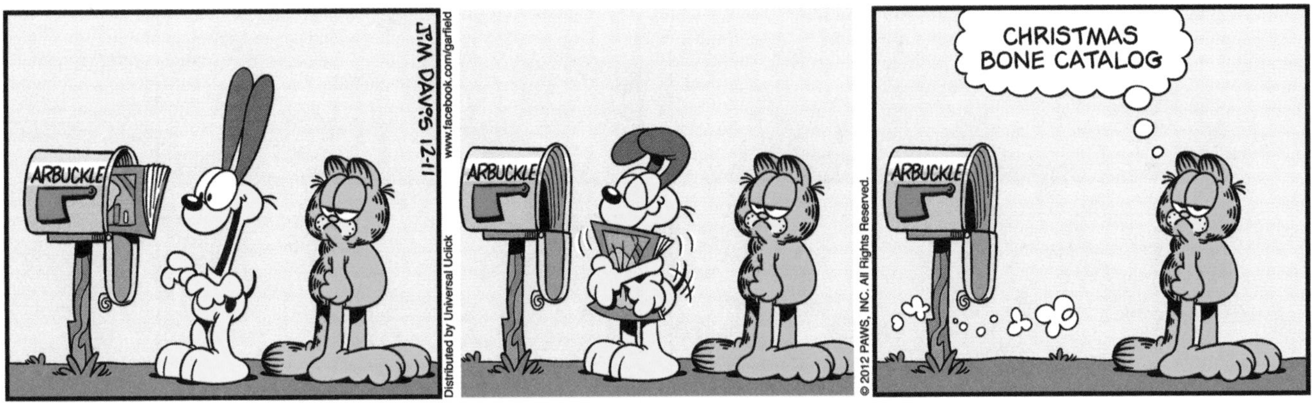
ARBUCKLE
JIM DAVIS 12-11
Distributed by Universal Uclick www.facebook.com/garfield
ARBUCKLE
© 2012 PAWS, INC. All Rights Reserved.
ARBUCKLE
CHRISTMAS BONE CATALOG

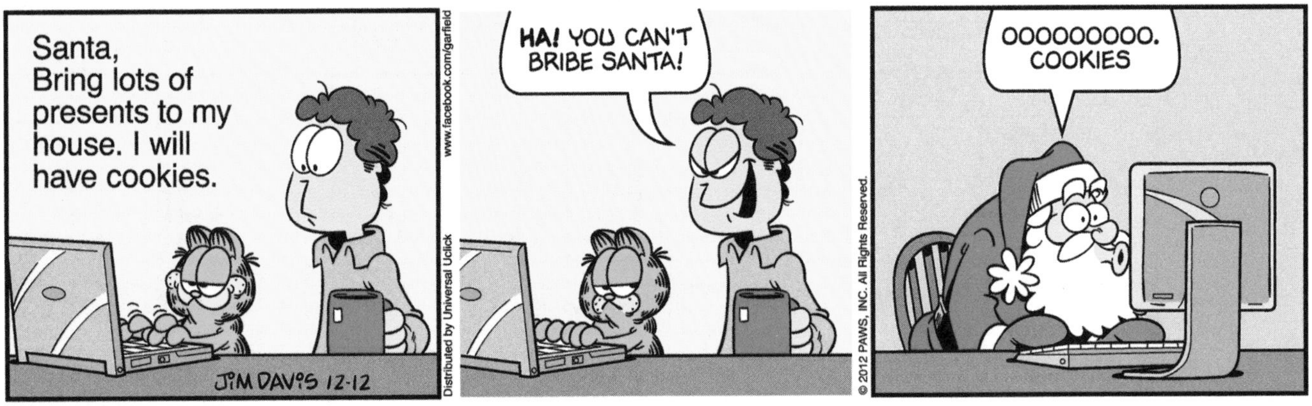
Santa,
Bring lots of presents to my house. I will have cookies.
JIM DAVIS 12-12
Distributed by Universal Uclick www.facebook.com/garfield
HA! YOU CAN'T BRIBE SANTA!
© 2012 PAWS, INC. All Rights Reserved.
OOOOOOOOO. COOKIES

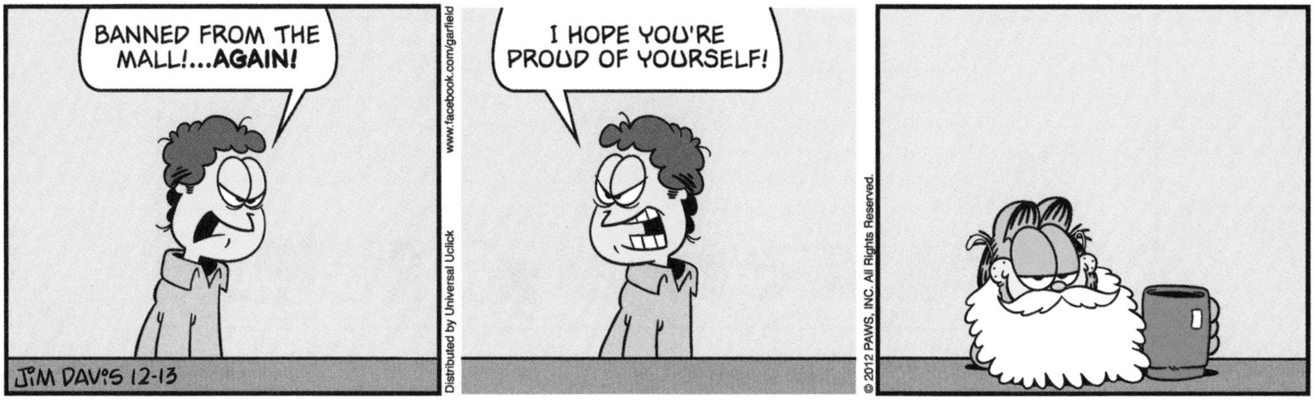
BANNED FROM THE MALL!...**AGAIN!**
JIM DAVIS 12-13
www.facebook.com/garfield
Distributed by Universal Uclick
I HOPE YOU'RE PROUD OF YOURSELF!
© 2012 PAWS, INC. All Rights Reserved.

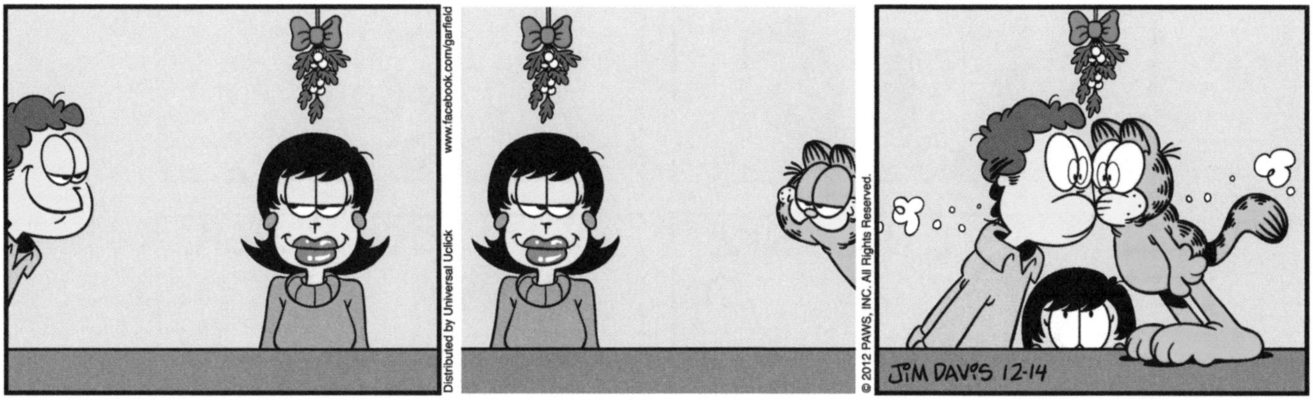
www.facebook.com/garfield
Distributed by Universal Uclick
© 2012 PAWS, INC. All Rights Reserved.
JIM DAVIS 12-14

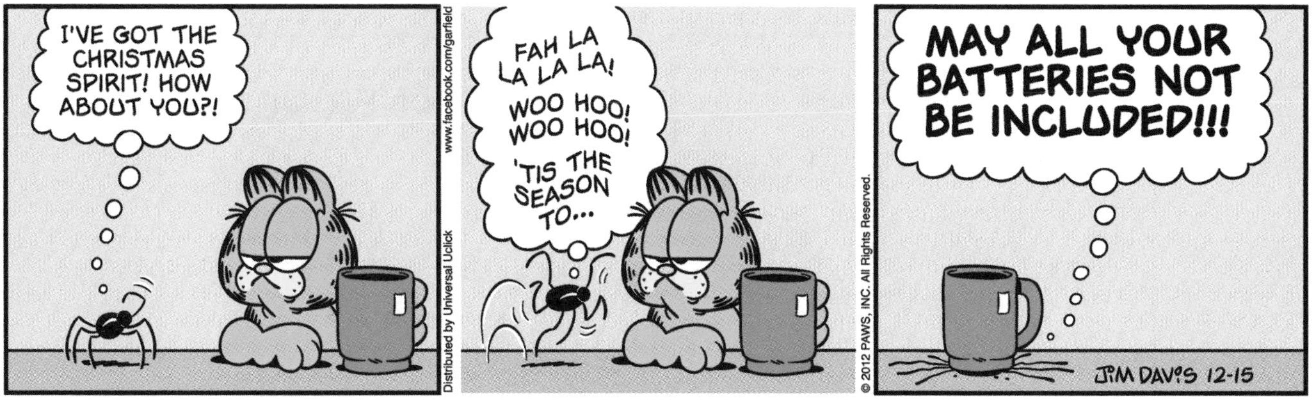
I'VE GOT THE CHRISTMAS SPIRIT! HOW ABOUT YOU?!
www.facebook.com/garfield
Distributed by Universal Uclick
FAH LA LA LA LA!
WOO HOO! WOO HOO!
'TIS THE SEASON TO...
© 2012 PAWS, INC. All Rights Reserved.
MAY ALL YOUR BATTERIES NOT BE INCLUDED!!!
JIM DAVIS 12-15

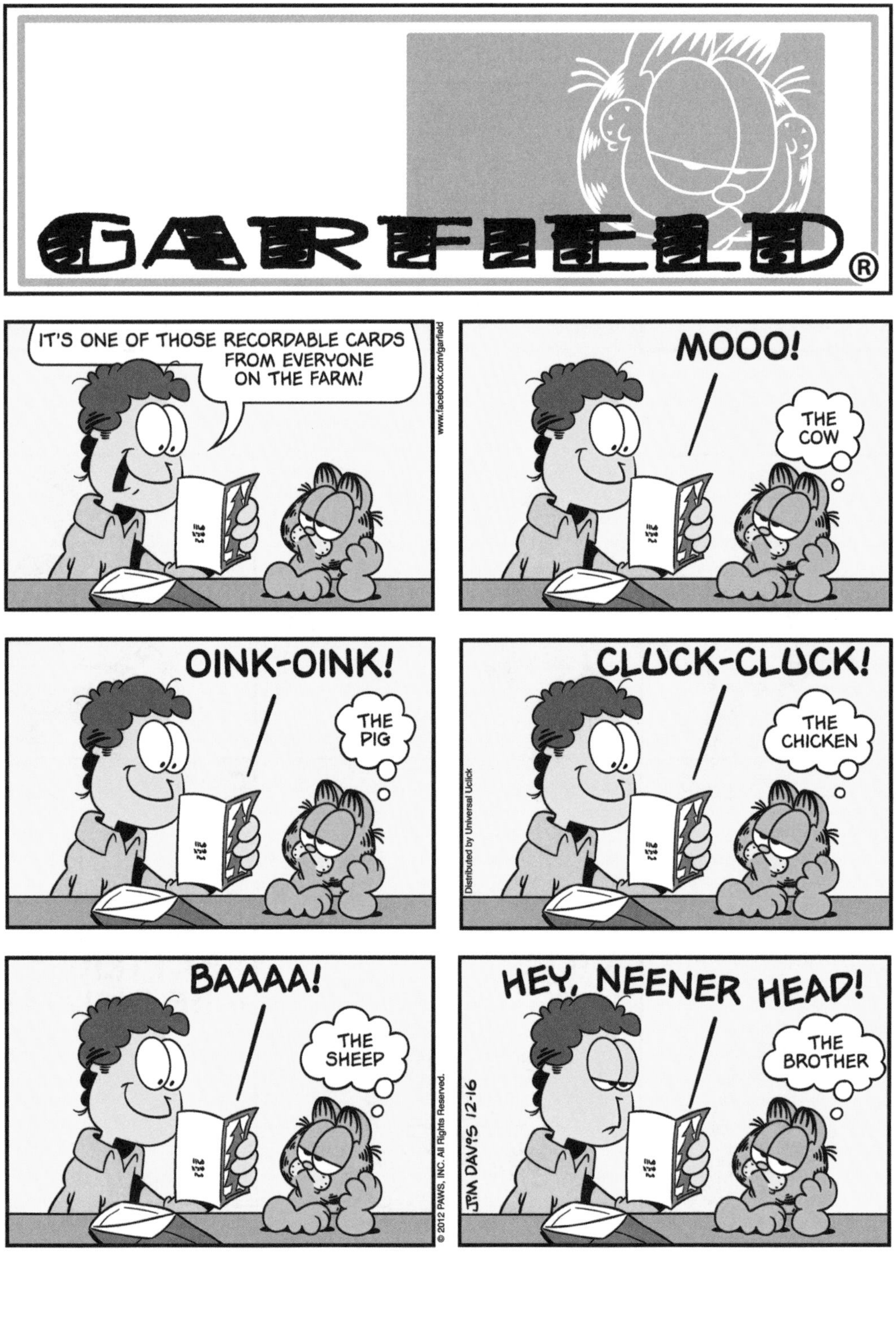
GARFIELD®
IT'S ONE OF THOSE RECORDABLE CARDS FROM EVERYONE ON THE FARM!
www.facebook.com/garfield
MOOO!
THE COW
OINK-OINK!
THE PIG
Distributed by Universal Uclick
CLUCK-CLUCK!
THE CHICKEN
BAAAA!
THE SHEEP
© 2012 PAWS, INC. All Rights Reserved.
JIM DAVIS 12-16
HEY, NEENER HEAD!
THE BROTHER

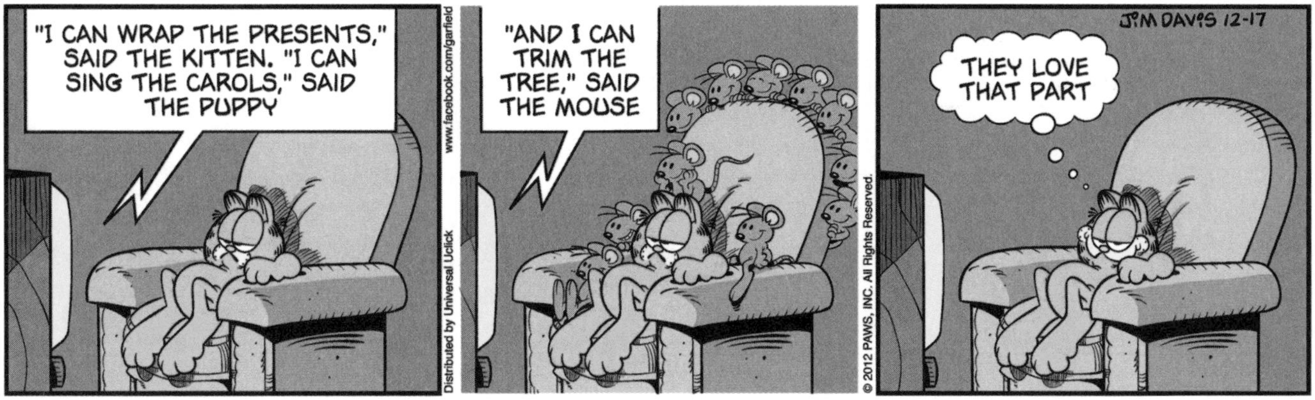
"I CAN WRAP THE PRESENTS," SAID THE KITTEN. "I CAN SING THE CAROLS," SAID THE PUPPY
Distributed by Universal Uclick www.facebook.com/garfield
"AND I CAN TRIM THE TREE," SAID THE MOUSE
© 2012 PAWS, INC. All Rights Reserved.
JIM DAVIS 12-17
THEY LOVE THAT PART

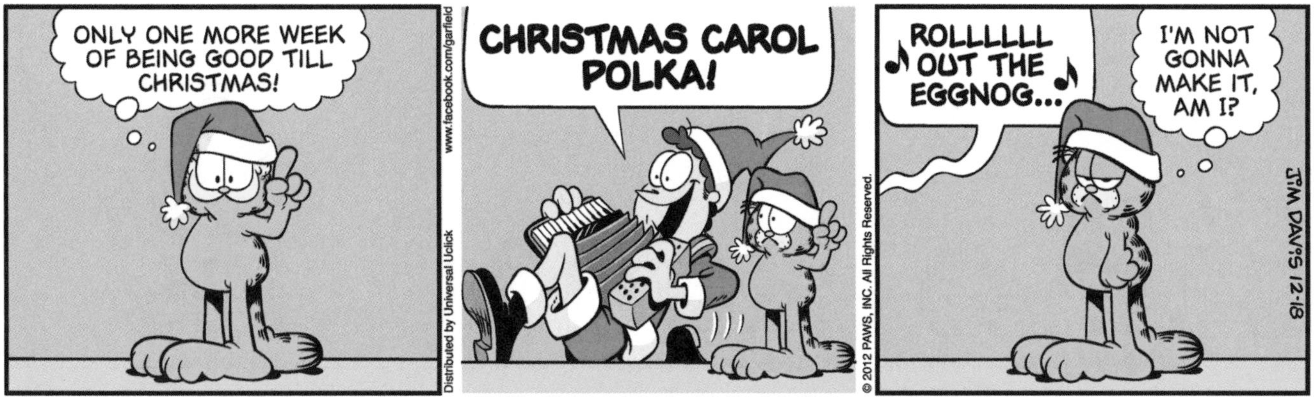
ONLY ONE MORE WEEK OF BEING GOOD TILL CHRISTMAS!
Distributed by Universal Uclick www.facebook.com/garfield
CHRISTMAS CAROL POLKA!
© 2012 PAWS, INC. All Rights Reserved.
ROLLLLLL OUT THE EGGNOG...
I'M NOT GONNA MAKE IT, AM I?
JIM DAVIS 12-18

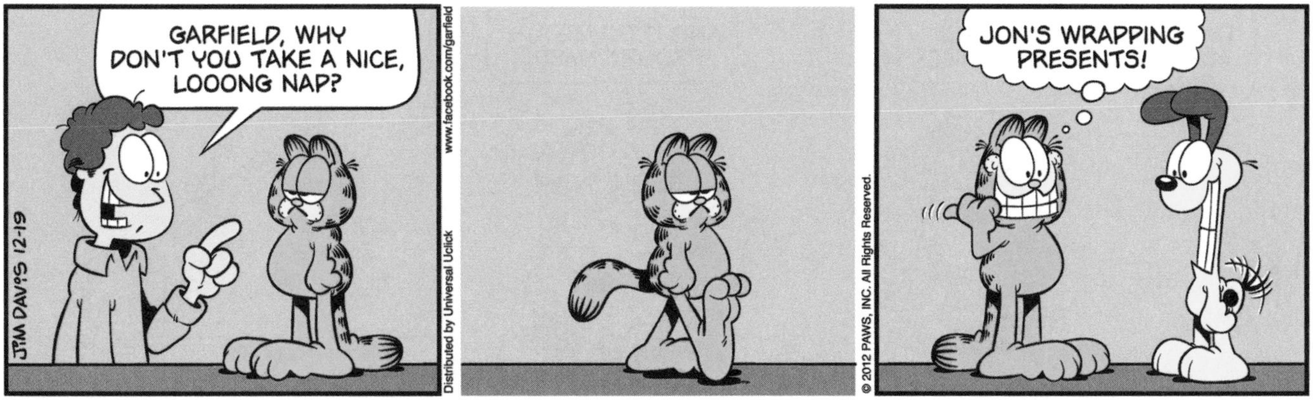
JIM DAVIS 12-19
GARFIELD, WHY DON'T YOU TAKE A NICE, LOOONG NAP?
Distributed by Universal Uclick www.facebook.com/garfield
© 2012 PAWS, INC. All Rights Reserved.
JON'S WRAPPING PRESENTS!

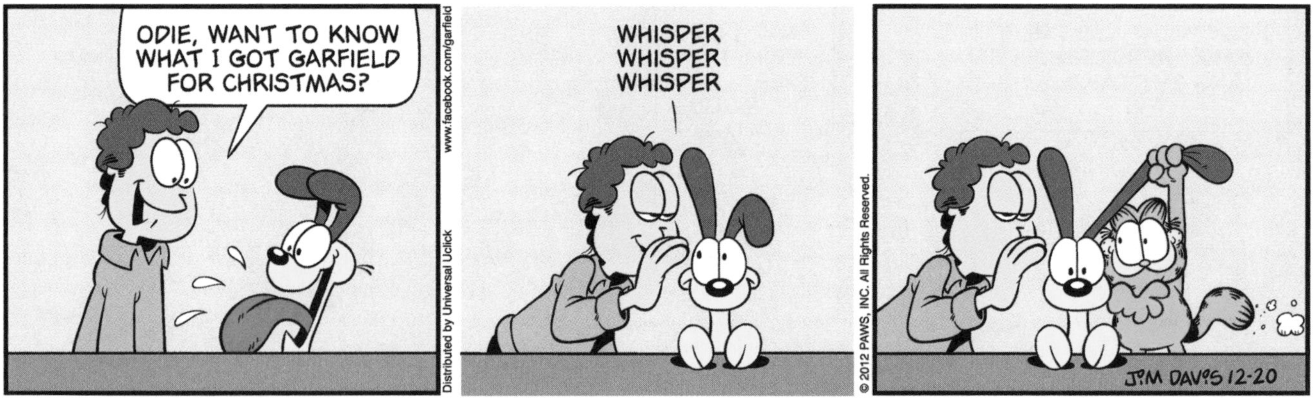
ODIE, WANT TO KNOW WHAT I GOT GARFIELD FOR CHRISTMAS?
WHISPER WHISPER WHISPER
JIM DAVIS 12-20
www.facebook.com/garfield
Distributed by Universal Uclick
© 2012 PAWS, INC. All Rights Reserved.

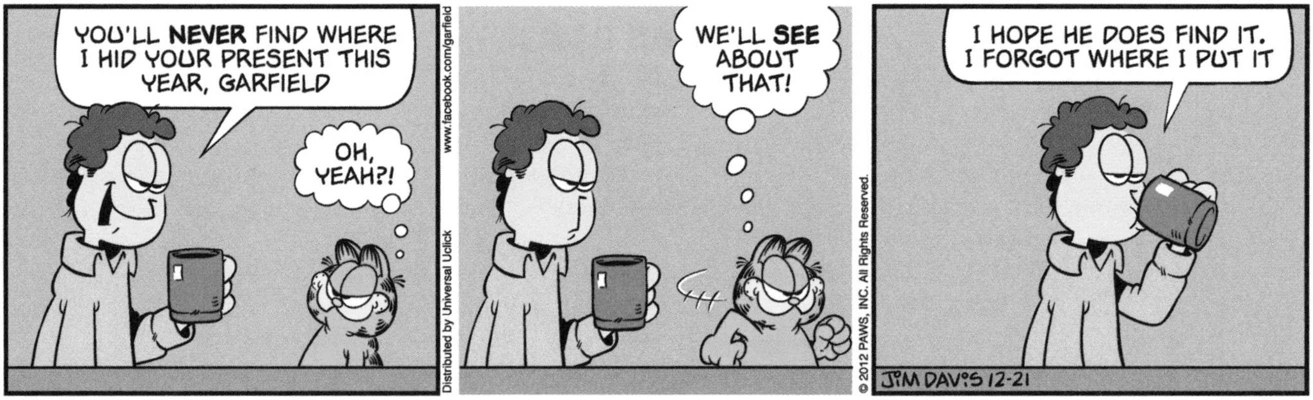
YOU'LL **NEVER** FIND WHERE I HID YOUR PRESENT THIS YEAR, GARFIELD
OH, YEAH?!
WE'LL **SEE** ABOUT THAT!
I HOPE HE DOES FIND IT. I FORGOT WHERE I PUT IT
JIM DAVIS 12-21
www.facebook.com/garfield
Distributed by Universal Uclick
© 2012 PAWS, INC. All Rights Reserved.

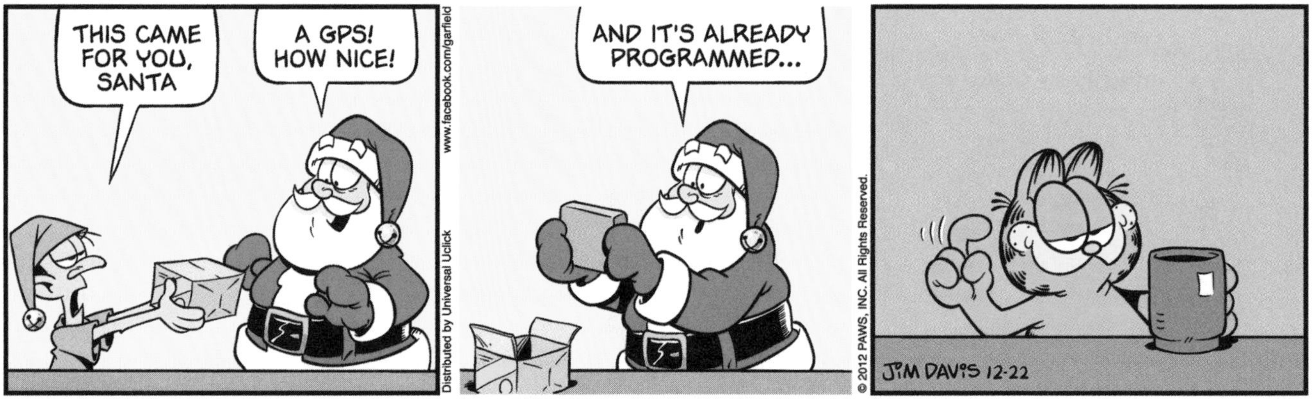
THIS CAME FOR YOU, SANTA
A GPS! HOW NICE!
AND IT'S ALREADY PROGRAMMED...
JIM DAVIS 12-22
www.facebook.com/garfield
Distributed by Universal Uclick
© 2012 PAWS, INC. All Rights Reserved.

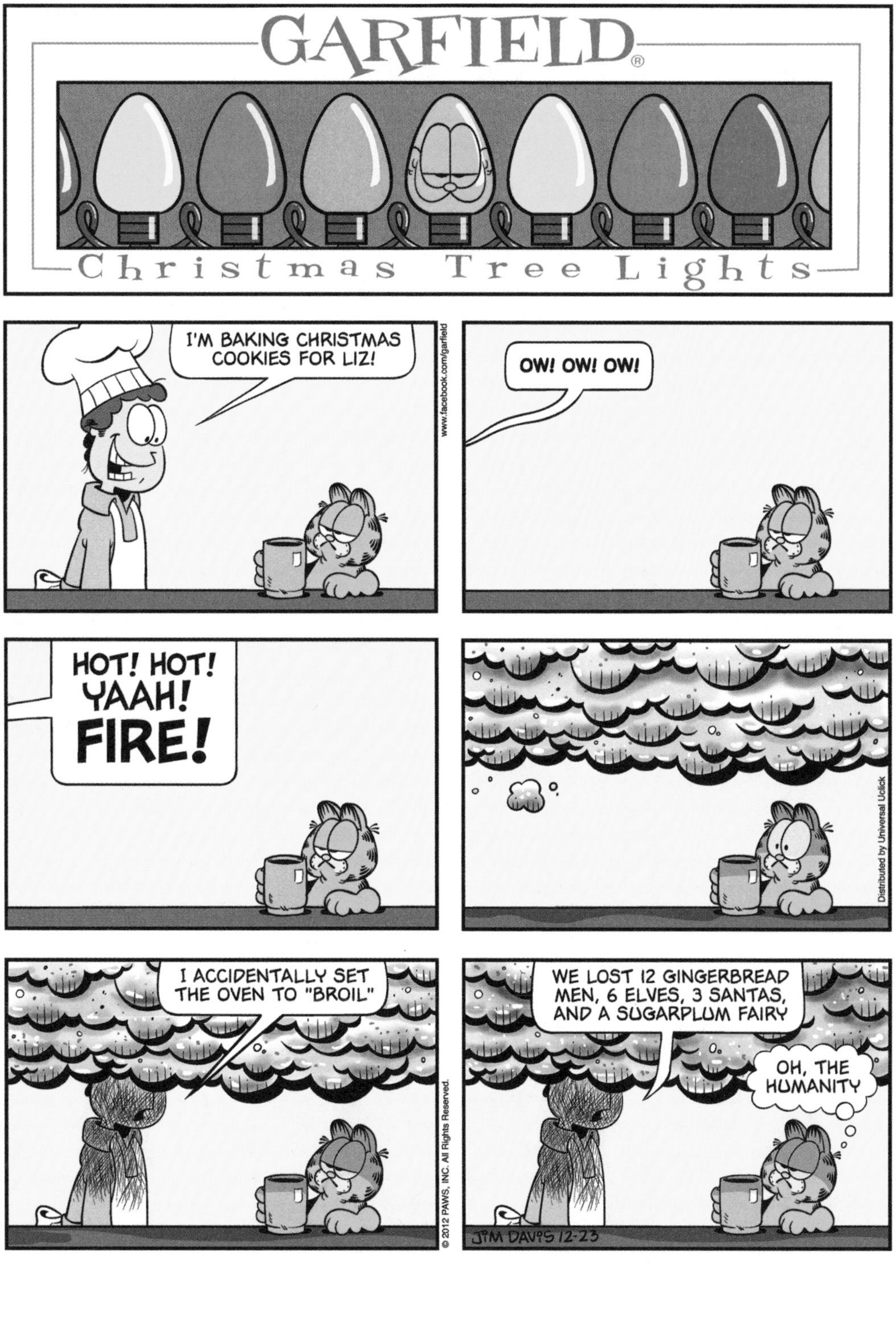
GARFIELD®
Christmas Tree Lights
I'M BAKING CHRISTMAS COOKIES FOR LIZ!
www.facebook.com/garfield
OW! OW! OW!
HOT! HOT! YAAH! FIRE!
Distributed by Universal Uclick
I ACCIDENTALLY SET THE OVEN TO "BROIL"
© 2012 PAWS, INC. All Rights Reserved.
WE LOST 12 GINGERBREAD MEN, 6 ELVES, 3 SANTAS, AND A SUGARPLUM FAIRY
OH, THE HUMANITY
JIM DAVIS 12-23

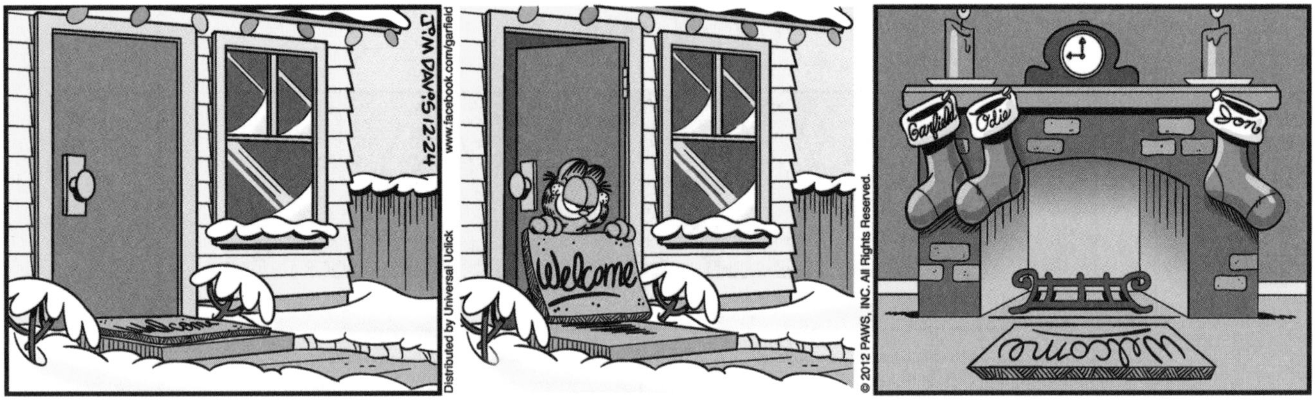
JIM DAVIS 12-24
www.facebook.com/garfield
Distributed by Universal Uclick
Welcome
© 2012 PAWS, INC. All Rights Reserved.
Garfield
Odie
Jon
Welcome

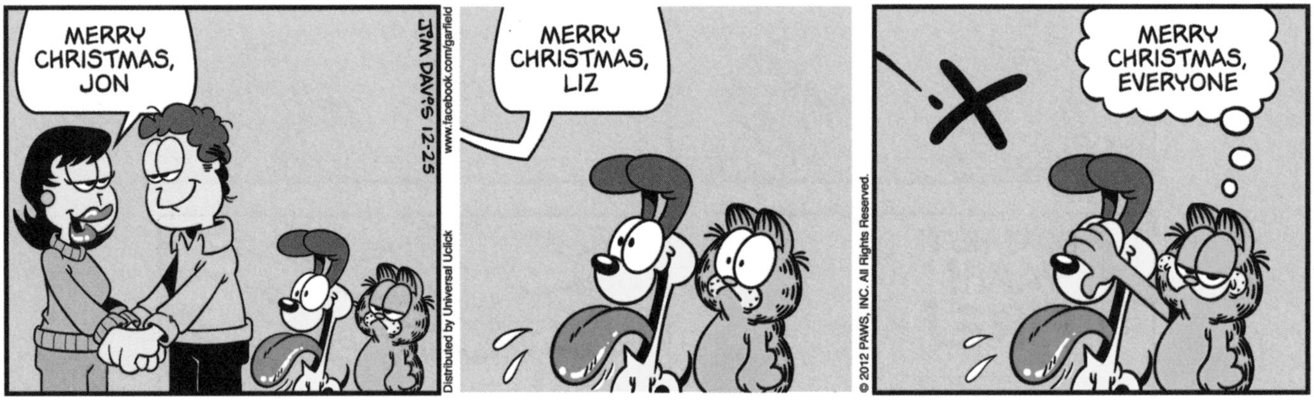
MERRY CHRISTMAS, JON
JIM DAVIS 12-25
www.facebook.com/garfield
Distributed by Universal Uclick
MERRY CHRISTMAS, LIZ
© 2012 PAWS, INC. All Rights Reserved.
MERRY CHRISTMAS, EVERYONE

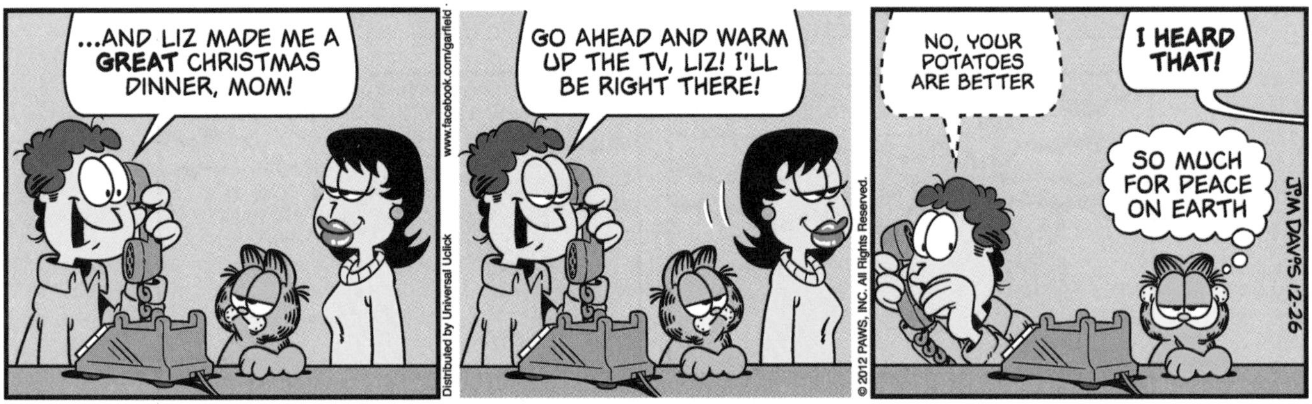
...AND LIZ MADE ME A **GREAT** CHRISTMAS DINNER, MOM!
www.facebook.com/garfield
Distributed by Universal Uclick
GO AHEAD AND WARM UP THE TV, LIZ! I'LL BE RIGHT THERE!
© 2012 PAWS, INC. All Rights Reserved.
NO, YOUR POTATOES ARE BETTER
I HEARD THAT!
SO MUCH FOR PEACE ON EARTH
JIM DAVIS 12-26

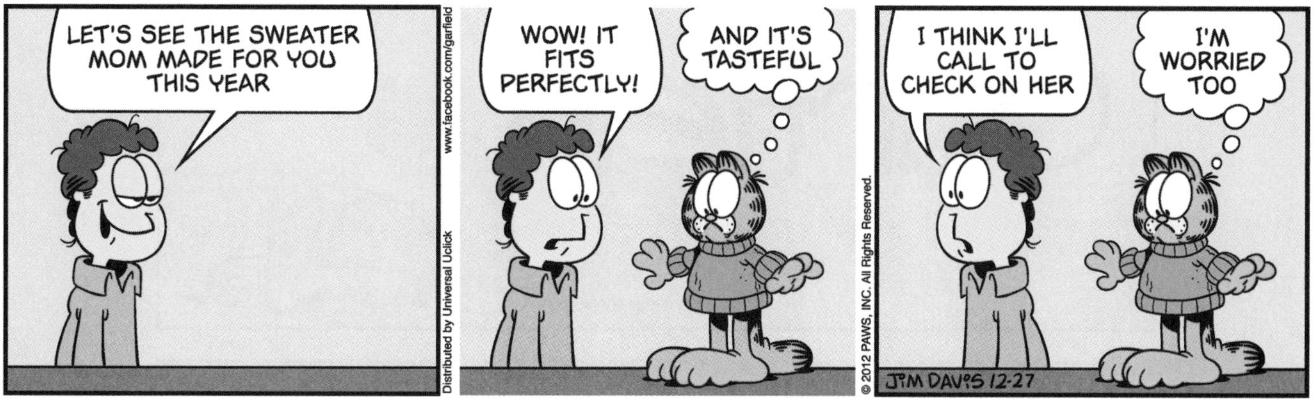
LET'S SEE THE SWEATER MOM MADE FOR YOU THIS YEAR
Distributed by Universal Uclick www.facebook.com/garfield
WOW! IT FITS PERFECTLY!
AND IT'S TASTEFUL
© 2012 PAWS, INC. All Rights Reserved.
I THINK I'LL CALL TO CHECK ON HER
I'M WORRIED TOO
JIM DAVIS 12-27

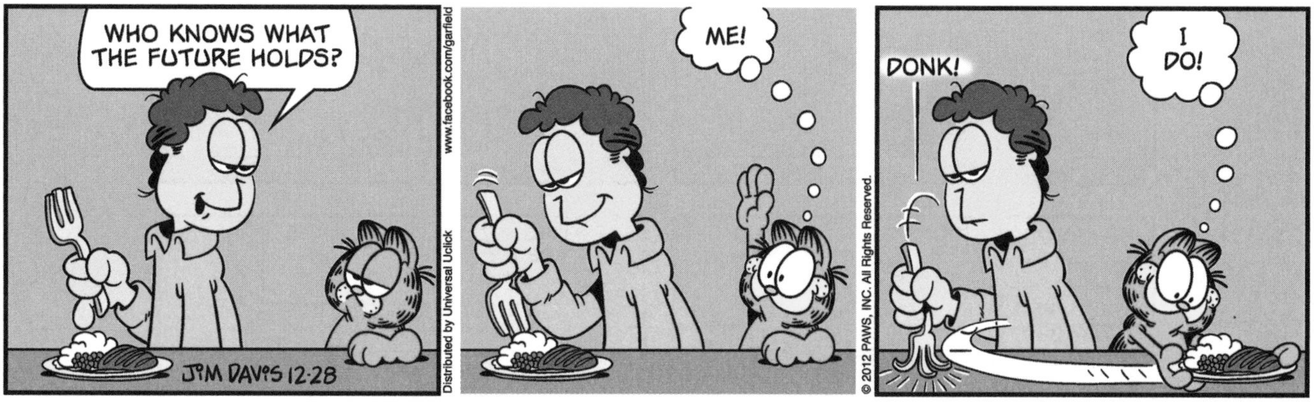
WHO KNOWS WHAT THE FUTURE HOLDS?
JIM DAVIS 12-28
Distributed by Universal Uclick www.facebook.com/garfield
ME!
© 2012 PAWS, INC. All Rights Reserved.
DONK!
I DO!

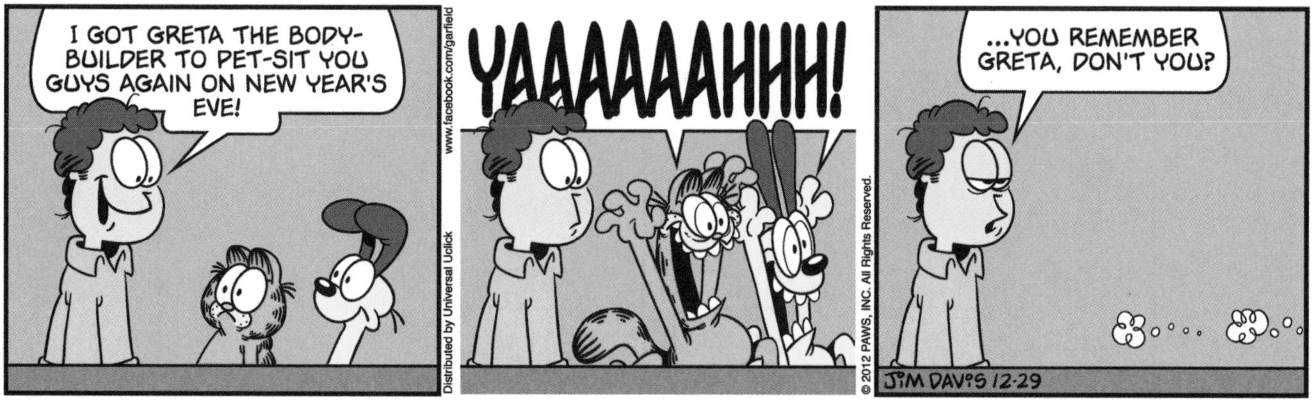
I GOT GRETA THE BODY-BUILDER TO PET-SIT YOU GUYS AGAIN ON NEW YEAR'S EVE!
Distributed by Universal Uclick www.facebook.com/garfield
YAAAAAAHHH!
© 2012 PAWS, INC. All Rights Reserved.
...YOU REMEMBER GRETA, DON'T YOU?
JIM DAVIS 12-29

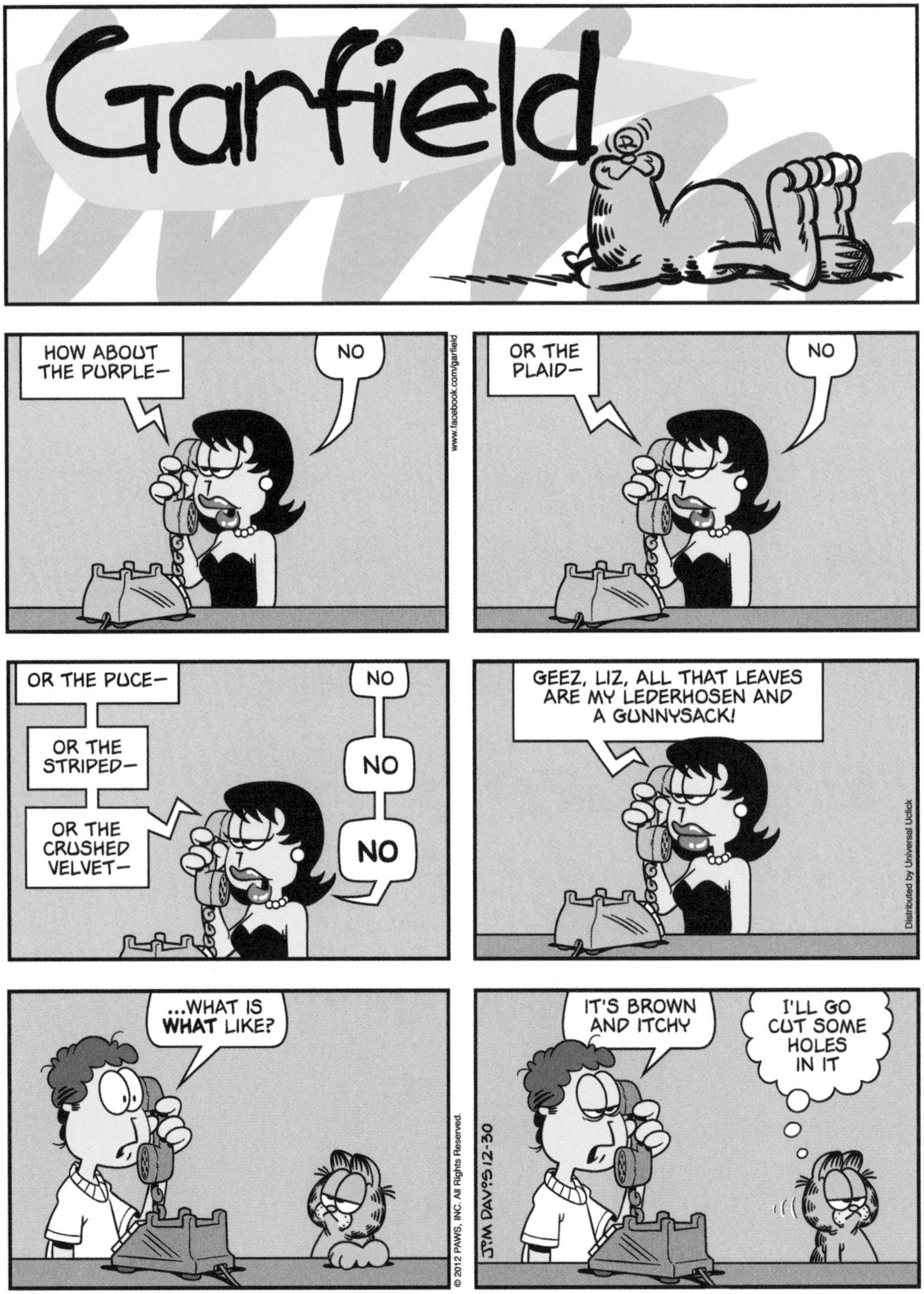
Garfield
HOW ABOUT THE PURPLE—
NO
www.facebook.com/garfield
OR THE PLAID—
NO
OR THE PUCE—
NO
OR THE STRIPED—
NO
OR THE CRUSHED VELVET—
NO
GEEZ, LIZ, ALL THAT LEAVES ARE MY LEDERHOSEN AND A GUNNYSACK!
Distributed by Universal Uclick
...WHAT IS WHAT LIKE?
© 2012 PAWS, INC. All Rights Reserved.
IT'S BROWN AND ITCHY
I'LL GO CUT SOME HOLES IN IT

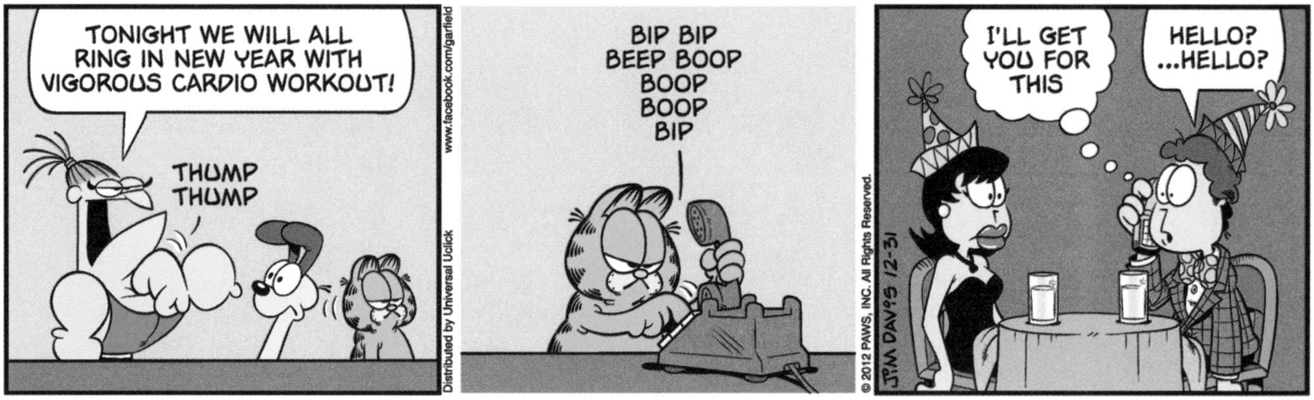
TONIGHT WE WILL ALL RING IN NEW YEAR WITH VIGOROUS CARDIO WORKOUT!
THUMP THUMP
BIP BIP BEEP BOOP BOOP BOOP BIP
I'LL GET YOU FOR THIS
HELLO? ...HELLO?
JIM DAVIS 12-31
Distributed by Universal Uclick www.facebook.com/garfield
© 2012 PAWS, INC. All Rights Reserved.

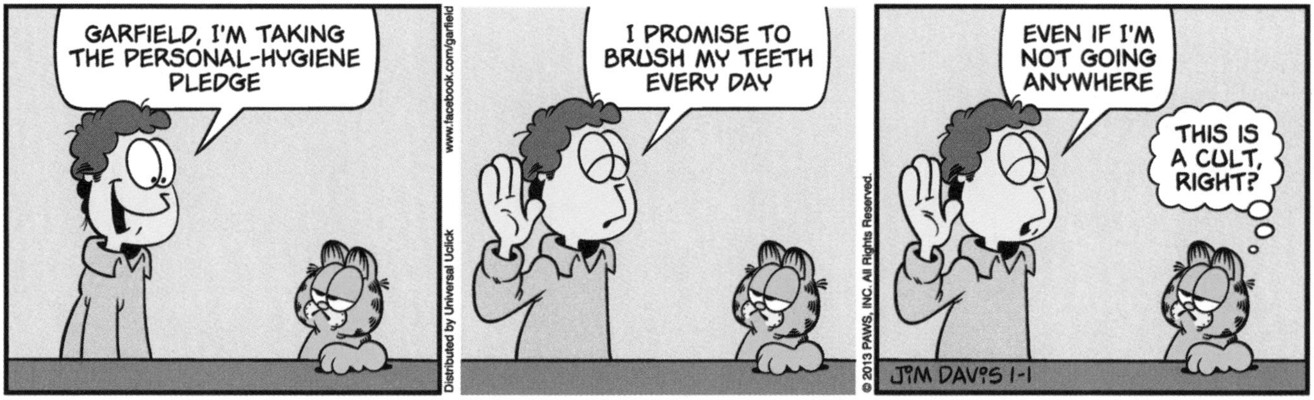
GARFIELD, I'M TAKING THE PERSONAL-HYGIENE PLEDGE
I PROMISE TO BRUSH MY TEETH EVERY DAY
EVEN IF I'M NOT GOING ANYWHERE
THIS IS A CULT, RIGHT?
JIM DAVIS 1-1
Distributed by Universal Uclick www.facebook.com/garfield
© 2013 PAWS, INC. All Rights Reserved.

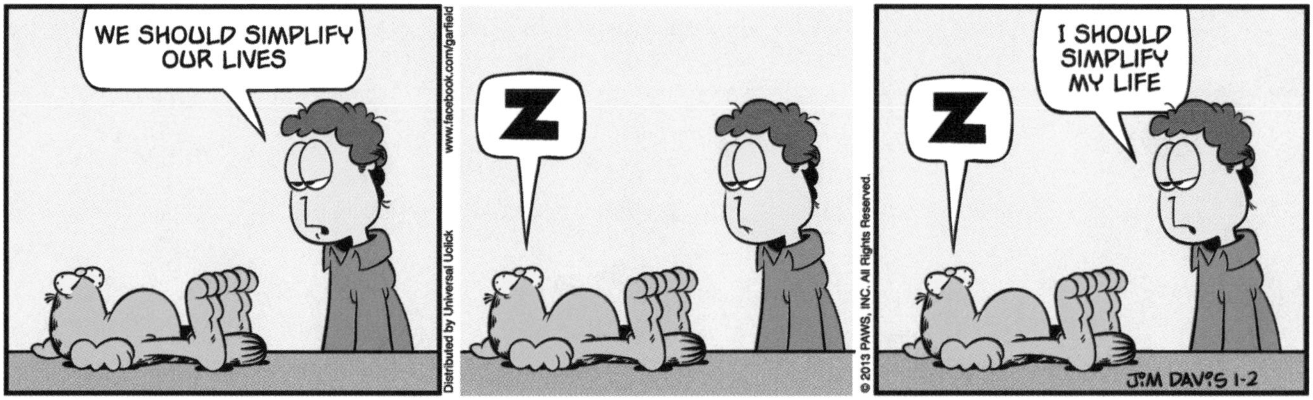
WE SHOULD SIMPLIFY OUR LIVES
Z
Z
I SHOULD SIMPLIFY MY LIFE
JIM DAVIS 1-2
Distributed by Universal Uclick www.facebook.com/garfield
© 2013 PAWS, INC. All Rights Reserved.

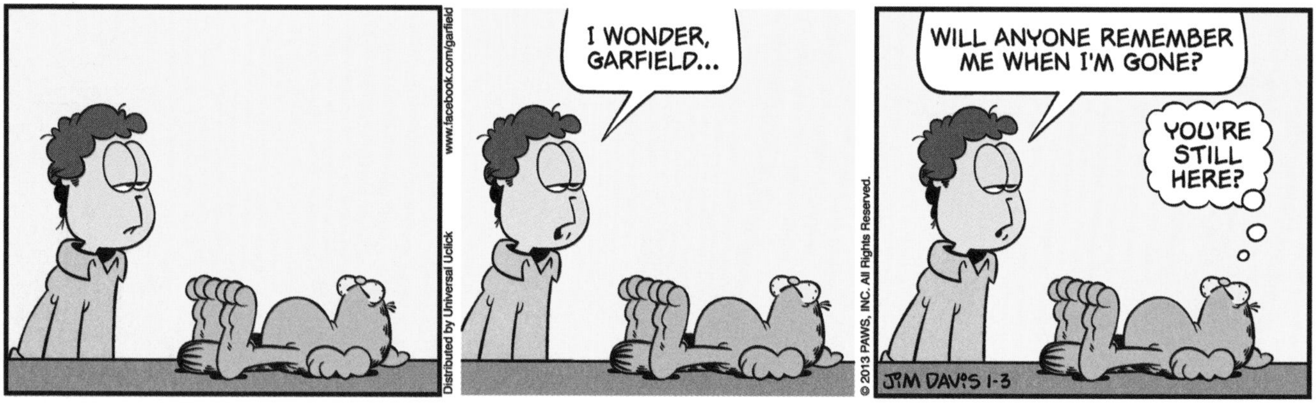
www.facebook.com/garfield
Distributed by Universal Uclick
I WONDER, GARFIELD...
WILL ANYONE REMEMBER ME WHEN I'M GONE?
YOU'RE STILL HERE?
© 2013 PAWS, INC. All Rights Reserved.
JIM DAVIS 1-3

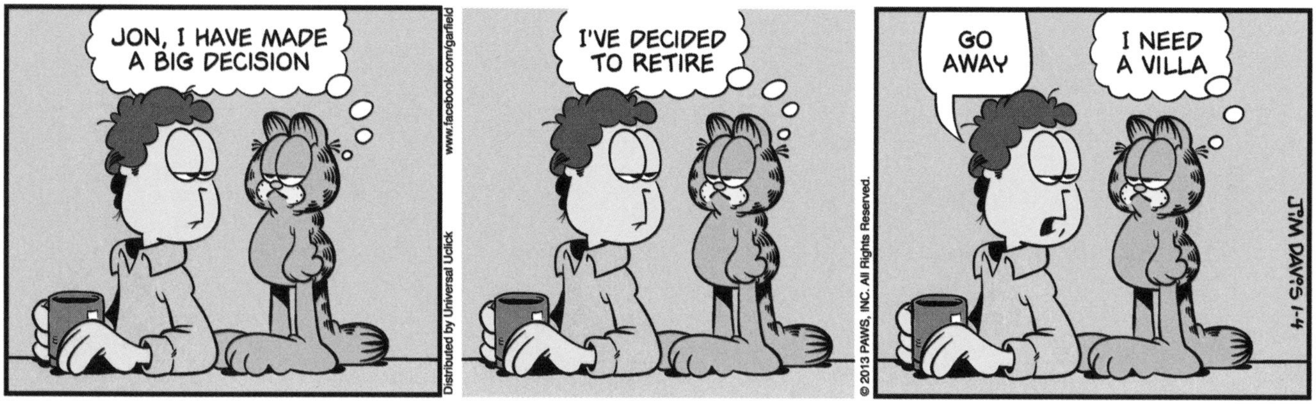
JON, I HAVE MADE A BIG DECISION
www.facebook.com/garfield
Distributed by Universal Uclick
I'VE DECIDED TO RETIRE
© 2013 PAWS, INC. All Rights Reserved.
GO AWAY
I NEED A VILLA
JIM DAVIS 1-4

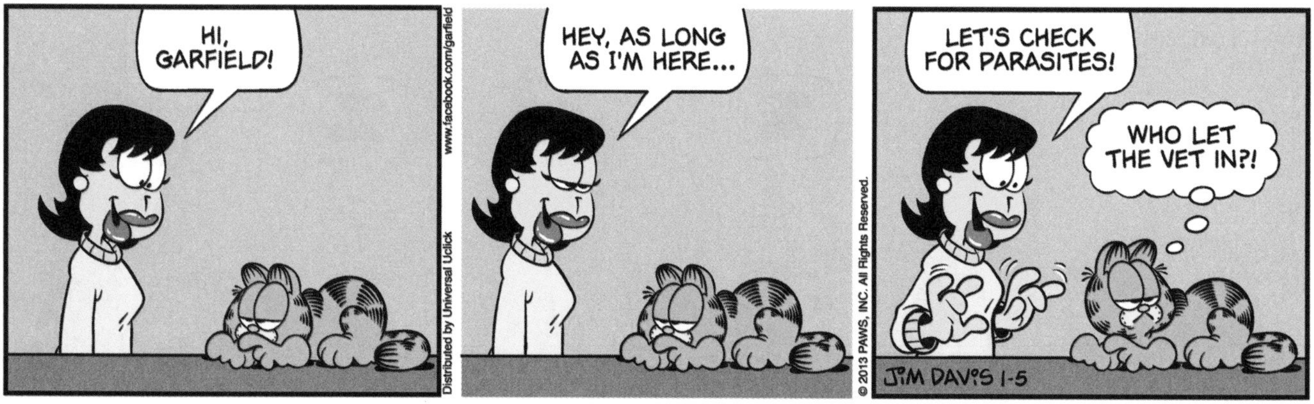
HI, GARFIELD!
www.facebook.com/garfield
Distributed by Universal Uclick
HEY, AS LONG AS I'M HERE...
© 2013 PAWS, INC. All Rights Reserved.
LET'S CHECK FOR PARASITES!
WHO LET THE VET IN?!
JIM DAVIS 1-5

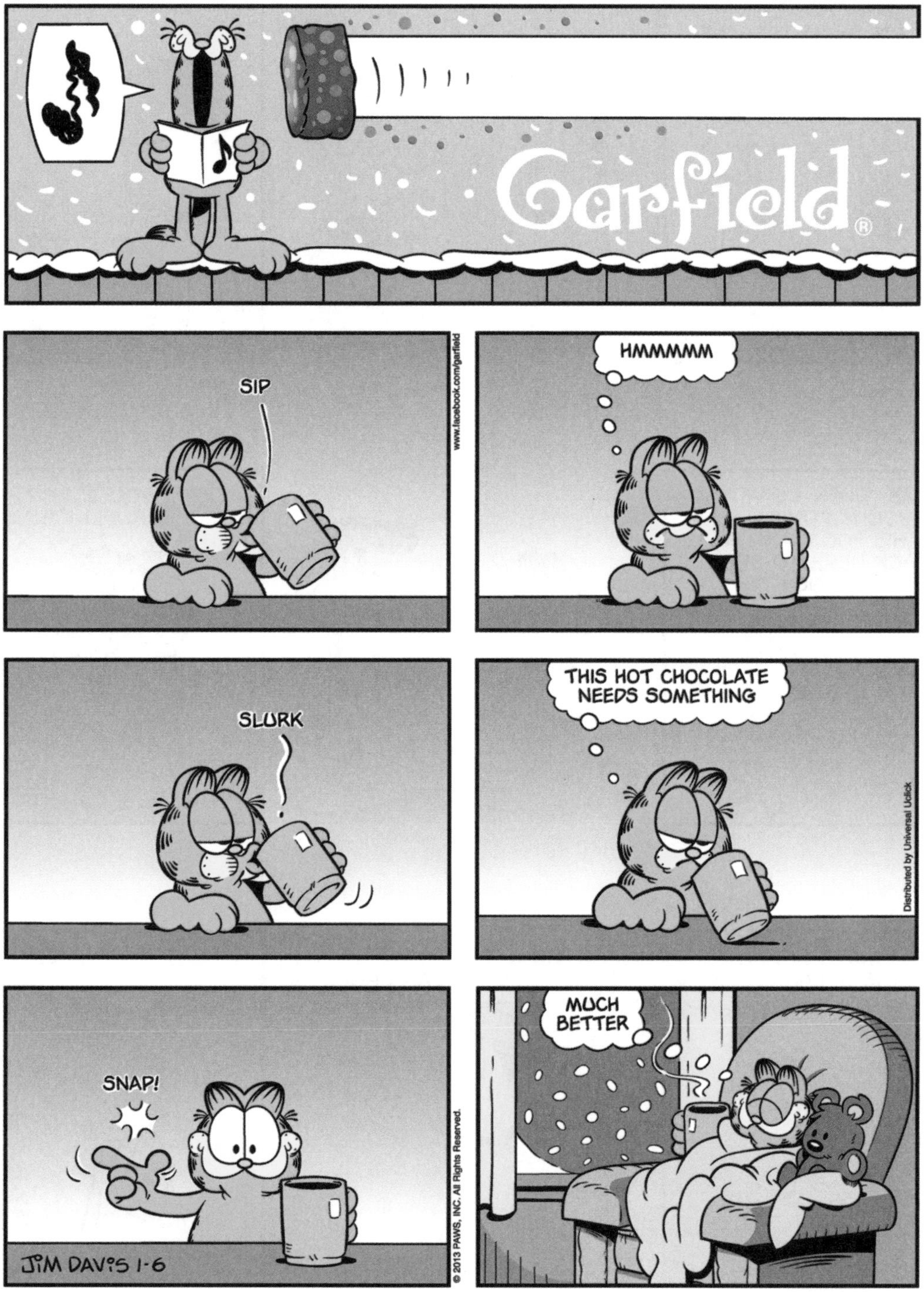
Garfield
SIP
www.facebook.com/garfield
HMMMMM
SLURK
THIS HOT CHOCOLATE NEEDS SOMETHING
Distributed by Universal Uclick
SNAP!
JIM DAVIS 1-6
© 2013 PAWS, INC. All Rights Reserved.
MUCH BETTER

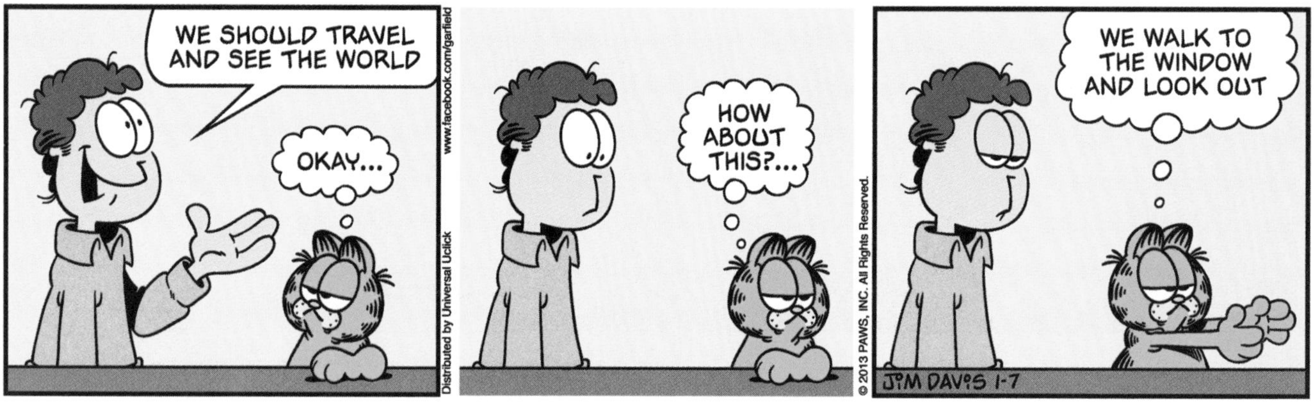
WE SHOULD TRAVEL AND SEE THE WORLD
OKAY...
HOW ABOUT THIS?...
WE WALK TO THE WINDOW AND LOOK OUT
JIM DAVIS 1-7
Distributed by Universal Uclick www.facebook.com/garfield
© 2013 PAWS, INC. All Rights Reserved.

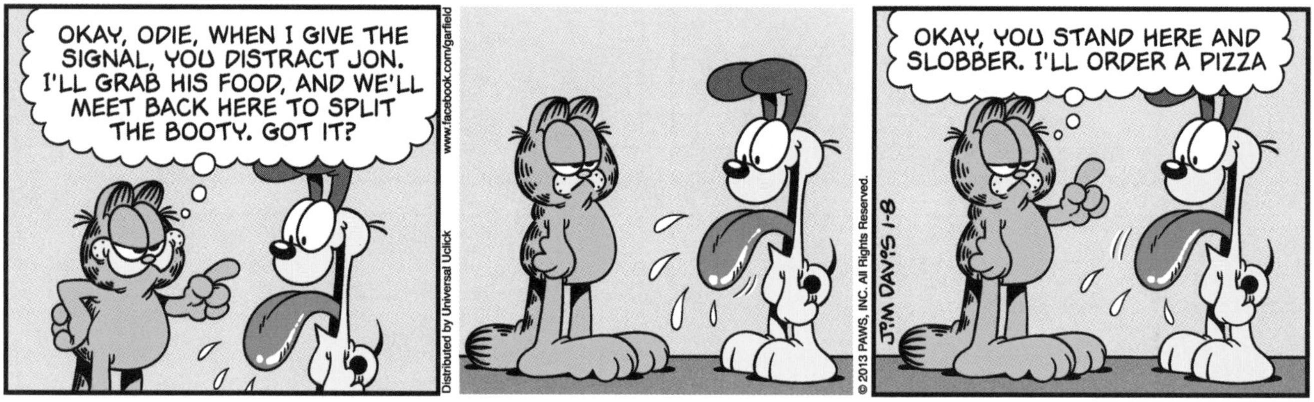
OKAY, ODIE, WHEN I GIVE THE SIGNAL, YOU DISTRACT JON. I'LL GRAB HIS FOOD, AND WE'LL MEET BACK HERE TO SPLIT THE BOOTY. GOT IT?
OKAY, YOU STAND HERE AND SLOBBER. I'LL ORDER A PIZZA
JIM DAVIS 1-8
Distributed by Universal Uclick www.facebook.com/garfield
© 2013 PAWS, INC. All Rights Reserved.

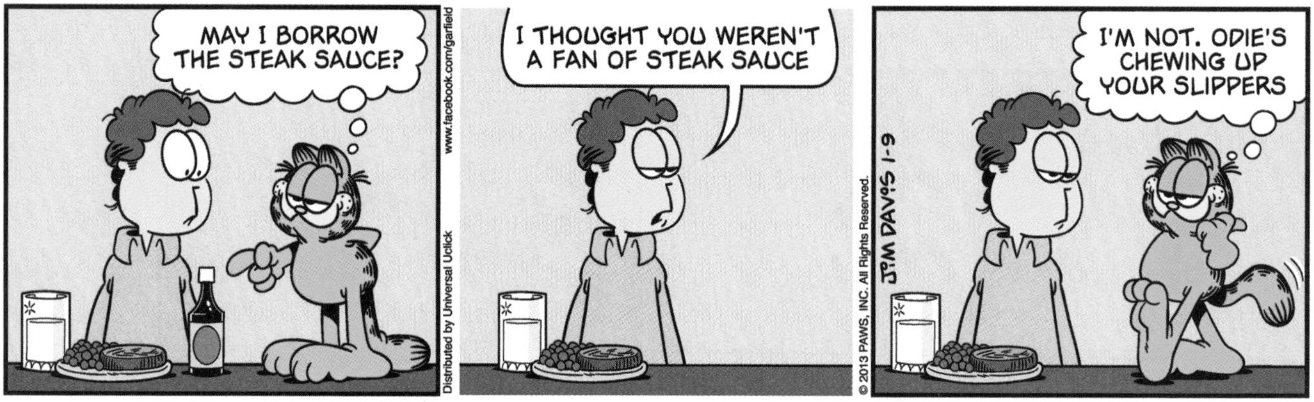
MAY I BORROW THE STEAK SAUCE?
I THOUGHT YOU WEREN'T A FAN OF STEAK SAUCE
I'M NOT. ODIE'S CHEWING UP YOUR SLIPPERS
JIM DAVIS 1-9
Distributed by Universal Uclick www.facebook.com/garfield
© 2013 PAWS, INC. All Rights Reserved.

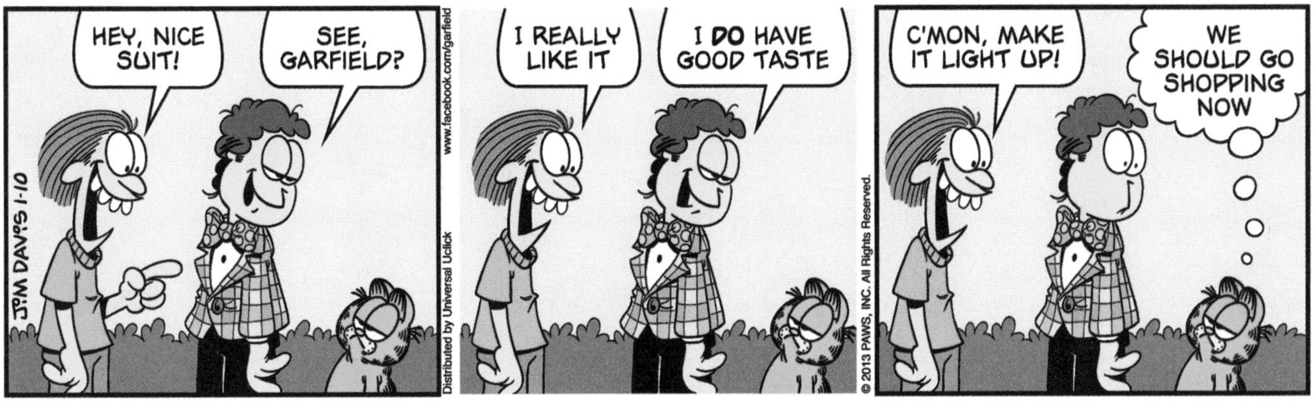
HEY, NICE SUIT!
SEE, GARFIELD?
JIM DAVIS 1-10
I REALLY LIKE IT
I DO HAVE GOOD TASTE
C'MON, MAKE IT LIGHT UP!
WE SHOULD GO SHOPPING NOW
www.facebook.com/garfield
Distributed by Universal Uclick
© 2013 PAWS, INC. All Rights Reserved.

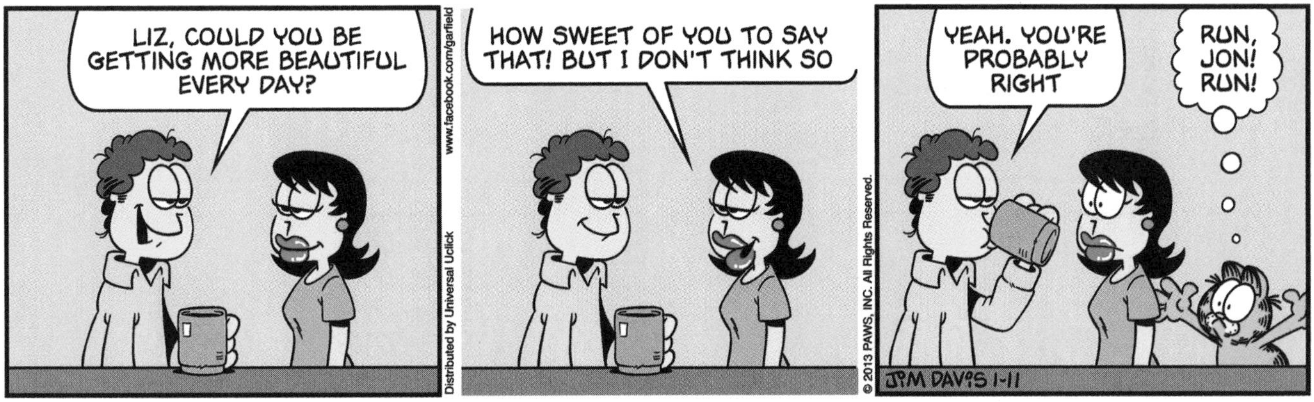
LIZ, COULD YOU BE GETTING MORE BEAUTIFUL EVERY DAY?
HOW SWEET OF YOU TO SAY THAT! BUT I DON'T THINK SO
YEAH. YOU'RE PROBABLY RIGHT
RUN, JON! RUN!
JIM DAVIS 1-11
www.facebook.com/garfield
Distributed by Universal Uclick
© 2013 PAWS, INC. All Rights Reserved.

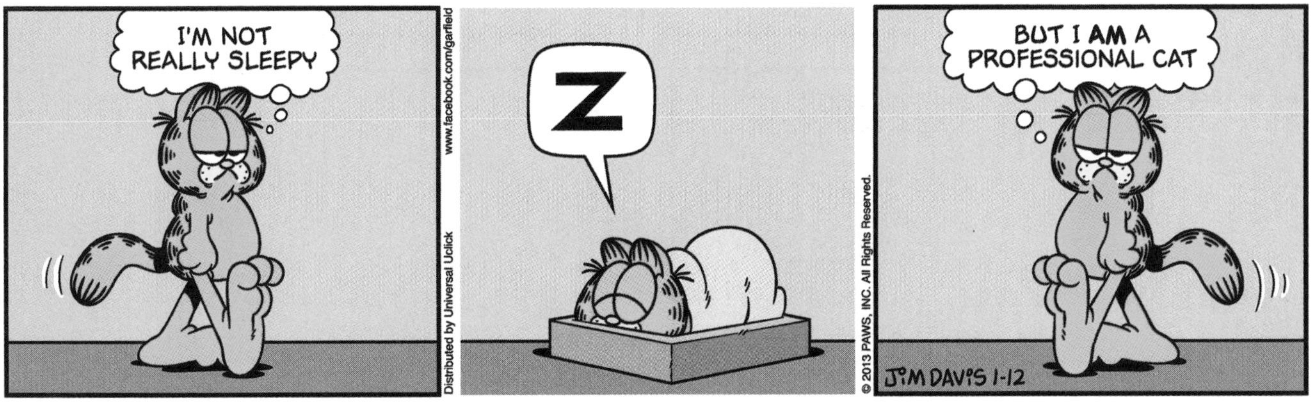
I'M NOT REALLY SLEEPY
Z
BUT I AM A PROFESSIONAL CAT
JIM DAVIS 1-12
www.facebook.com/garfield
Distributed by Universal Uclick
© 2013 PAWS, INC. All Rights Reserved.

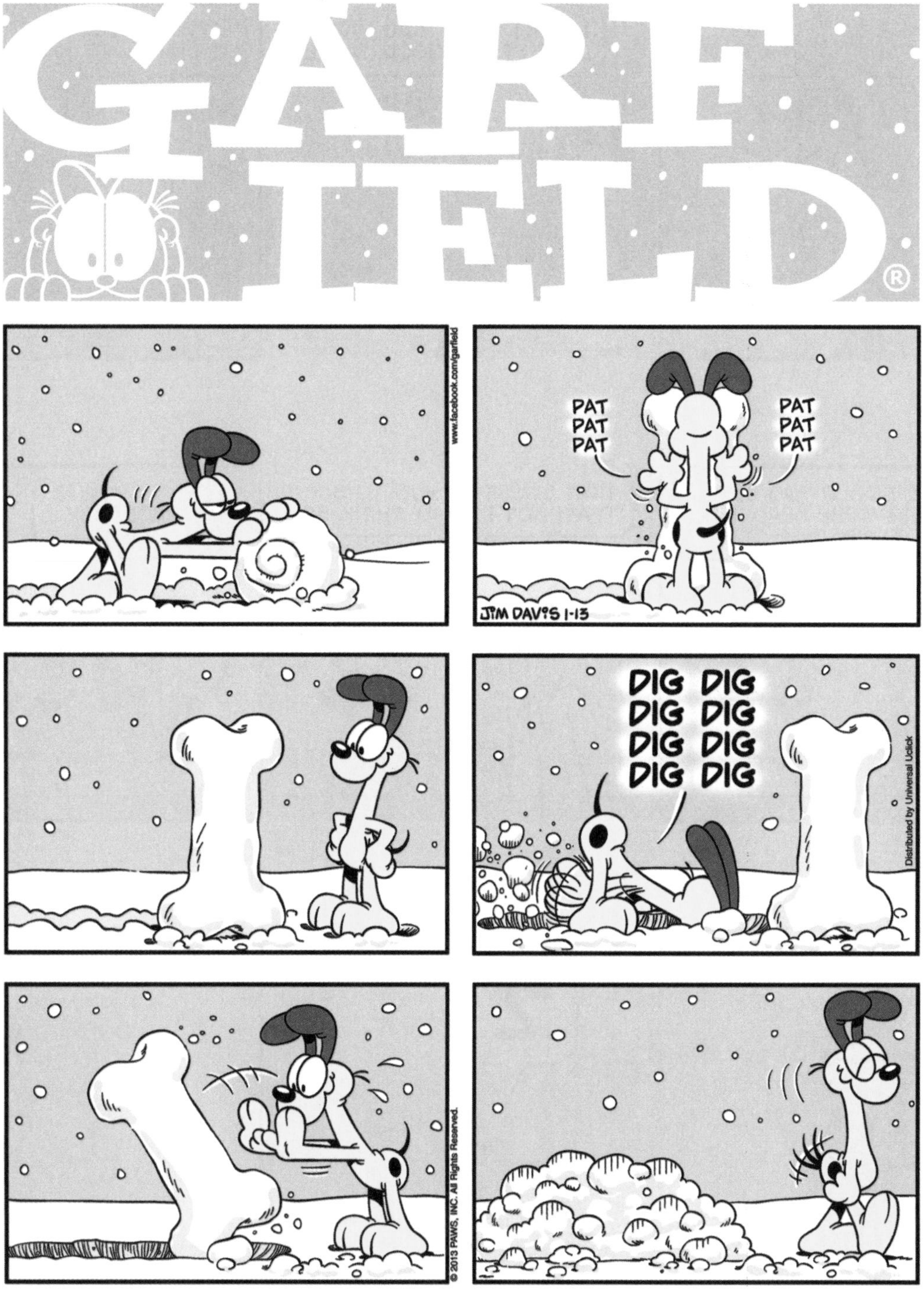
GARFIELD
www.facebook.com/garfield
PAT PAT PAT
PAT PAT PAT
JIM DAVIS 1-13
DIG DIG DIG DIG DIG DIG DIG DIG
Distributed by Universal Uclick
© 2013 PAWS, INC. All Rights Reserved.

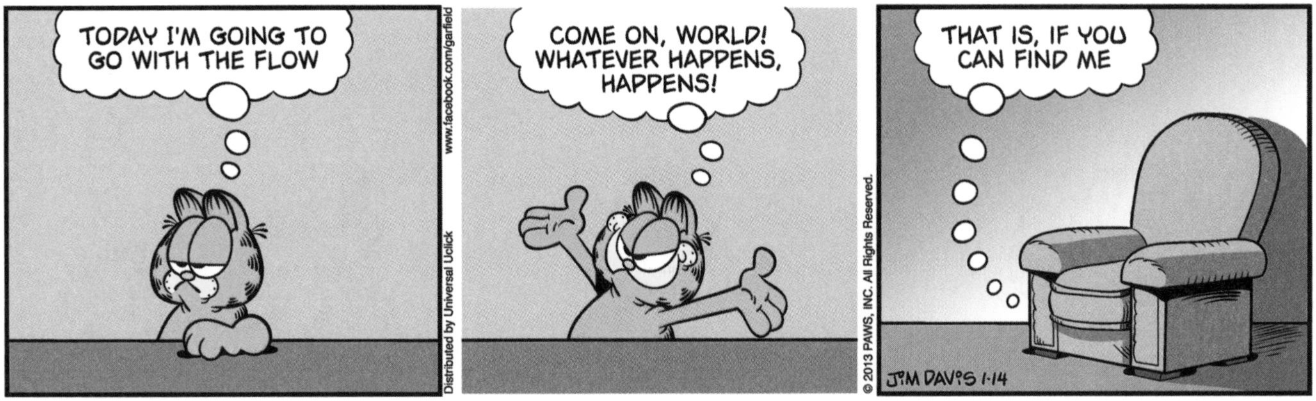
TODAY I'M GOING TO GO WITH THE FLOW
www.facebook.com/garfield
Distributed by Universal Uclick
COME ON, WORLD! WHATEVER HAPPENS, HAPPENS!
© 2013 PAWS, INC. All Rights Reserved.
THAT IS, IF YOU CAN FIND ME
JIM DAVIS 1-14

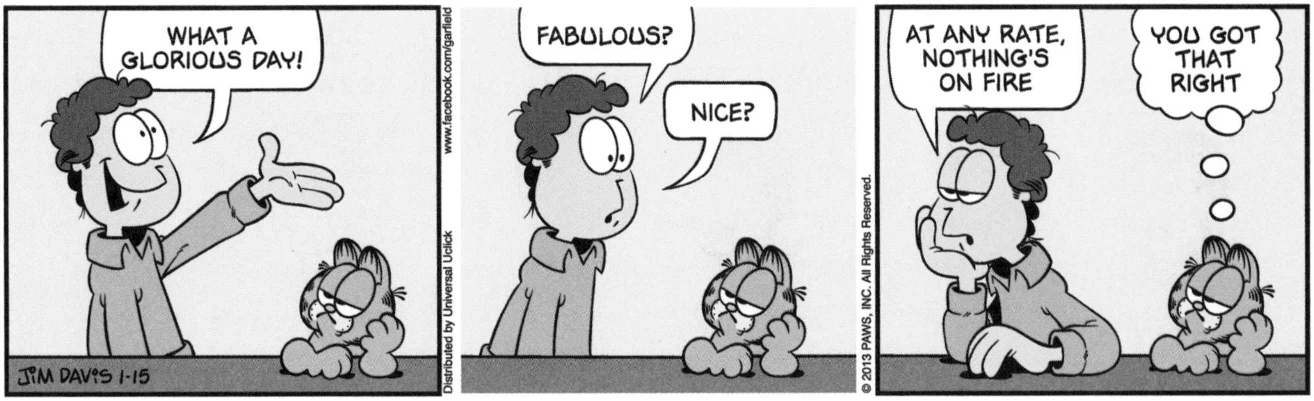
WHAT A GLORIOUS DAY!
JIM DAVIS 1-15
www.facebook.com/garfield
Distributed by Universal Uclick
FABULOUS?
NICE?
© 2013 PAWS, INC. All Rights Reserved.
AT ANY RATE, NOTHING'S ON FIRE
YOU GOT THAT RIGHT

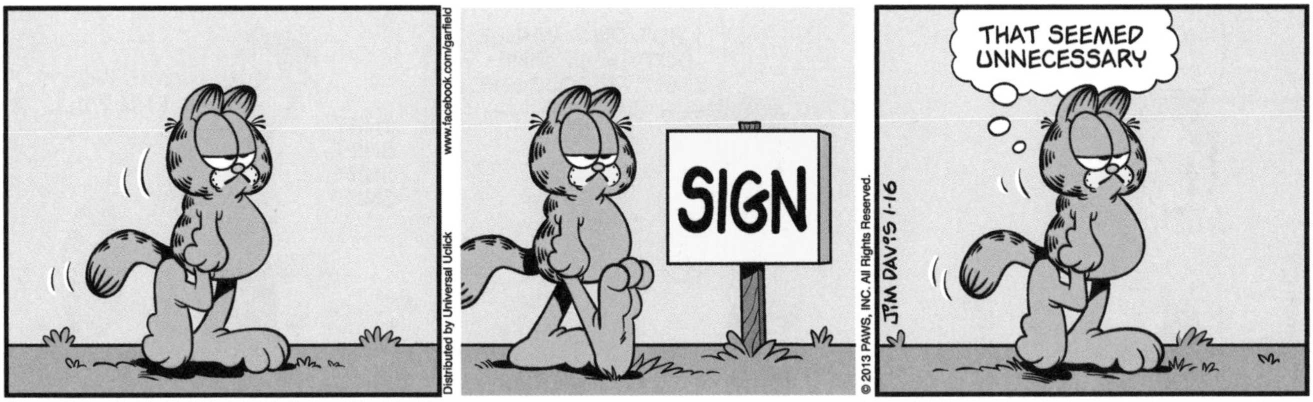
www.facebook.com/garfield
Distributed by Universal Uclick
SIGN
© 2013 PAWS, INC. All Rights Reserved.
JIM DAVIS 1-16
THAT SEEMED UNNECESSARY

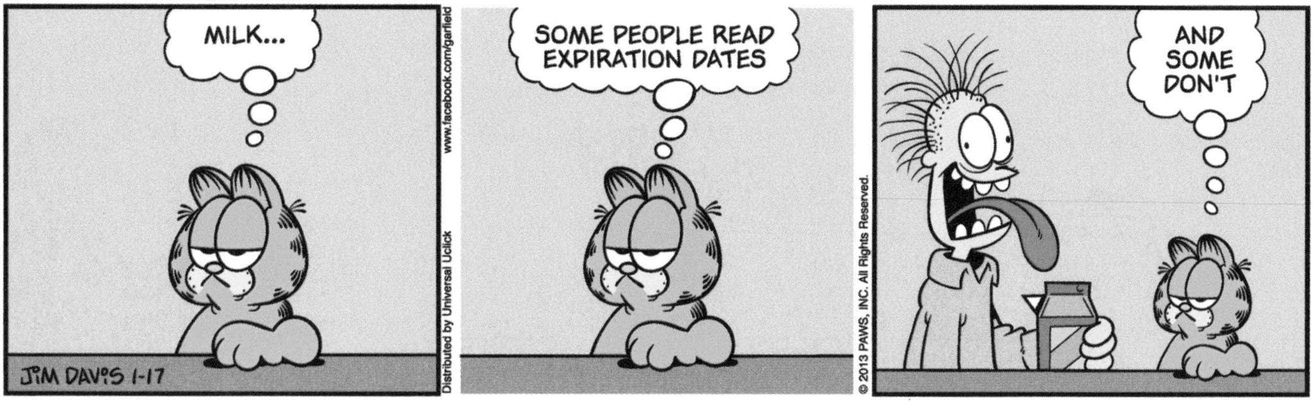
MILK...
JIM DAVIS 1-17
www.facebook.com/garfield
Distributed by Universal Uclick
SOME PEOPLE READ EXPIRATION DATES
© 2013 PAWS, INC. All Rights Reserved.
AND SOME DON'T

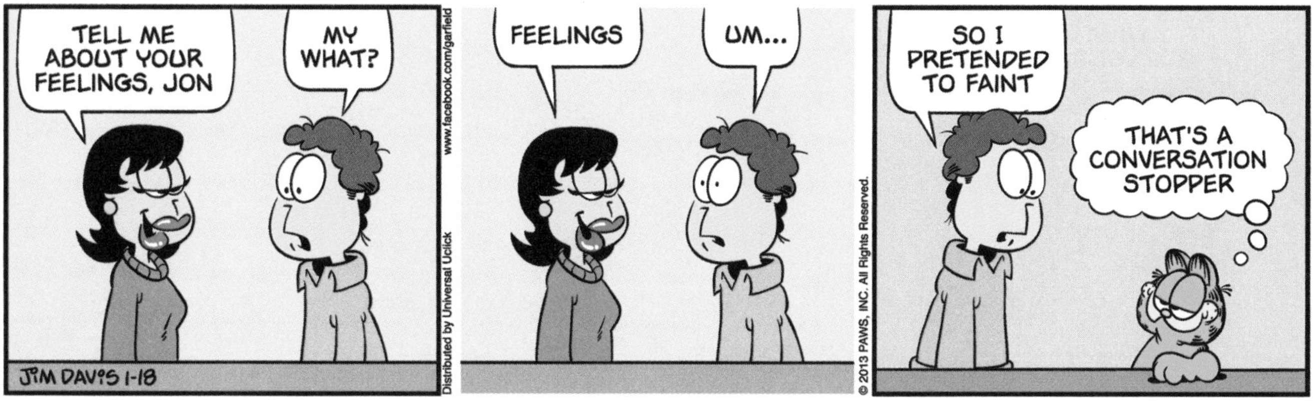
TELL ME ABOUT YOUR FEELINGS, JON
MY WHAT?
JIM DAVIS 1-18
www.facebook.com/garfield
Distributed by Universal Uclick
FEELINGS
UM...
© 2013 PAWS, INC. All Rights Reserved.
SO I PRETENDED TO FAINT
THAT'S A CONVERSATION STOPPER

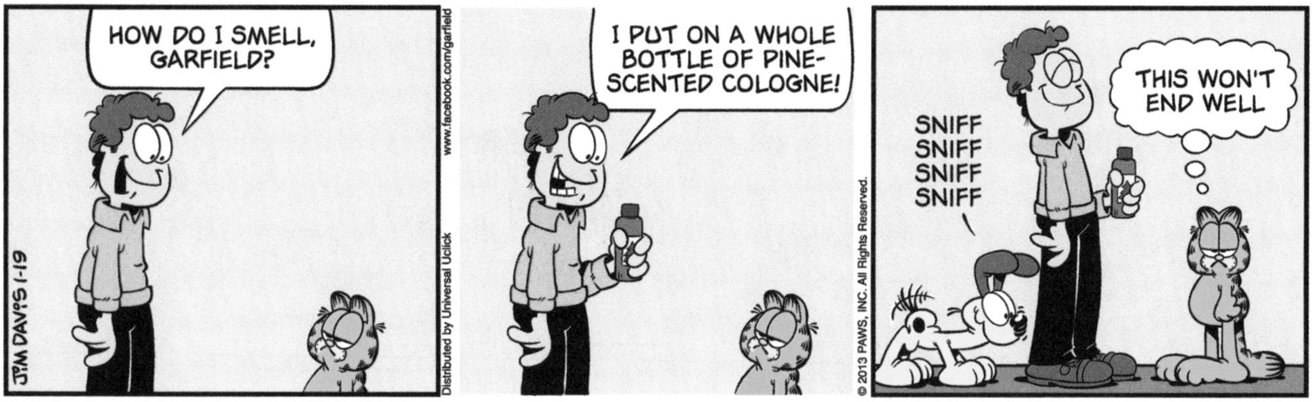
HOW DO I SMELL, GARFIELD?
JIM DAVIS 1-19
www.facebook.com/garfield
Distributed by Universal Uclick
I PUT ON A WHOLE BOTTLE OF PINE-SCENTED COLOGNE!
© 2013 PAWS, INC. All Rights Reserved.
SNIFF SNIFF SNIFF SNIFF
THIS WON'T END WELL

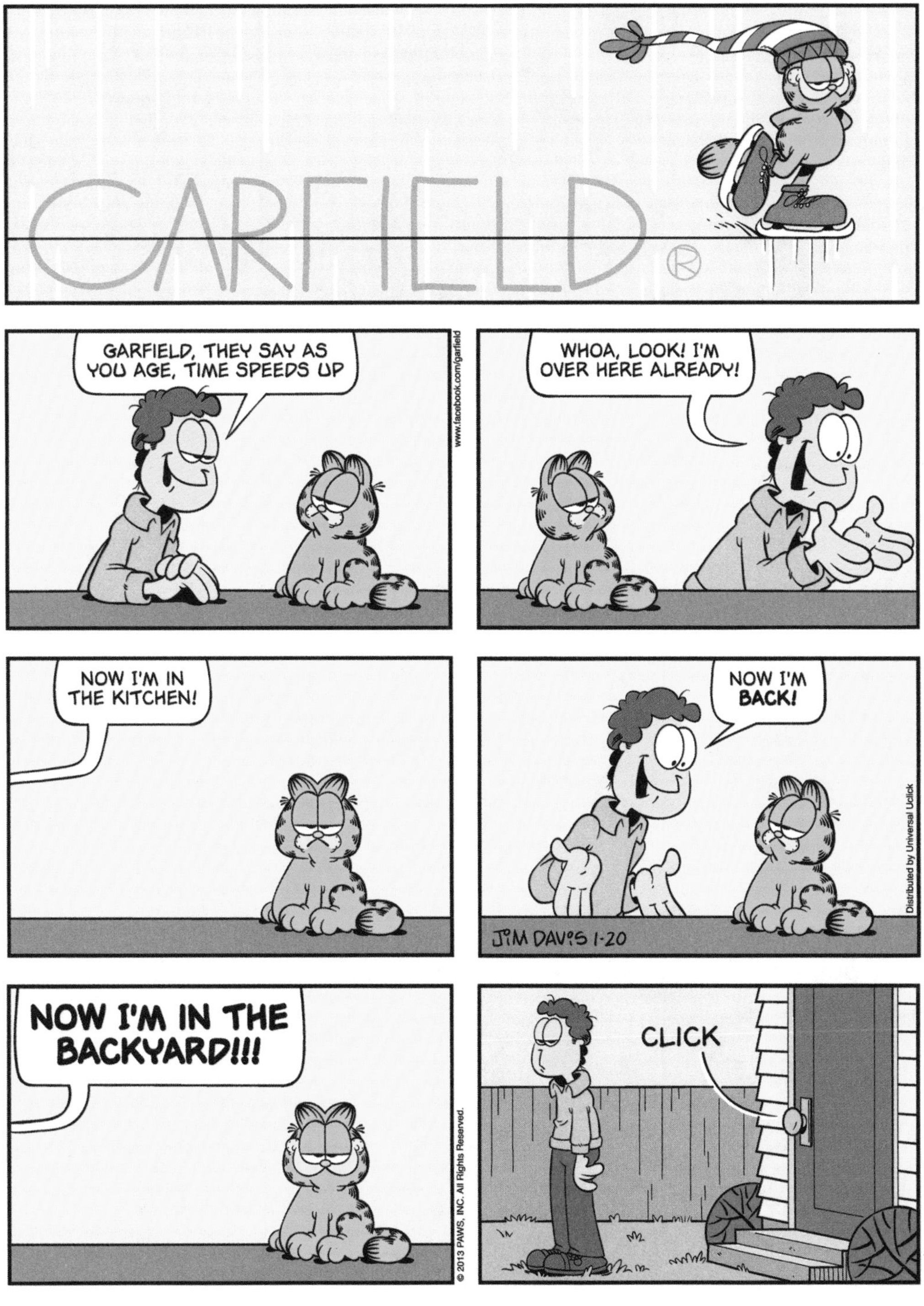
GARFIELD®
GARFIELD, THEY SAY AS YOU AGE, TIME SPEEDS UP
www.facebook.com/garfield
WHOA, LOOK! I'M OVER HERE ALREADY!
NOW I'M IN THE KITCHEN!
NOW I'M BACK!
JIM DAVIS 1-20
Distributed by Universal Uclick
NOW I'M IN THE BACKYARD!!!
© 2013 PAWS, INC. All Rights Reserved.
CLICK

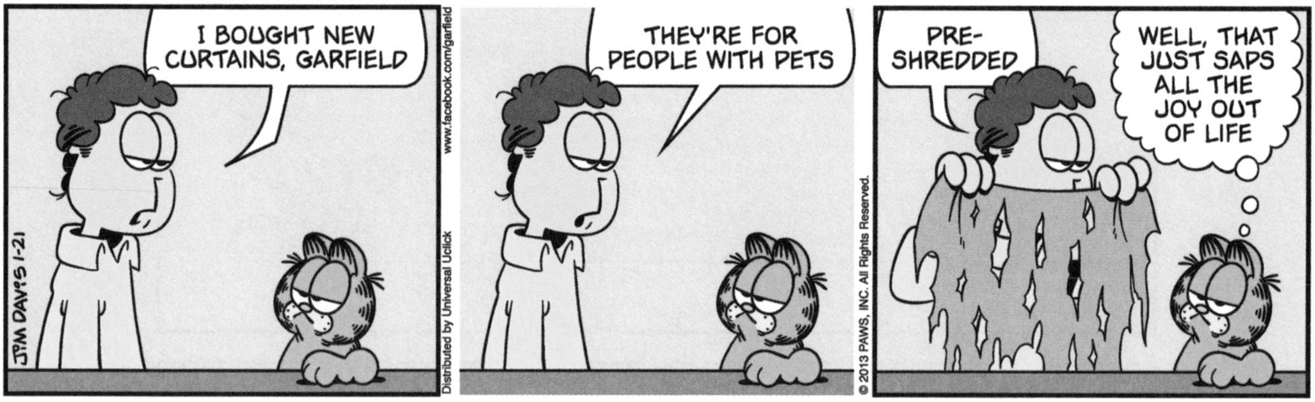
JIM DAVIS 1-21
I BOUGHT NEW CURTAINS, GARFIELD
www.facebook.com/garfield
Distributed by Universal Uclick
THEY'RE FOR PEOPLE WITH PETS
© 2013 PAWS, INC. All Rights Reserved.
PRE-SHREDDED
WELL, THAT JUST SAPS ALL THE JOY OUT OF LIFE

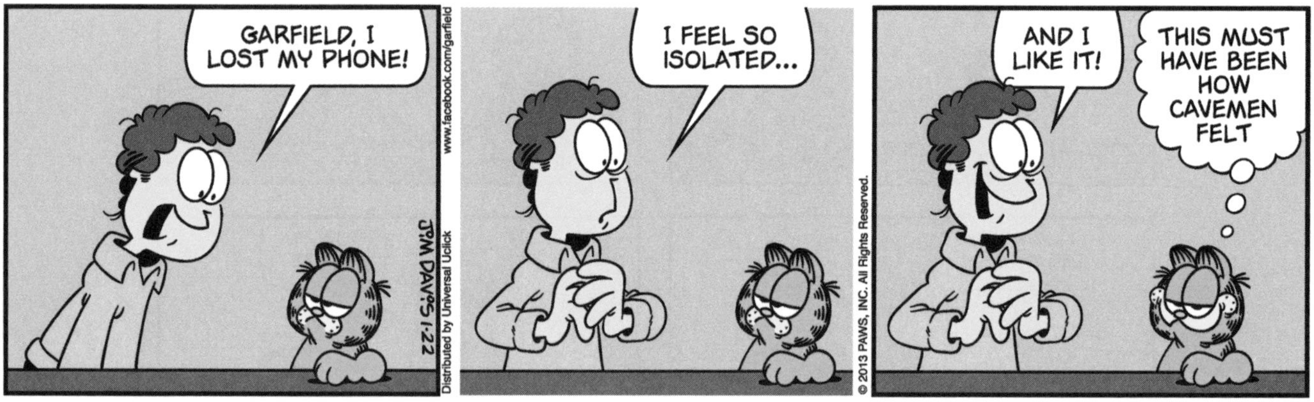
GARFIELD, I LOST MY PHONE!
JIM DAVIS 1-22
www.facebook.com/garfield
Distributed by Universal Uclick
I FEEL SO ISOLATED...
© 2013 PAWS, INC. All Rights Reserved.
AND I LIKE IT!
THIS MUST HAVE BEEN HOW CAVEMEN FELT

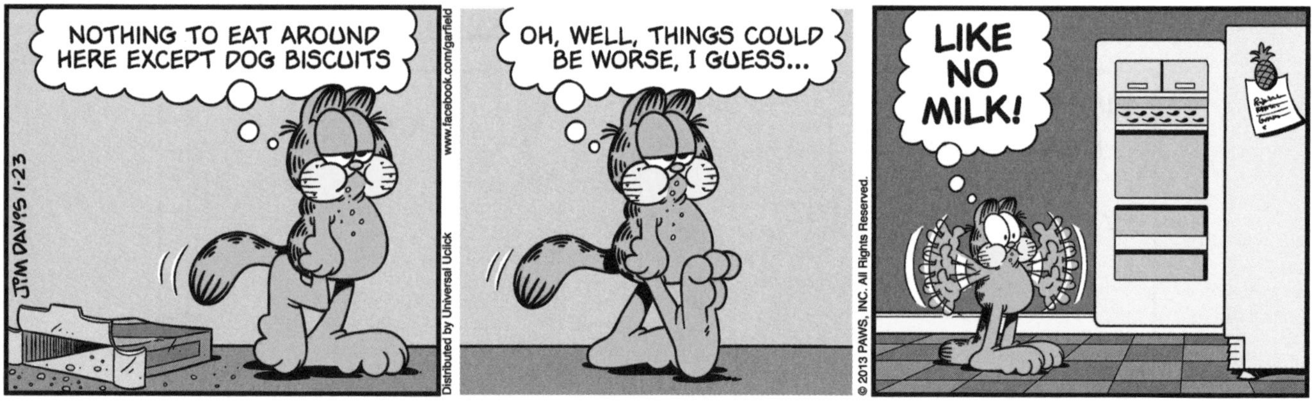
JIM DAVIS 1-23
NOTHING TO EAT AROUND HERE EXCEPT DOG BISCUITS
www.facebook.com/garfield
Distributed by Universal Uclick
OH, WELL, THINGS COULD BE WORSE, I GUESS...
© 2013 PAWS, INC. All Rights Reserved.
LIKE NO MILK!

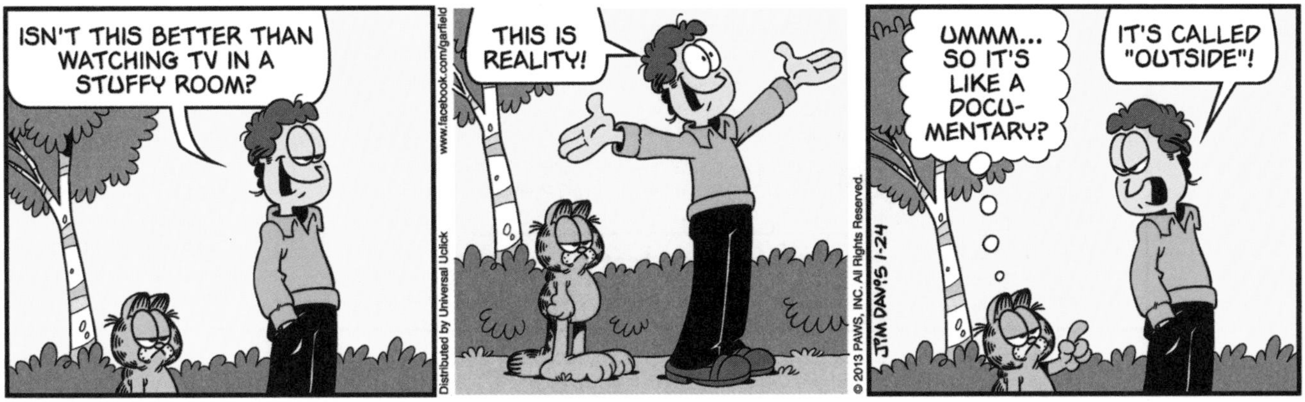
ISN'T THIS BETTER THAN WATCHING TV IN A STUFFY ROOM?
THIS IS REALITY!
UMMM... SO IT'S LIKE A DOCU-MENTARY?
IT'S CALLED "OUTSIDE"!
Distributed by Universal Uclick www.facebook.com/garfield
© 2013 PAWS, INC. All Rights Reserved.
JIM DAVIS 1-24

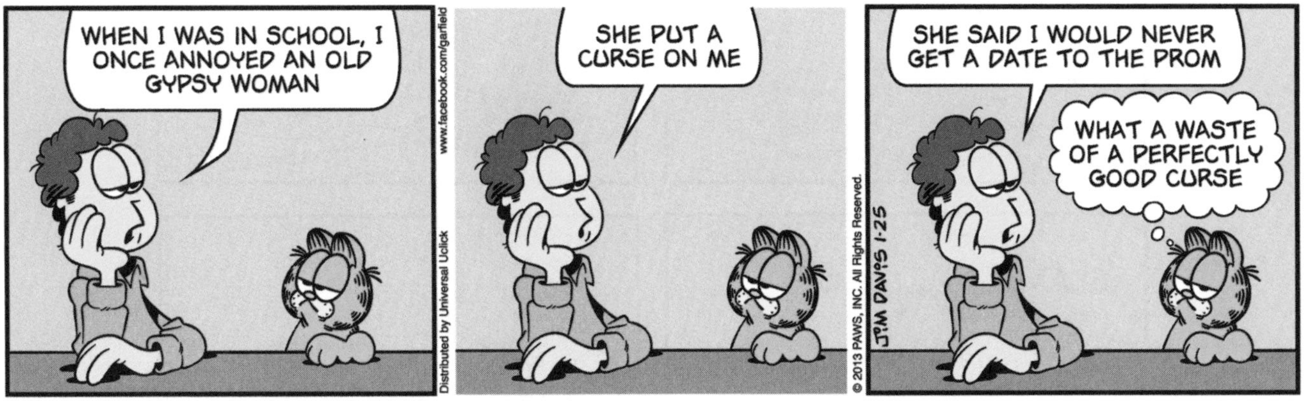
WHEN I WAS IN SCHOOL, I ONCE ANNOYED AN OLD GYPSY WOMAN
SHE PUT A CURSE ON ME
SHE SAID I WOULD NEVER GET A DATE TO THE PROM
WHAT A WASTE OF A PERFECTLY GOOD CURSE
Distributed by Universal Uclick www.facebook.com/garfield
© 2013 PAWS, INC. All Rights Reserved.
JIM DAVIS 1-25

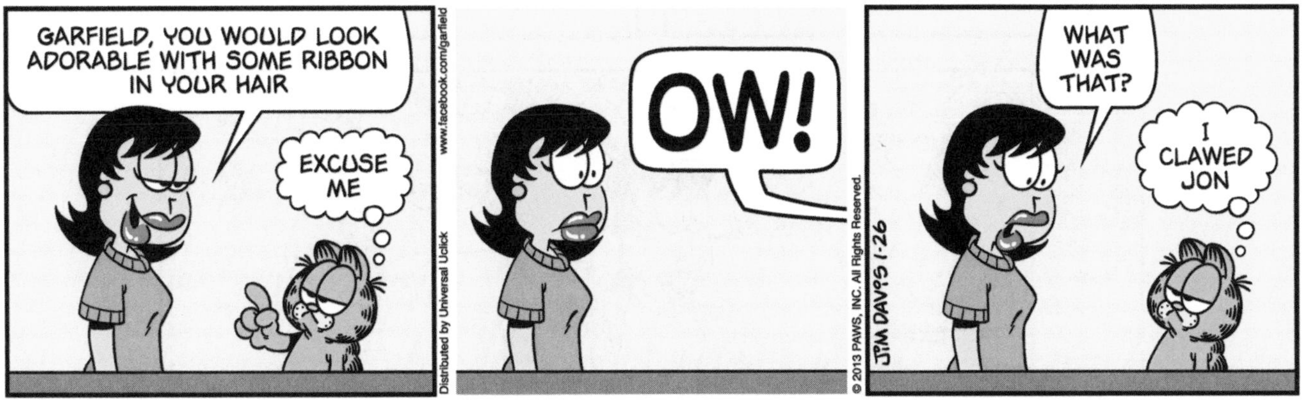
GARFIELD, YOU WOULD LOOK ADORABLE WITH SOME RIBBON IN YOUR HAIR
EXCUSE ME
OW!
WHAT WAS THAT?
I CLAWED JON
Distributed by Universal Uclick www.facebook.com/garfield
© 2013 PAWS, INC. All Rights Reserved.
JIM DAVIS 1-26

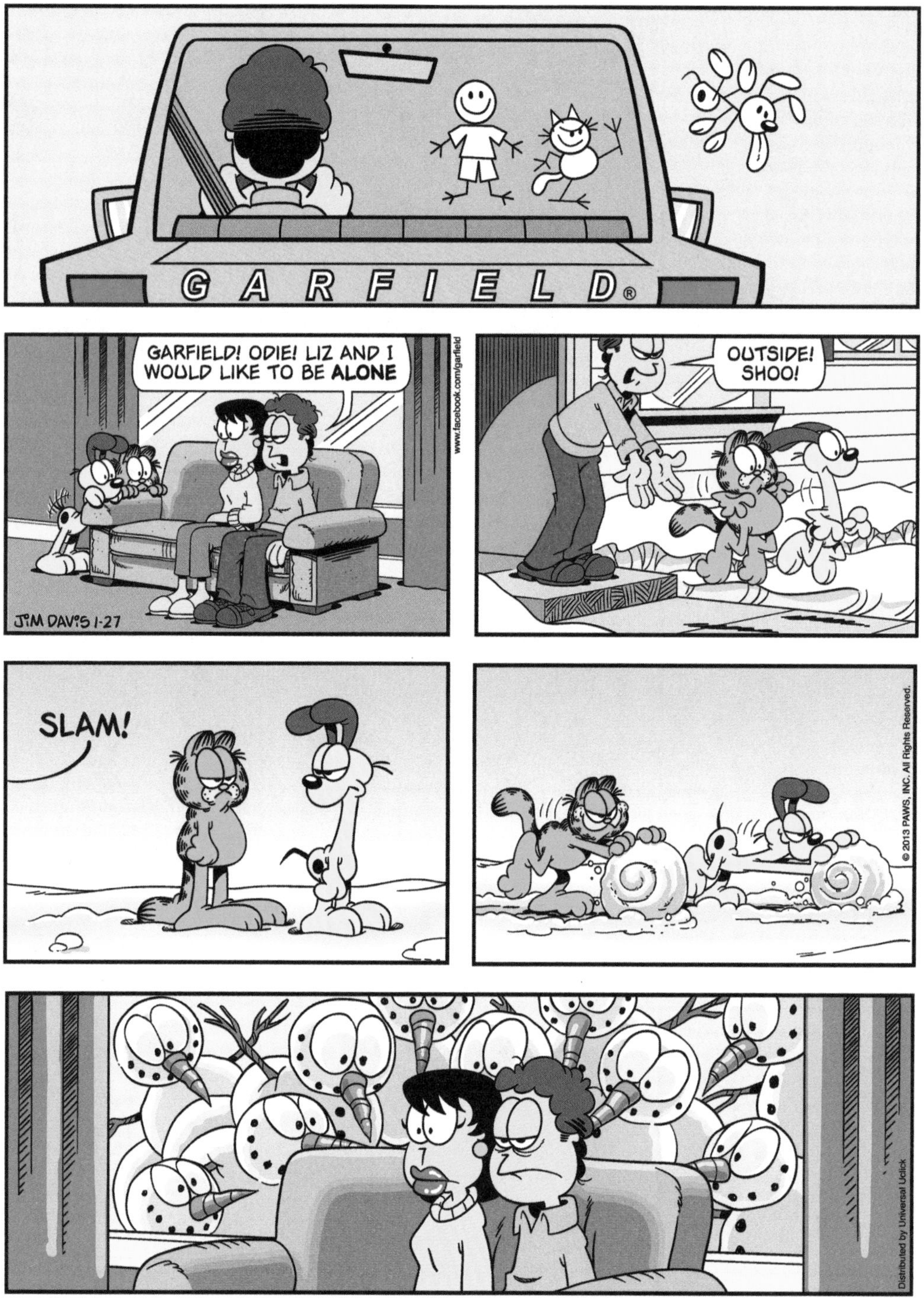
GARFIELD®
GARFIELD! ODIE! LIZ AND I WOULD LIKE TO BE ALONE
www.facebook.com/garfield
JIM DAVIS 1-27
OUTSIDE! SHOO!
SLAM!
© 2013 PAWS, INC. All Rights Reserved.
Distributed by Universal Uclick

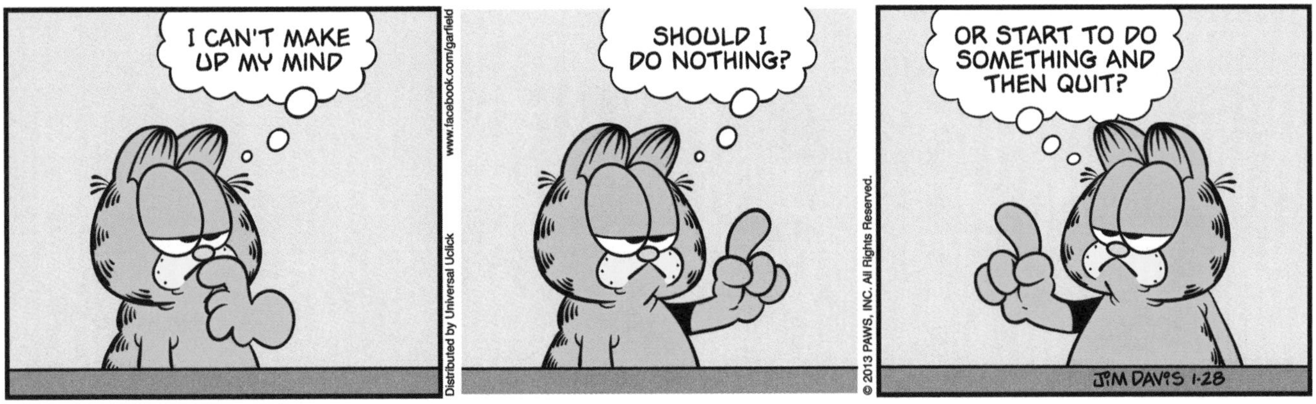
I CAN'T MAKE UP MY MIND
Distributed by Universal Uclick www.facebook.com/garfield
SHOULD I DO NOTHING?
© 2013 PAWS, INC. All Rights Reserved.
OR START TO DO SOMETHING AND THEN QUIT?
JIM DAVIS 1-28

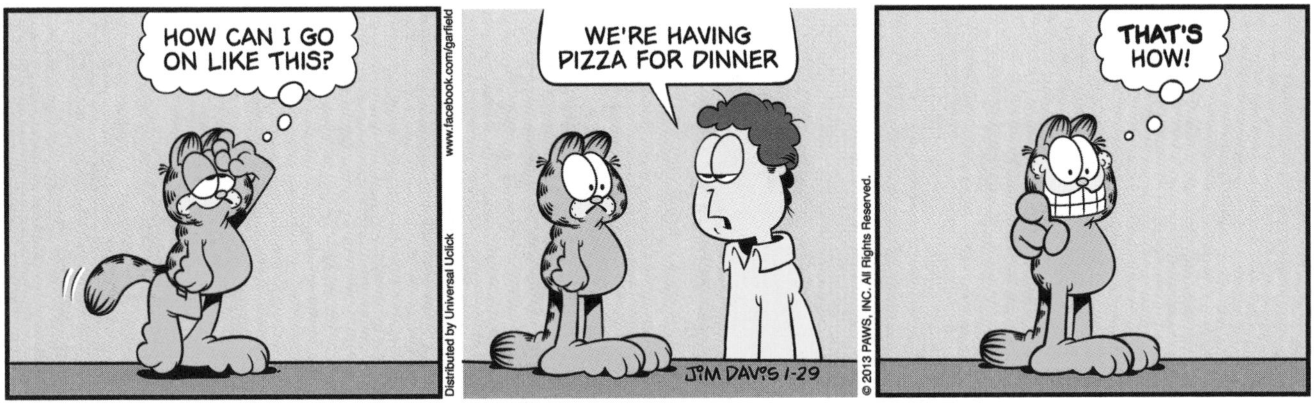
HOW CAN I GO ON LIKE THIS?
Distributed by Universal Uclick www.facebook.com/garfield
WE'RE HAVING PIZZA FOR DINNER
JIM DAVIS 1-29
© 2013 PAWS, INC. All Rights Reserved.
THAT'S HOW!

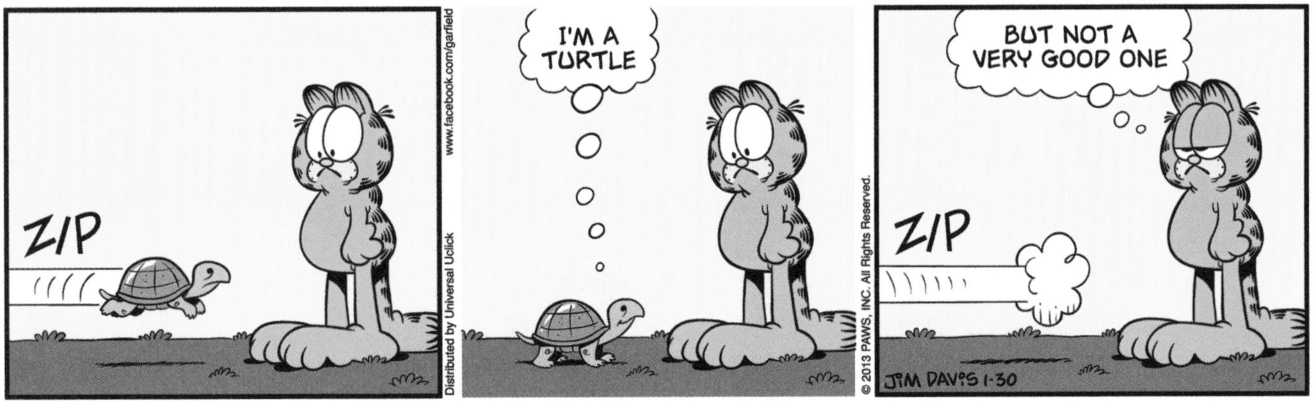
ZIP
Distributed by Universal Uclick www.facebook.com/garfield
I'M A TURTLE
© 2013 PAWS, INC. All Rights Reserved.
ZIP
BUT NOT A VERY GOOD ONE
JIM DAVIS 1-30

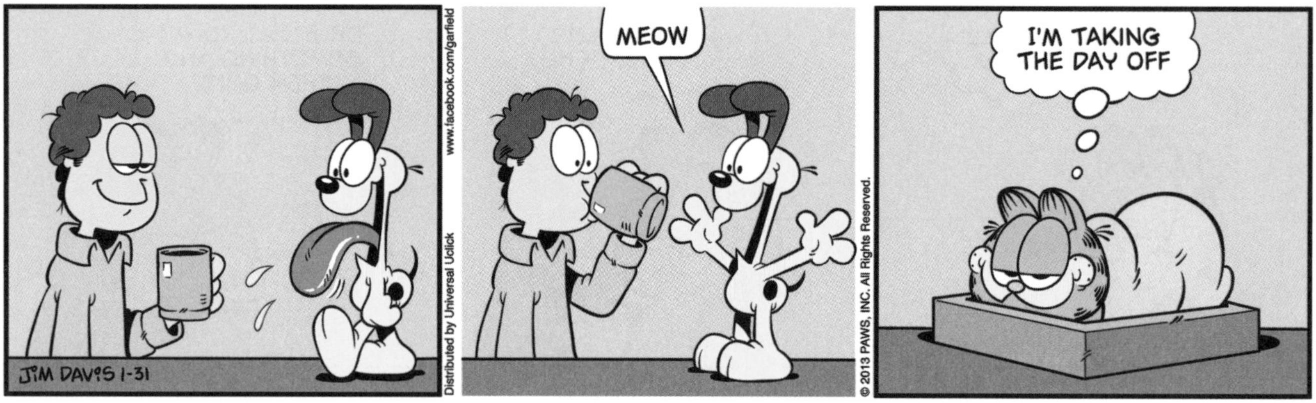
JIM DAVIS 1-31
Distributed by Universal Uclick
www.facebook.com/garfield
MEOW
© 2013 PAWS, INC. All Rights Reserved.
I'M TAKING THE DAY OFF

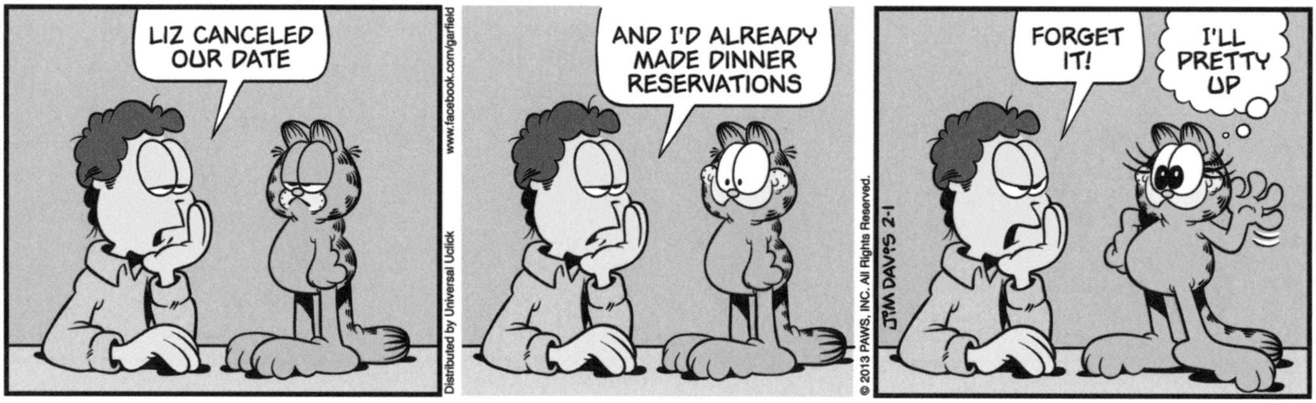
LIZ CANCELED OUR DATE
Distributed by Universal Uclick
www.facebook.com/garfield
AND I'D ALREADY MADE DINNER RESERVATIONS
© 2013 PAWS, INC. All Rights Reserved.
JIM DAVIS 2-1
FORGET IT!
I'LL PRETTY UP

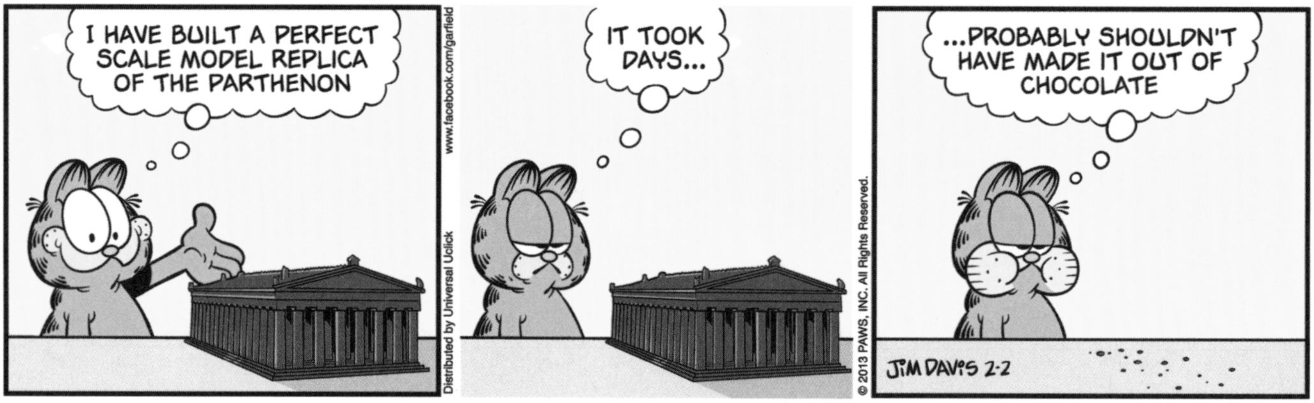
I HAVE BUILT A PERFECT SCALE MODEL REPLICA OF THE PARTHENON
Distributed by Universal Uclick
www.facebook.com/garfield
IT TOOK DAYS...
© 2013 PAWS, INC. All Rights Reserved.
...PROBABLY SHOULDN'T HAVE MADE IT OUT OF CHOCOLATE
JIM DAVIS 2-2

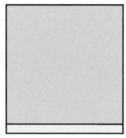

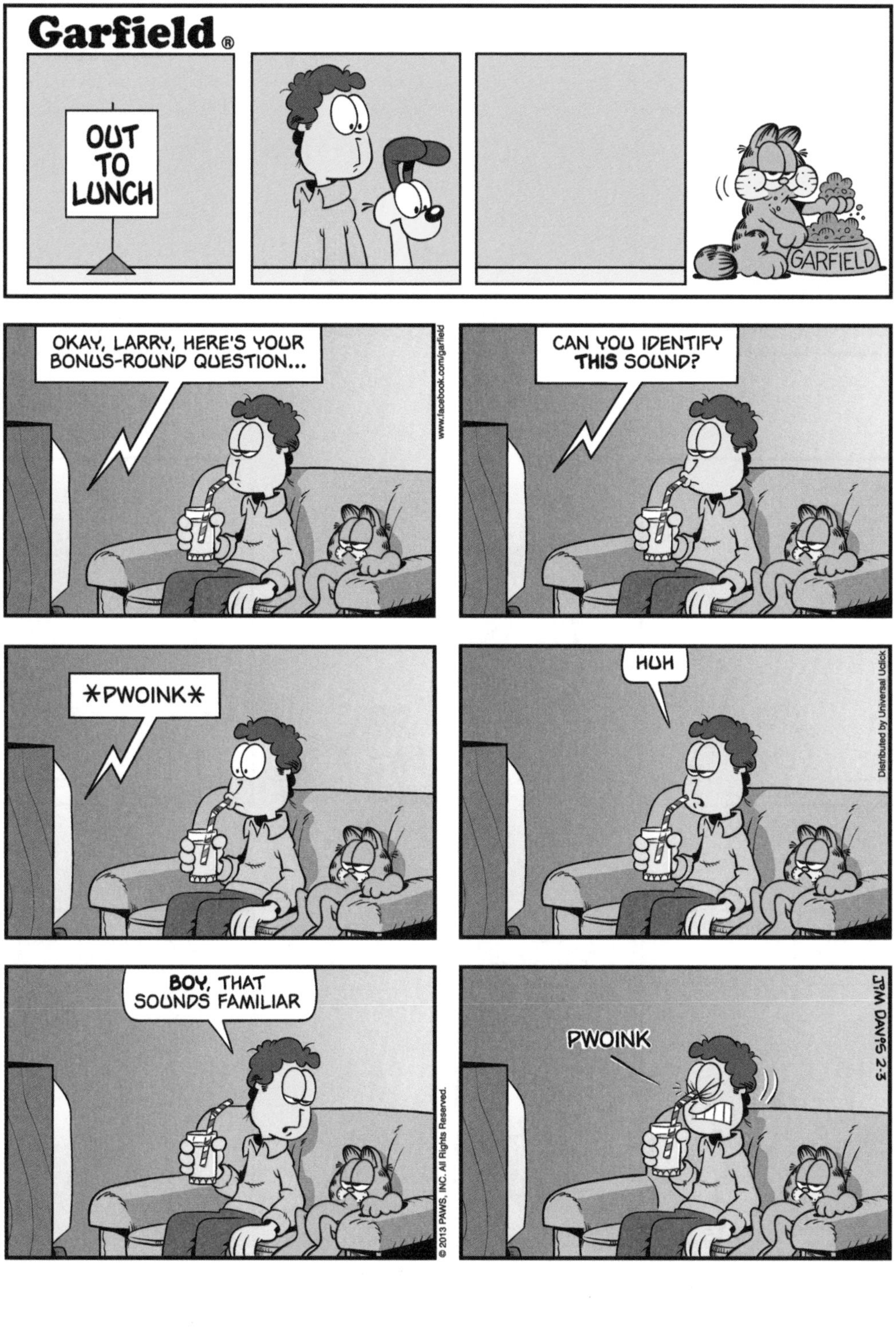
Garfield®
OUT TO LUNCH
GARFIELD
OKAY, LARRY, HERE'S YOUR BONUS-ROUND QUESTION...
www.facebook.com/garfield
CAN YOU IDENTIFY **THIS** SOUND?
PWOINK
HUH
Distributed by Universal Uclick
BOY, THAT SOUNDS FAMILIAR
© 2013 PAWS, INC. All Rights Reserved.
PWOINK
JIM DAVIS 2-3

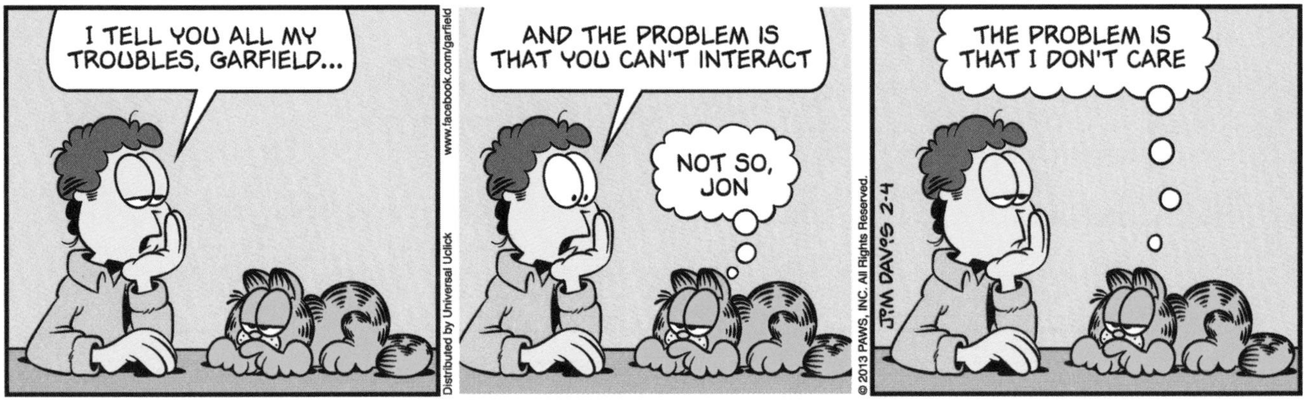
I TELL YOU ALL MY TROUBLES, GARFIELD...
AND THE PROBLEM IS THAT YOU CAN'T INTERACT
NOT SO, JON
THE PROBLEM IS THAT I DON'T CARE
JIM DAVIS 2-4
Distributed by Universal Uclick
www.facebook.com/garfield
© 2013 PAWS, INC. All Rights Reserved.

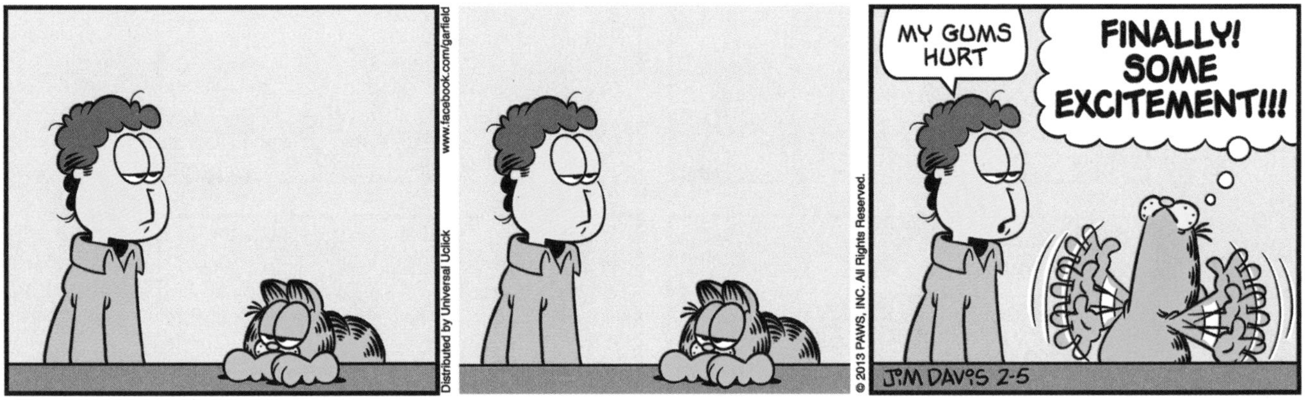
MY GUMS HURT
FINALLY! SOME EXCITEMENT!!!
JIM DAVIS 2-5
Distributed by Universal Uclick
www.facebook.com/garfield
© 2013 PAWS, INC. All Rights Reserved.

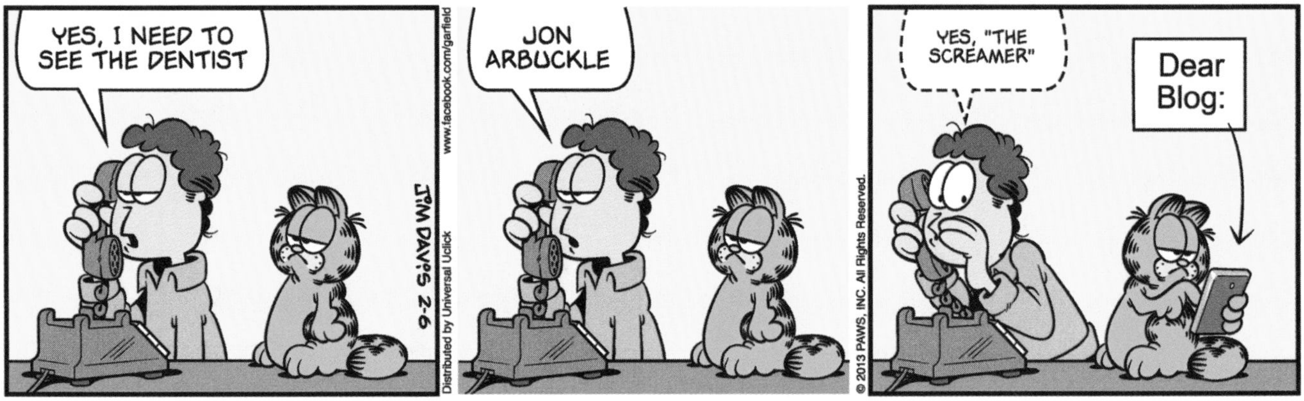
YES, I NEED TO SEE THE DENTIST
JON ARBUCKLE
YES, "THE SCREAMER"
Dear Blog:
JIM DAVIS 2-6
Distributed by Universal Uclick
www.facebook.com/garfield
© 2013 PAWS, INC. All Rights Reserved.

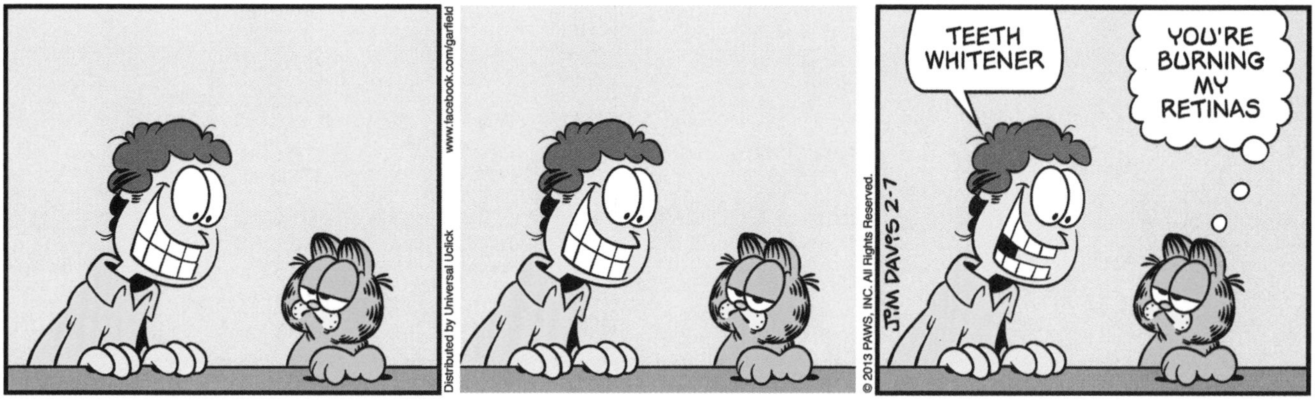
Distributed by Universal Uclick www.facebook.com/garfield
TEETH WHITENER
YOU'RE BURNING MY RETINAS
© 2013 PAWS, INC. All Rights Reserved.
JIM DAVIS 2-7

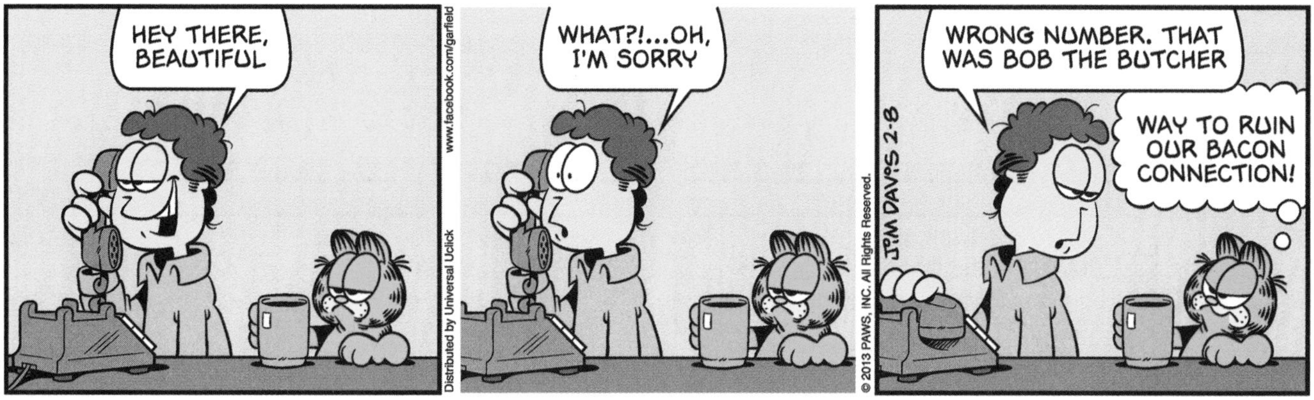
HEY THERE, BEAUTIFUL
Distributed by Universal Uclick www.facebook.com/garfield
WHAT?!...OH, I'M SORRY
© 2013 PAWS, INC. All Rights Reserved.
WRONG NUMBER. THAT WAS BOB THE BUTCHER
WAY TO RUIN OUR BACON CONNECTION!
JIM DAVIS 2-8

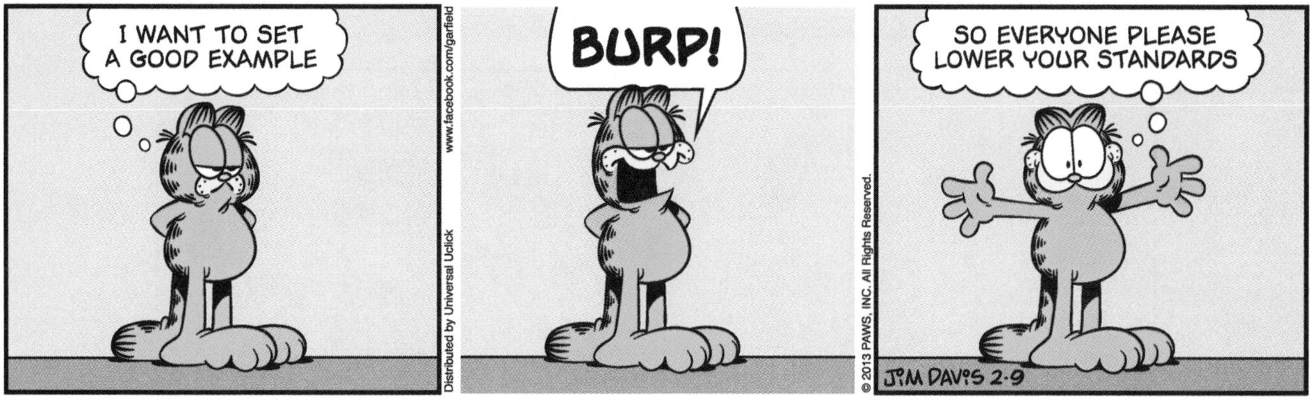
I WANT TO SET A GOOD EXAMPLE
Distributed by Universal Uclick www.facebook.com/garfield
BURP!
© 2013 PAWS, INC. All Rights Reserved.
SO EVERYONE PLEASE LOWER YOUR STANDARDS
JIM DAVIS 2-9

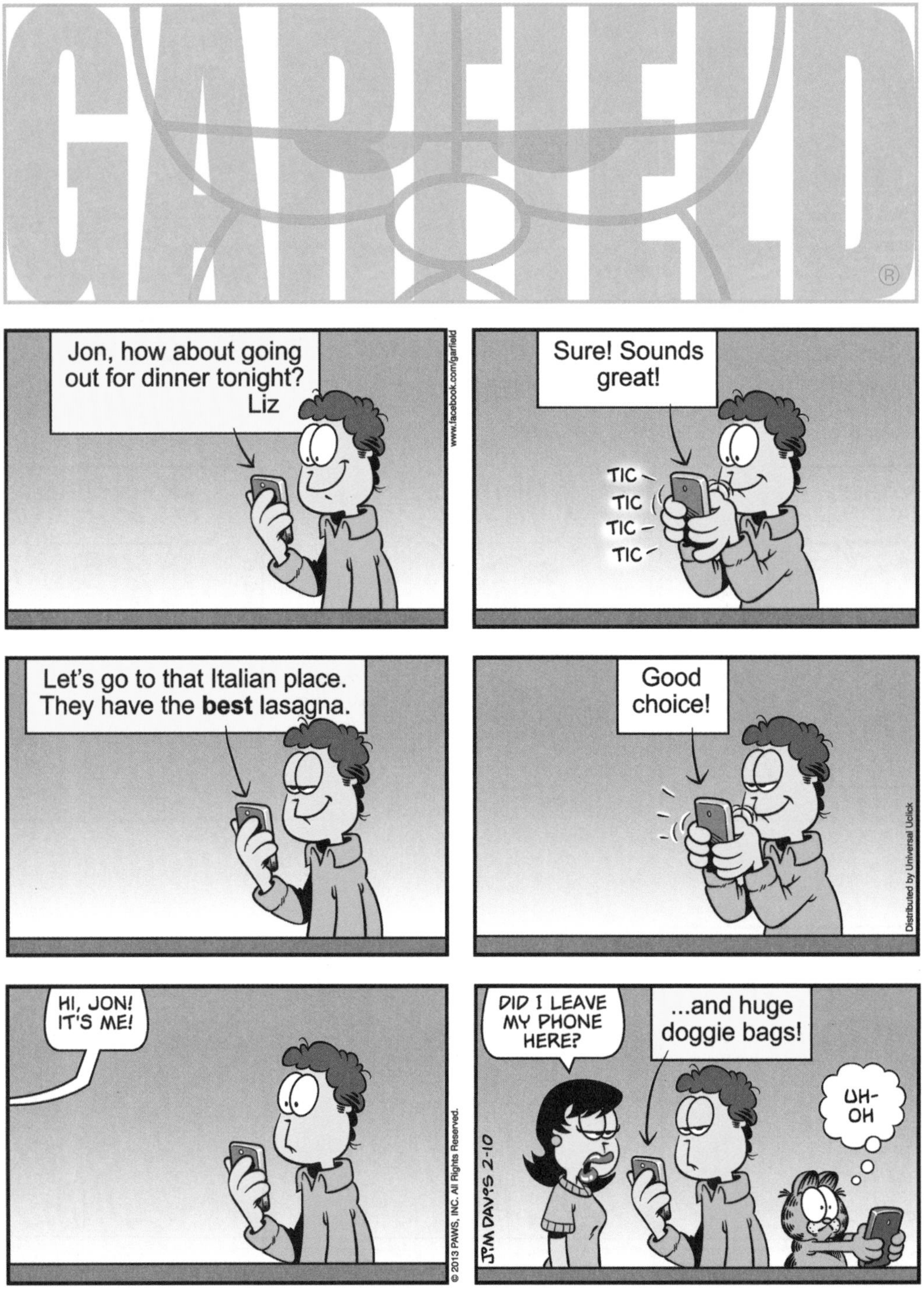
GARFIELD
Jon, how about going out for dinner tonight? Liz
www.facebook.com/garfield
Sure! Sounds great!
TIC TIC TIC TIC
Let's go to that Italian place. They have the **best** lasagna.
Good choice!
Distributed by Universal Uclick
HI, JON! IT'S ME!
© 2013 PAWS, INC. All Rights Reserved.
JIM DAVIS 2-10
DID I LEAVE MY PHONE HERE?
...and huge doggie bags!
UH-OH

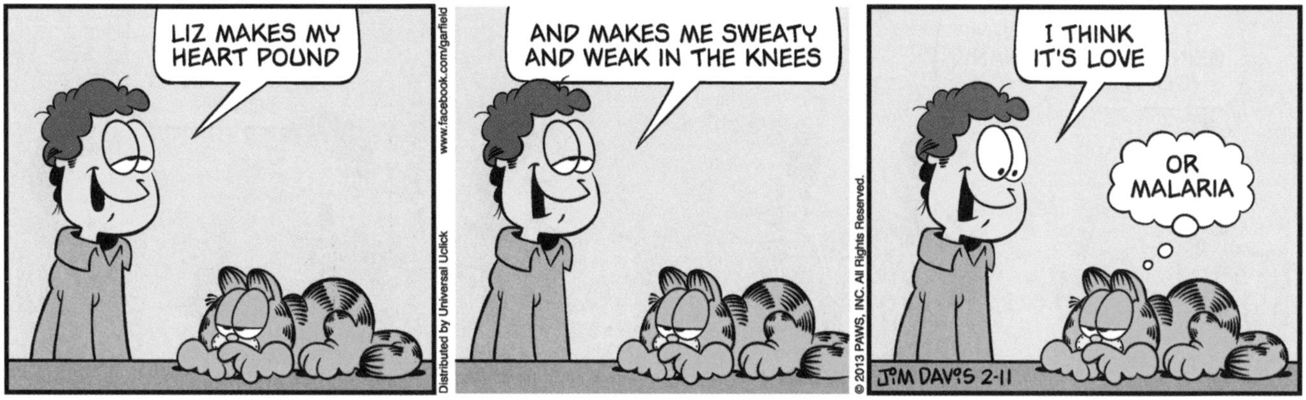
LIZ MAKES MY HEART POUND
AND MAKES ME SWEATY AND WEAK IN THE KNEES
I THINK IT'S LOVE
OR MALARIA
JIM DAVIS 2-11
Distributed by Universal Uclick
www.facebook.com/garfield
© 2013 PAWS, INC. All Rights Reserved.

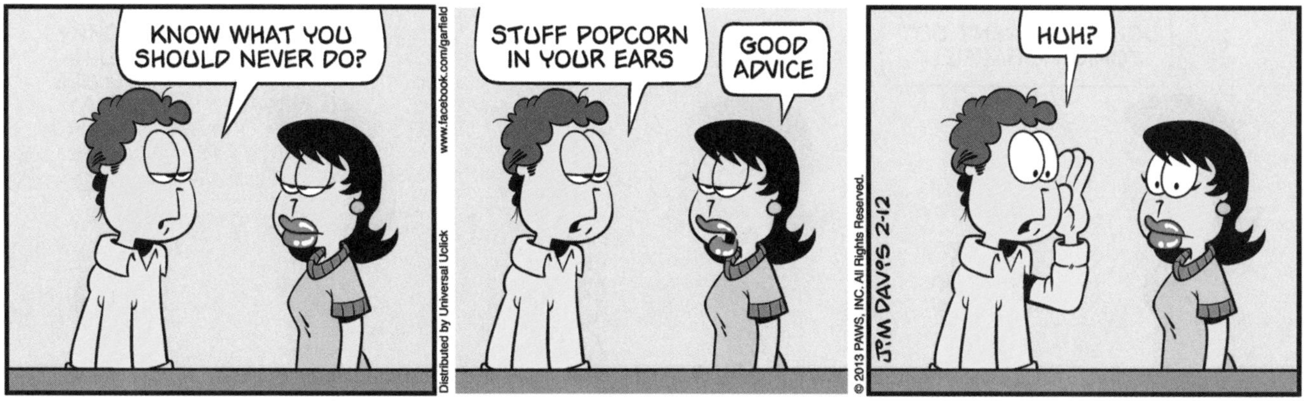
KNOW WHAT YOU SHOULD NEVER DO?
STUFF POPCORN IN YOUR EARS
GOOD ADVICE
HUH?
JIM DAVIS 2-12
Distributed by Universal Uclick
www.facebook.com/garfield
© 2013 PAWS, INC. All Rights Reserved.

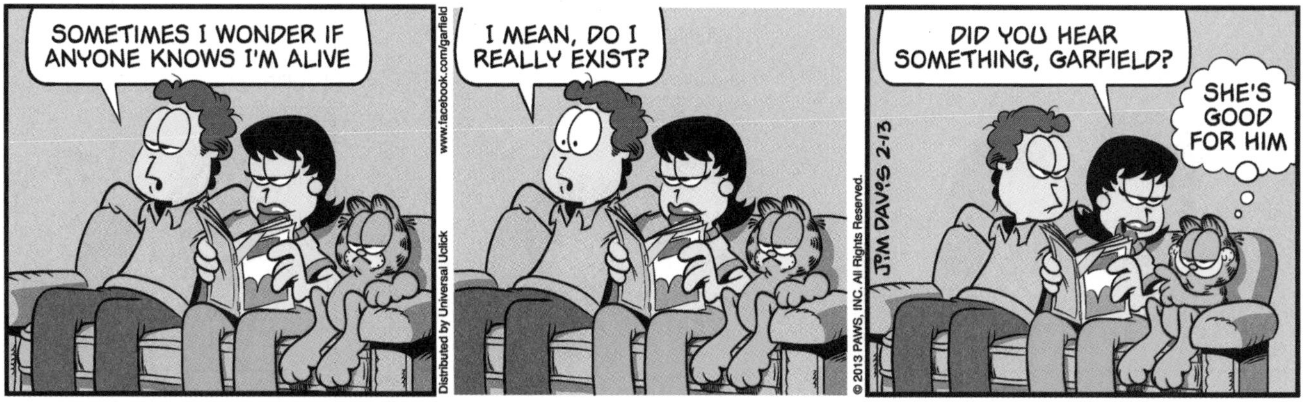
SOMETIMES I WONDER IF ANYONE KNOWS I'M ALIVE
I MEAN, DO I REALLY EXIST?
DID YOU HEAR SOMETHING, GARFIELD?
SHE'S GOOD FOR HIM
JIM DAVIS 2-13
Distributed by Universal Uclick
www.facebook.com/garfield
© 2013 PAWS, INC. All Rights Reserved.

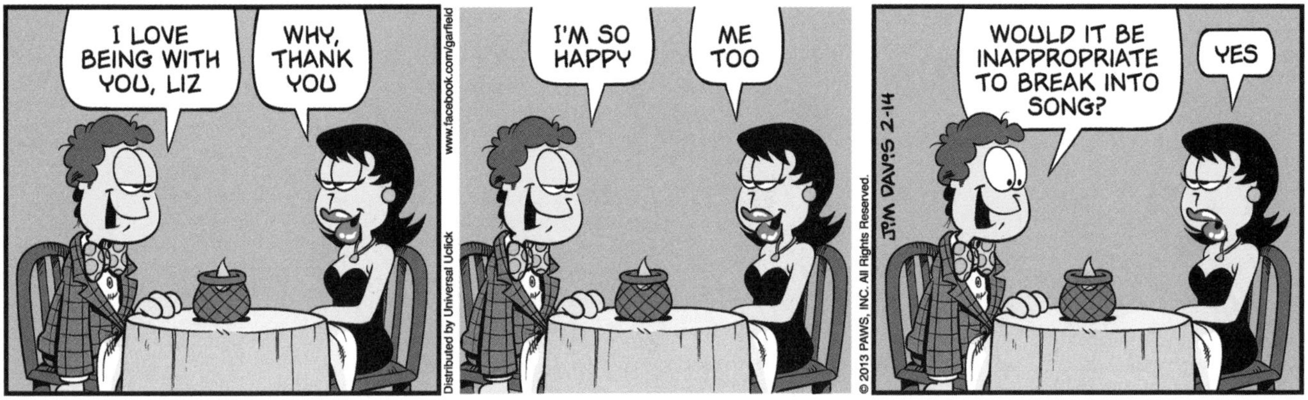
I LOVE BEING WITH YOU, LIZ
WHY, THANK YOU
I'M SO HAPPY
ME TOO
WOULD IT BE INAPPROPRIATE TO BREAK INTO SONG?
YES
JIM DAVIS 2-14
Distributed by Universal Uclick
www.facebook.com/garfield
© 2013 PAWS, INC. All Rights Reserved.

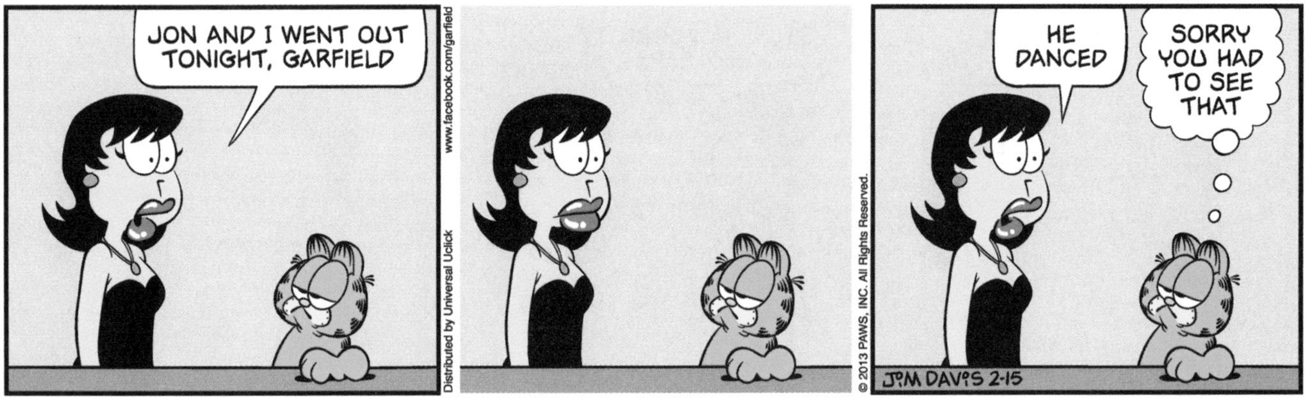
JON AND I WENT OUT TONIGHT, GARFIELD
HE DANCED
SORRY YOU HAD TO SEE THAT
JIM DAVIS 2-15
Distributed by Universal Uclick
www.facebook.com/garfield
© 2013 PAWS, INC. All Rights Reserved.

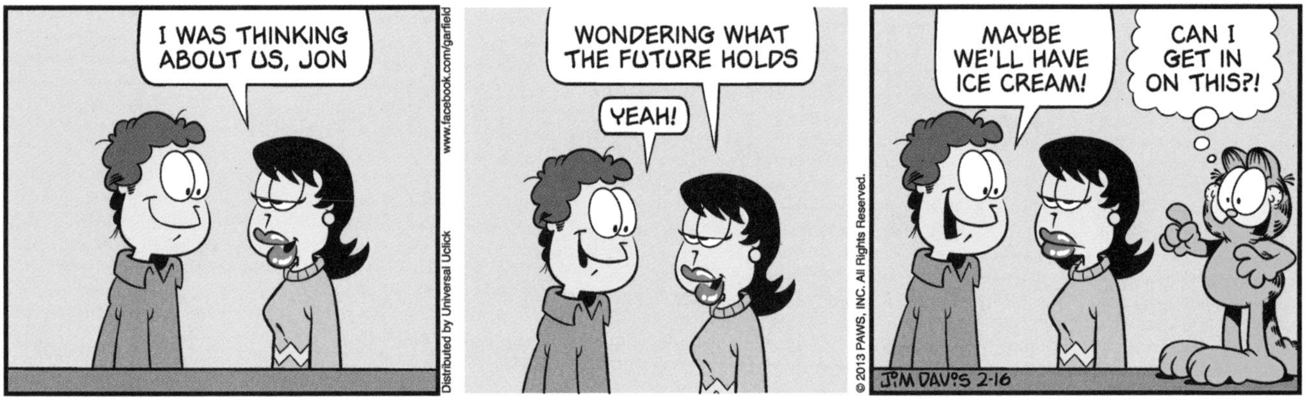
I WAS THINKING ABOUT US, JON
WONDERING WHAT THE FUTURE HOLDS
YEAH!
MAYBE WE'LL HAVE ICE CREAM!
CAN I GET IN ON THIS?!
JIM DAVIS 2-16
Distributed by Universal Uclick
www.facebook.com/garfield
© 2013 PAWS, INC. All Rights Reserved.

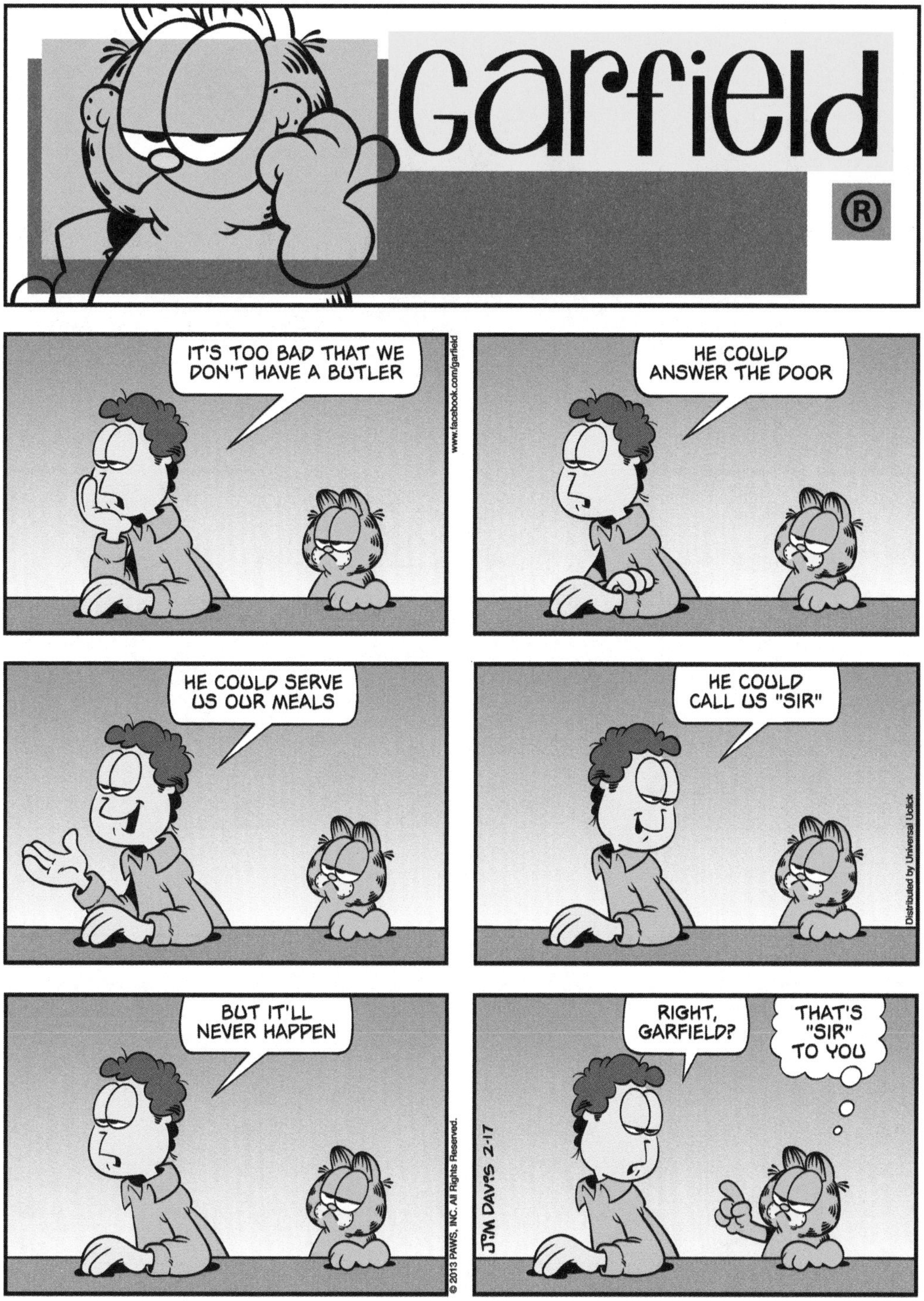
Garfield ®
IT'S TOO BAD THAT WE DON'T HAVE A BUTLER
www.facebook.com/garfield
HE COULD ANSWER THE DOOR
HE COULD SERVE US OUR MEALS
HE COULD CALL US "SIR"
Distributed by Universal Uclick
BUT IT'LL NEVER HAPPEN
© 2013 PAWS, INC. All Rights Reserved.
JPM DAVPS 2-17
RIGHT, GARFIELD?
THAT'S "SIR" TO YOU

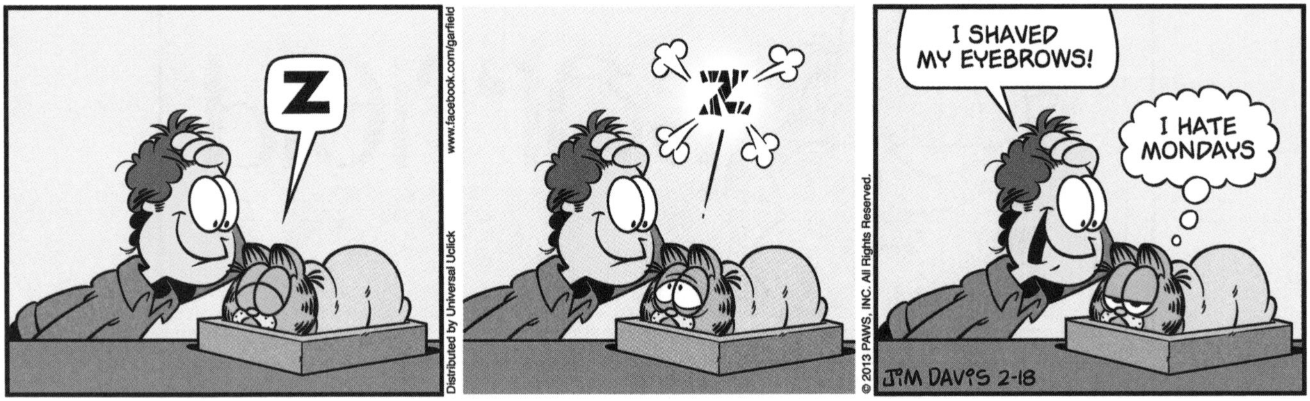
Z
Z
I SHAVED MY EYEBROWS!
I HATE MONDAYS
JIM DAVIS 2-18
www.facebook.com/garfield
Distributed by Universal Uclick
© 2013 PAWS, INC. All Rights Reserved.

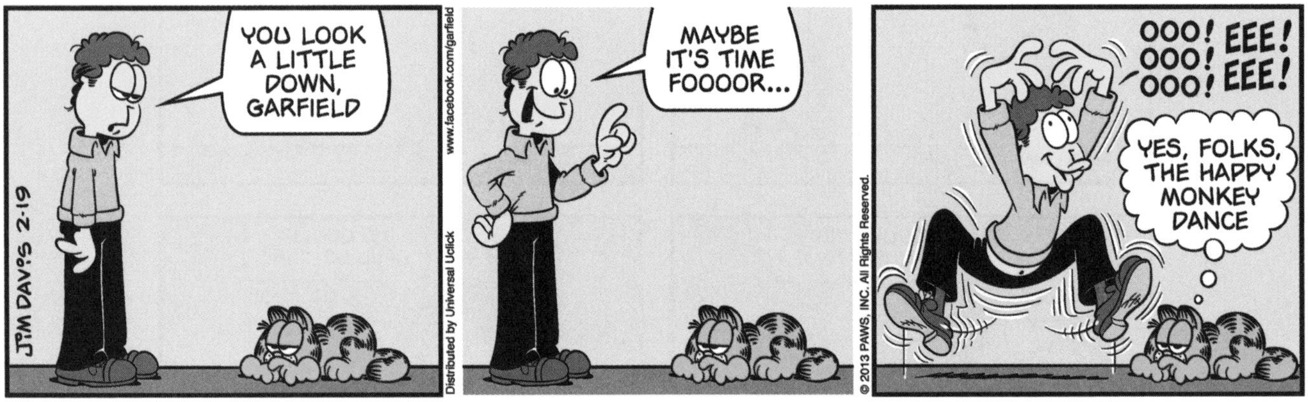
YOU LOOK A LITTLE DOWN, GARFIELD
MAYBE IT'S TIME FOOOOR...
OOO! EEE! OOO! EEE! OOO!
YES, FOLKS, THE HAPPY MONKEY DANCE
JIM DAVIS 2-19
www.facebook.com/garfield
Distributed by Universal Uclick
© 2013 PAWS, INC. All Rights Reserved.

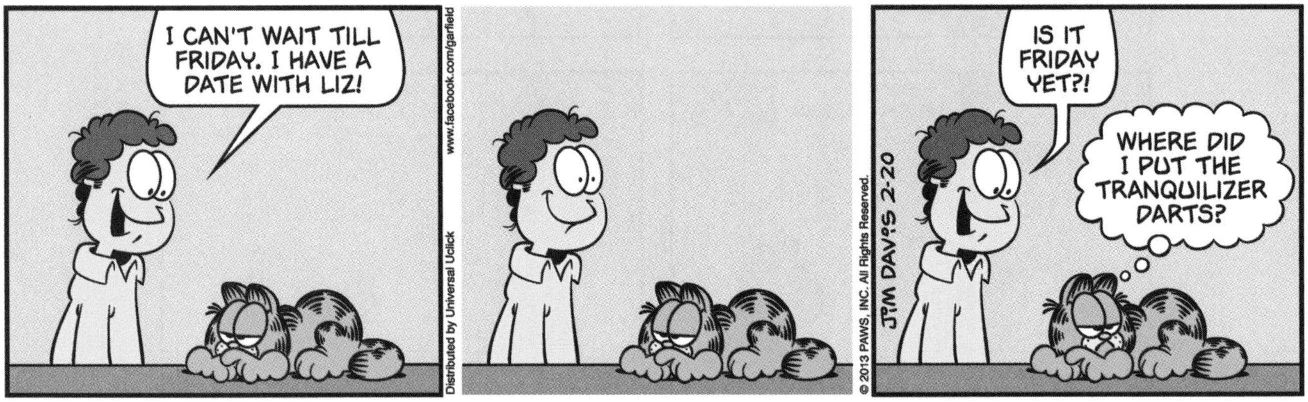
I CAN'T WAIT TILL FRIDAY. I HAVE A DATE WITH LIZ!
IS IT FRIDAY YET?!
WHERE DID I PUT THE TRANQUILIZER DARTS?
JIM DAVIS 2-20
www.facebook.com/garfield
Distributed by Universal Uclick
© 2013 PAWS, INC. All Rights Reserved.

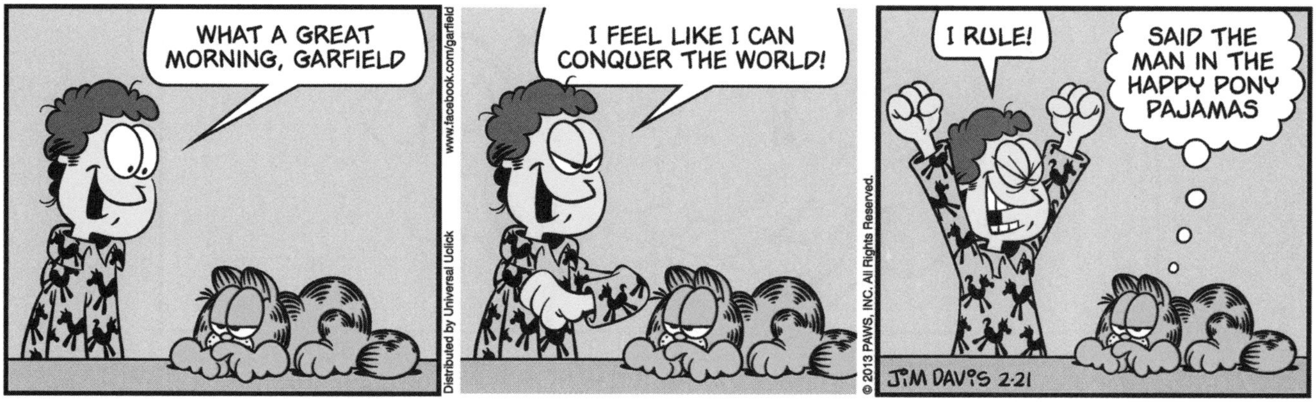
WHAT A GREAT MORNING, GARFIELD
I FEEL LIKE I CAN CONQUER THE WORLD!
I RULE!
SAID THE MAN IN THE HAPPY PONY PAJAMAS
JIM DAVIS 2-21
Distributed by Universal Uclick www.facebook.com/garfield
© 2013 PAWS, INC. All Rights Reserved.

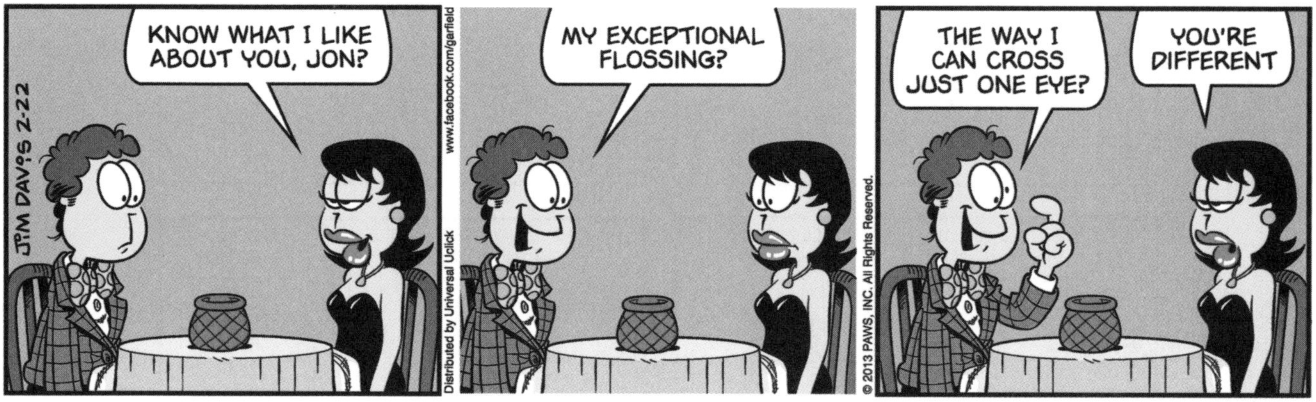
KNOW WHAT I LIKE ABOUT YOU, JON?
MY EXCEPTIONAL FLOSSING?
THE WAY I CAN CROSS JUST ONE EYE?
YOU'RE DIFFERENT
JIM DAVIS 2-22
Distributed by Universal Uclick www.facebook.com/garfield
© 2013 PAWS, INC. All Rights Reserved.

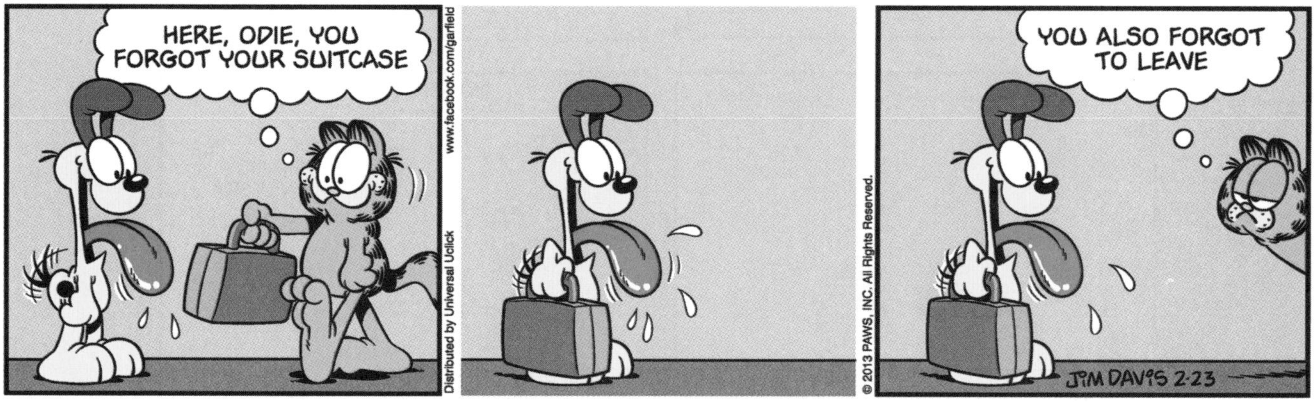
HERE, ODIE, YOU FORGOT YOUR SUITCASE
YOU ALSO FORGOT TO LEAVE
JIM DAVIS 2-23
Distributed by Universal Uclick www.facebook.com/garfield
© 2013 PAWS, INC. All Rights Reserved.

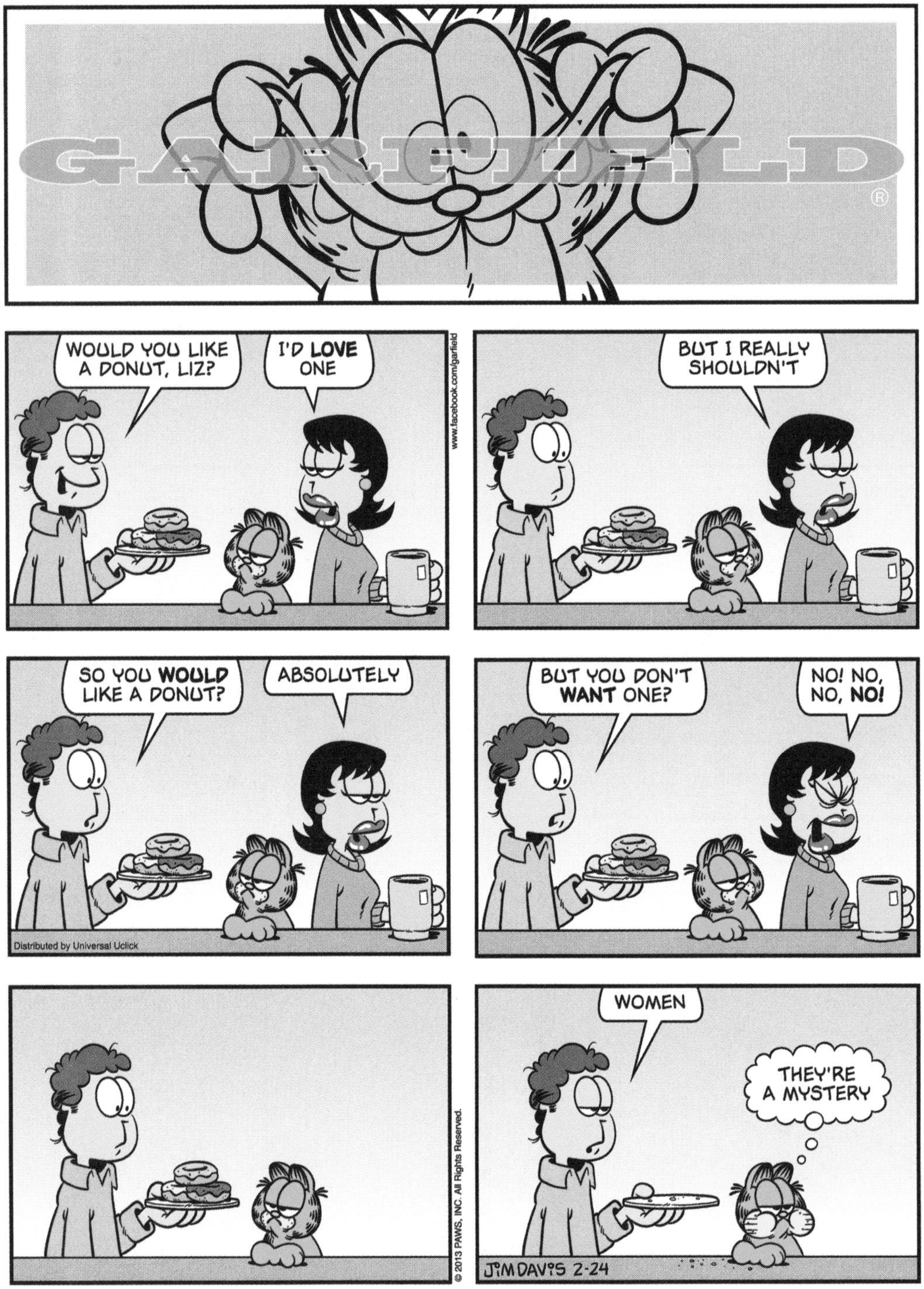
GARFIELD®
WOULD YOU LIKE A DONUT, LIZ?
I'D LOVE ONE
www.facebook.com/garfield
BUT I REALLY SHOULDN'T
SO YOU WOULD LIKE A DONUT?
ABSOLUTELY
Distributed by Universal Uclick
BUT YOU DON'T WANT ONE?
NO! NO, NO, NO!
© 2013 PAWS, INC. All Rights Reserved.
WOMEN
THEY'RE A MYSTERY
JIM DAVIS 2-24

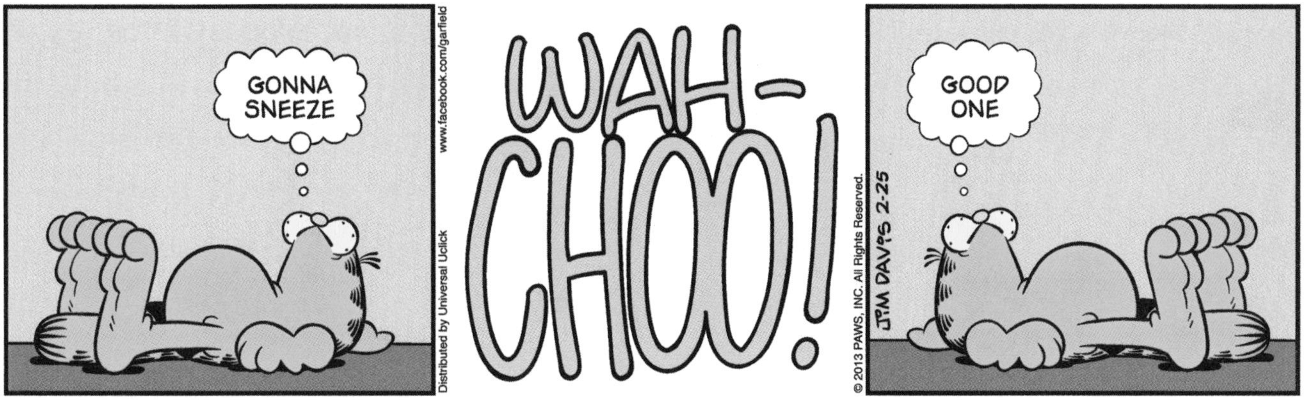
GONNA SNEEZE
WAH-CHOO!
GOOD ONE
JIM DAVIS 2-25
Distributed by Universal Uclick www.facebook.com/garfield
© 2013 PAWS, INC. All Rights Reserved.

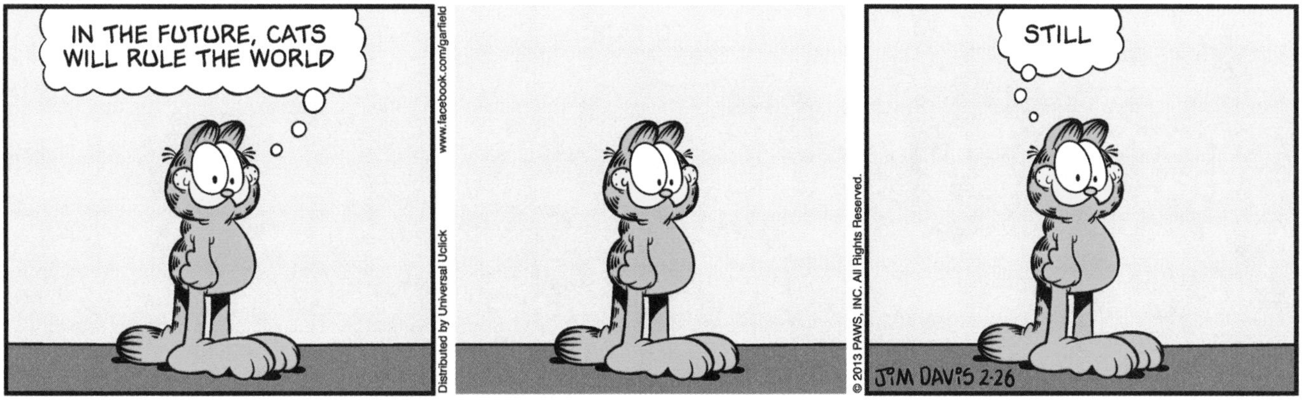
IN THE FUTURE, CATS WILL RULE THE WORLD
STILL
JIM DAVIS 2-26
Distributed by Universal Uclick www.facebook.com/garfield
© 2013 PAWS, INC. All Rights Reserved.

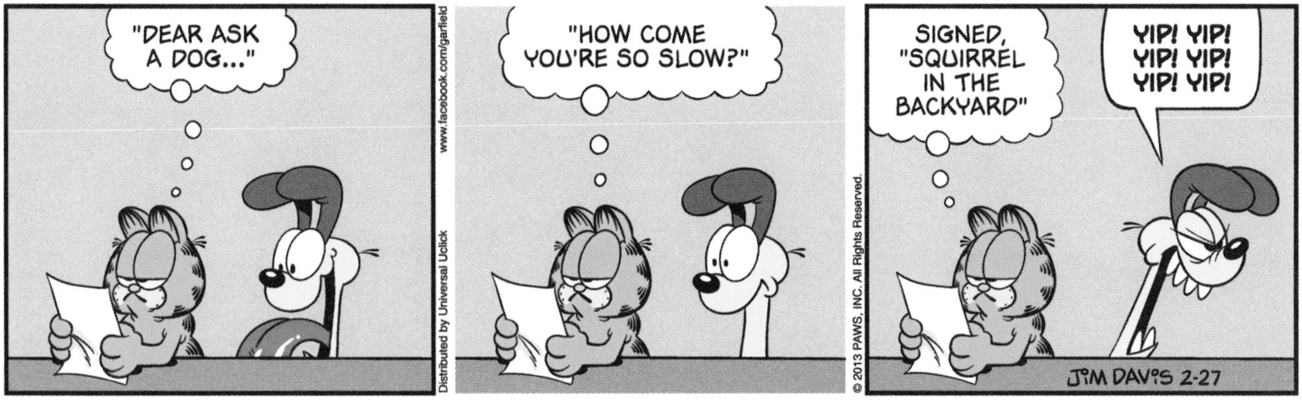
"DEAR ASK A DOG..."
"HOW COME YOU'RE SO SLOW?"
SIGNED, "SQUIRREL IN THE BACKYARD"
YIP! YIP! YIP! YIP! YIP! YIP!
JIM DAVIS 2-27
Distributed by Universal Uclick www.facebook.com/garfield
© 2013 PAWS, INC. All Rights Reserved.

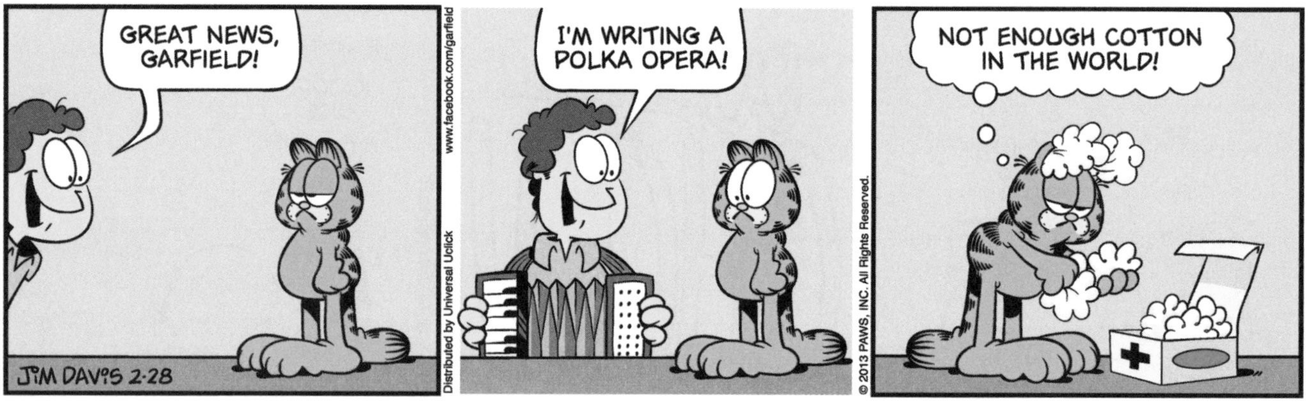
GREAT NEWS, GARFIELD!
JIM DAVIS 2-28
Distributed by Universal Uclick www.facebook.com/garfield
I'M WRITING A POLKA OPERA!
© 2013 PAWS, INC. All Rights Reserved.
NOT ENOUGH COTTON IN THE WORLD!

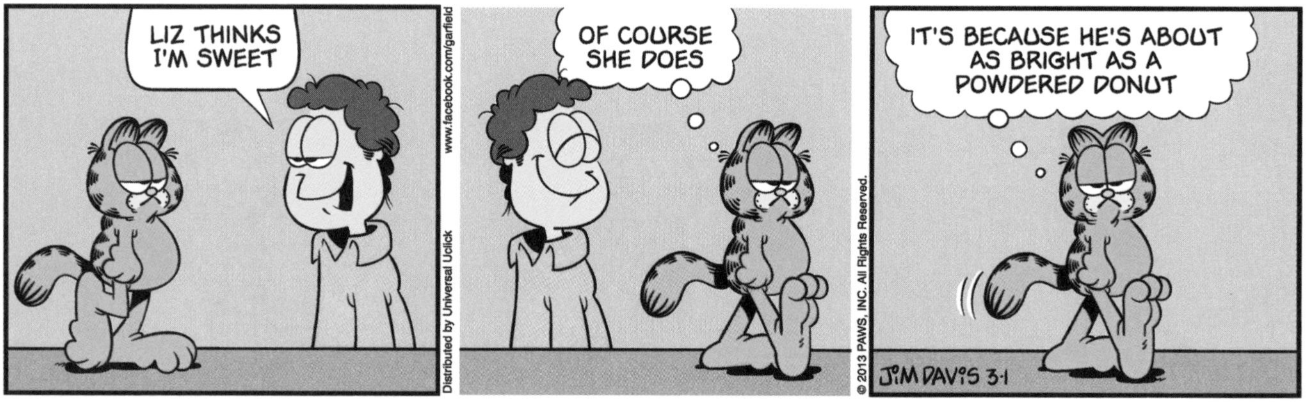
LIZ THINKS I'M SWEET
Distributed by Universal Uclick www.facebook.com/garfield
OF COURSE SHE DOES
© 2013 PAWS, INC. All Rights Reserved.
IT'S BECAUSE HE'S ABOUT AS BRIGHT AS A POWDERED DONUT
JIM DAVIS 3-1

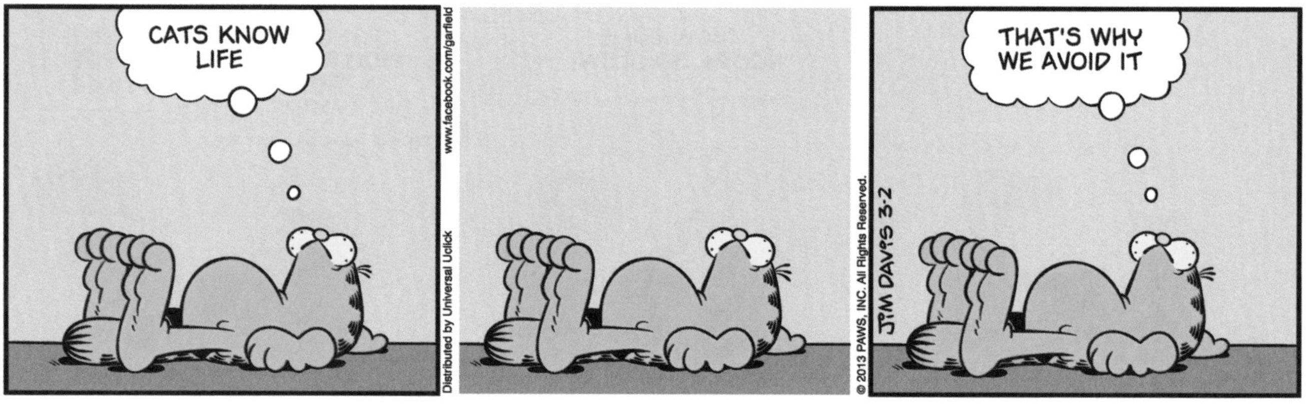
CATS KNOW LIFE
Distributed by Universal Uclick www.facebook.com/garfield
© 2013 PAWS, INC. All Rights Reserved.
JIM DAVIS 3-2
THAT'S WHY WE AVOID IT

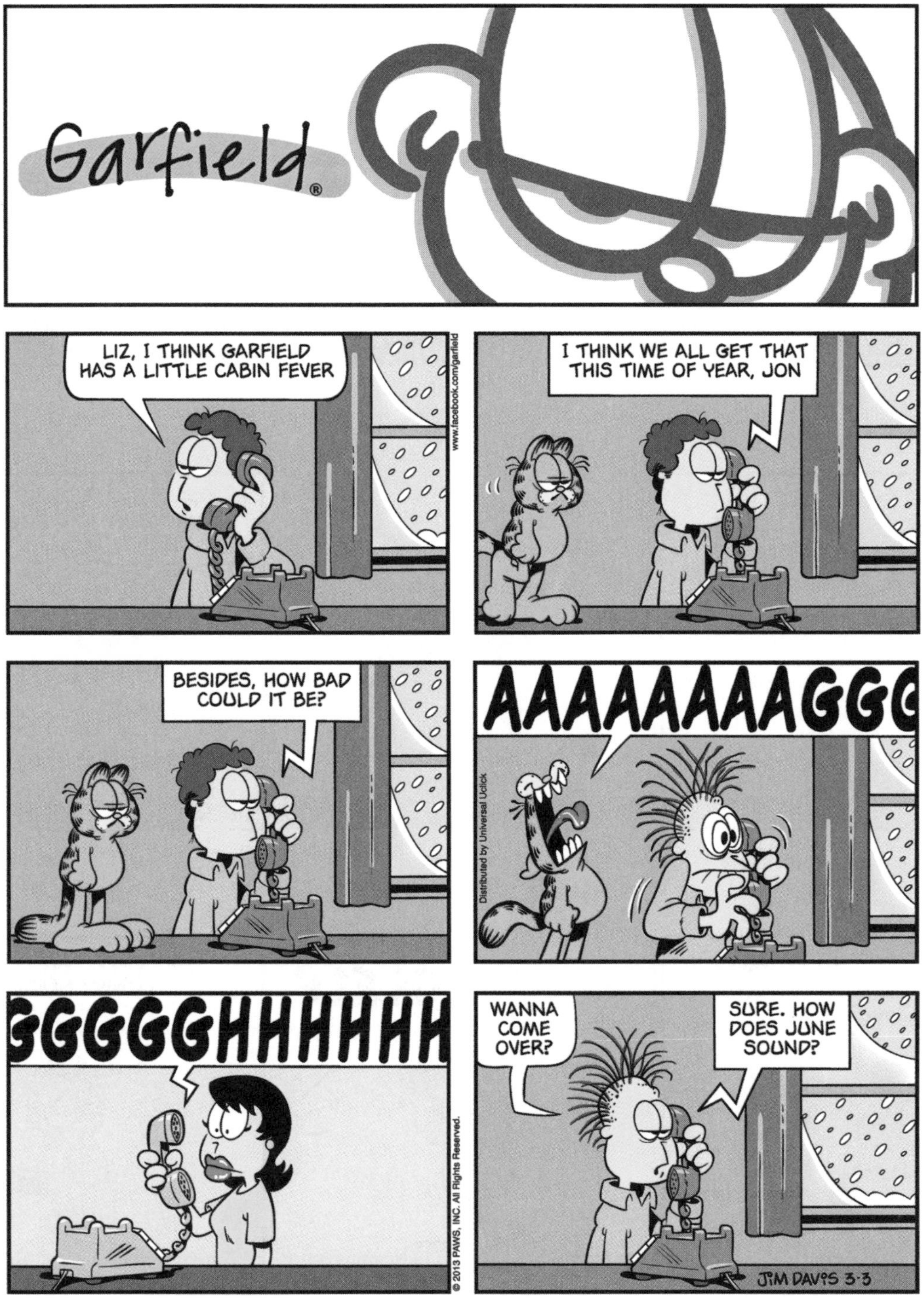
Garfield®
www.facebook.com/garfield
LIZ, I THINK GARFIELD HAS A LITTLE CABIN FEVER
I THINK WE ALL GET THAT THIS TIME OF YEAR, JON
BESIDES, HOW BAD COULD IT BE?
Distributed by Universal Uclick
AAAAAAAAGGG
GGGGGHHHHHH
© 2013 PAWS, INC. All Rights Reserved.
WANNA COME OVER?
SURE. HOW DOES JUNE SOUND?
JIM DAVIS 3-3

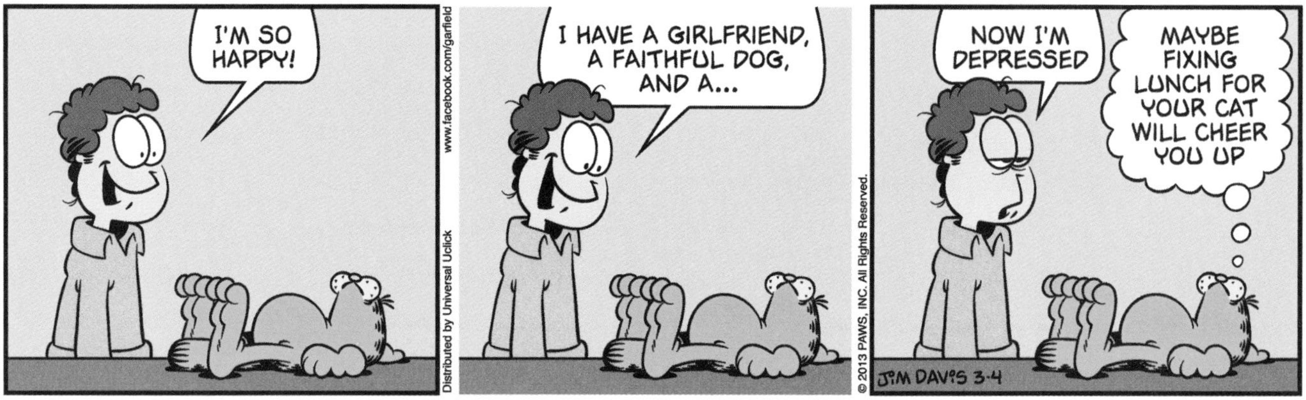
I'M SO HAPPY!
I HAVE A GIRLFRIEND, A FAITHFUL DOG, AND A...
NOW I'M DEPRESSED
MAYBE FIXING LUNCH FOR YOUR CAT WILL CHEER YOU UP
Distributed by Universal Uclick www.facebook.com/garfield
© 2013 PAWS, INC. All Rights Reserved.
JIM DAVIS 3-4

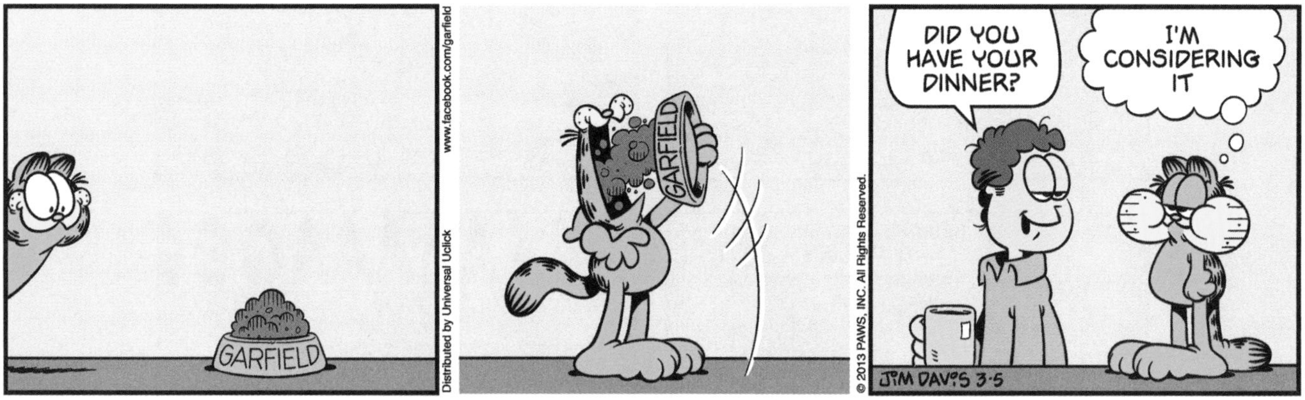
GARFIELD
GARFIELD
DID YOU HAVE YOUR DINNER?
I'M CONSIDERING IT
Distributed by Universal Uclick www.facebook.com/garfield
© 2013 PAWS, INC. All Rights Reserved.
JIM DAVIS 3-5

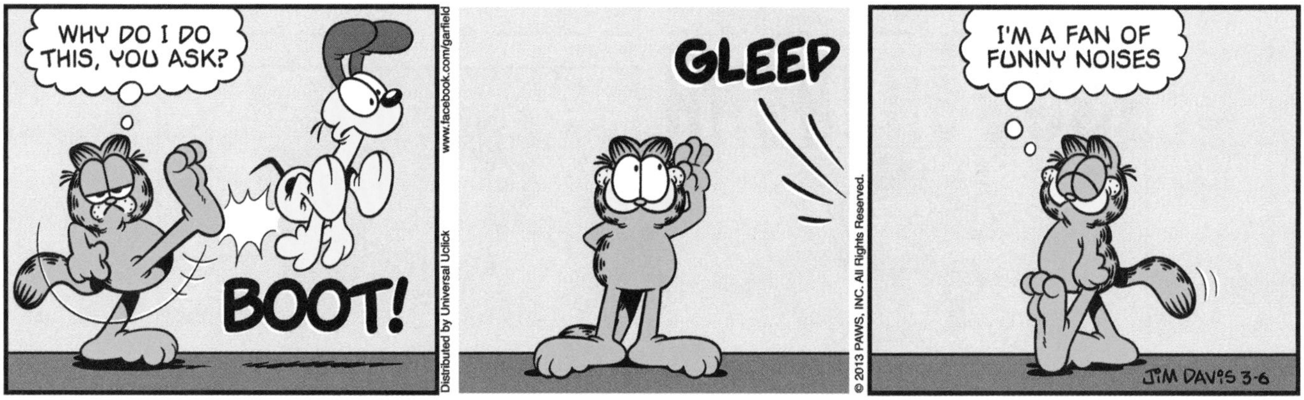
WHY DO I DO THIS, YOU ASK?
BOOT!
GLEEP
I'M A FAN OF FUNNY NOISES
Distributed by Universal Uclick www.facebook.com/garfield
© 2013 PAWS, INC. All Rights Reserved.
JIM DAVIS 3-6

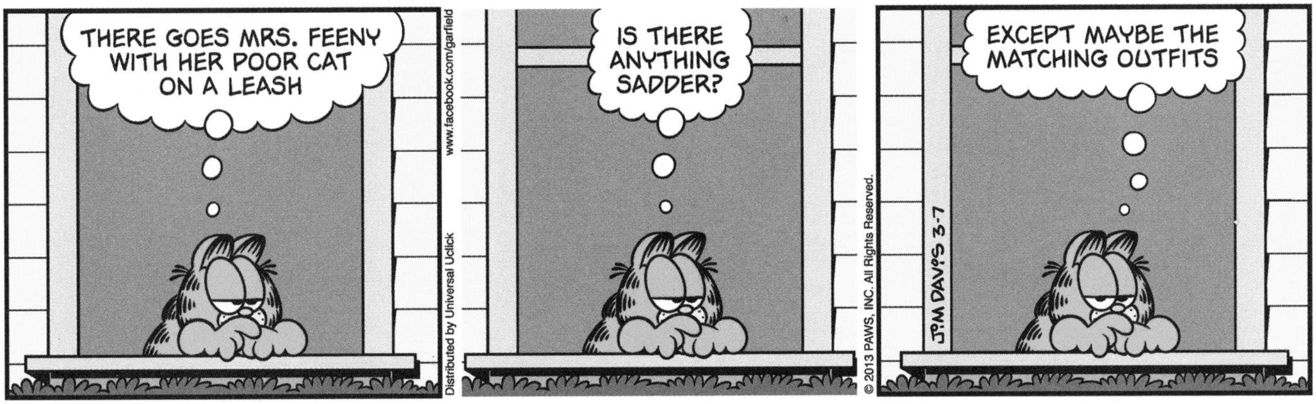

THERE GOES MRS. FEENY WITH HER POOR CAT ON A LEASH
IS THERE ANYTHING SADDER?
EXCEPT MAYBE THE MATCHING OUTFITS
JIM DAVIS 3-7
Distributed by Universal Uclick www.facebook.com/garfield
© 2013 PAWS, INC. All Rights Reserved.

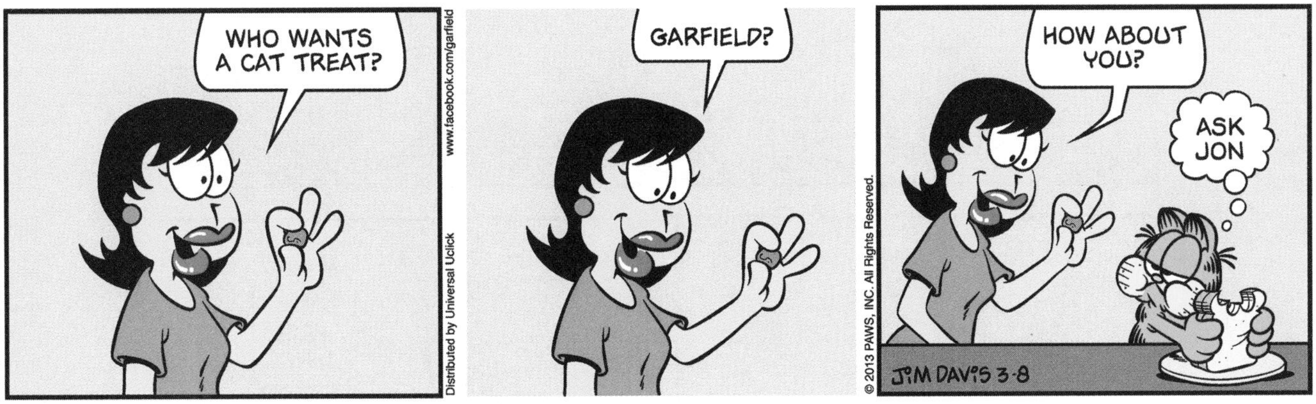

WHO WANTS A CAT TREAT?
GARFIELD?
HOW ABOUT YOU?
ASK JON
JIM DAVIS 3-8
Distributed by Universal Uclick www.facebook.com/garfield
© 2013 PAWS, INC. All Rights Reserved.

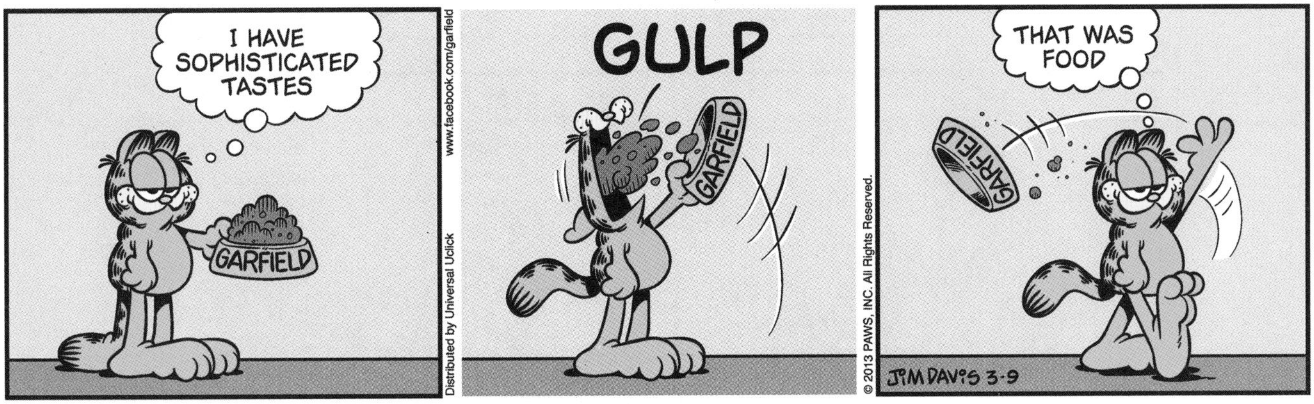

I HAVE SOPHISTICATED TASTES
GARFIELD
GULP
GARFIELD
THAT WAS FOOD
GARFIELD
JIM DAVIS 3-9
Distributed by Universal Uclick www.facebook.com/garfield
© 2013 PAWS, INC. All Rights Reserved.

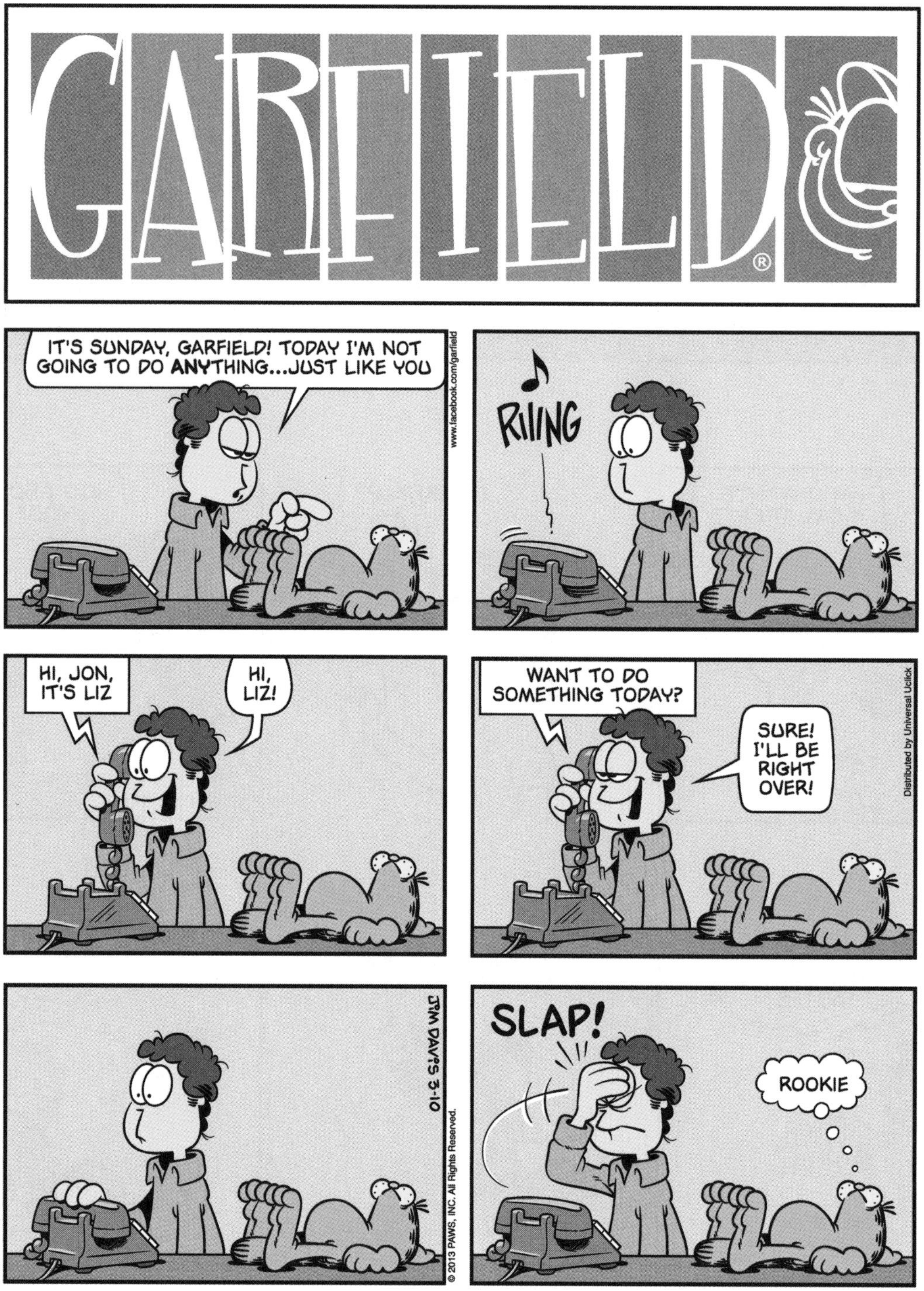
GARFIELD®
IT'S SUNDAY, GARFIELD! TODAY I'M NOT GOING TO DO ANYTHING...JUST LIKE YOU
www.facebook.com/garfield
RIIING
HI, JON, IT'S LIZ
HI, LIZ!
WANT TO DO SOMETHING TODAY?
SURE! I'LL BE RIGHT OVER!
Distributed by Universal Uclick
JIM DAVIS 3-10
© 2013 PAWS, INC. All Rights Reserved.
SLAP!
ROOKIE

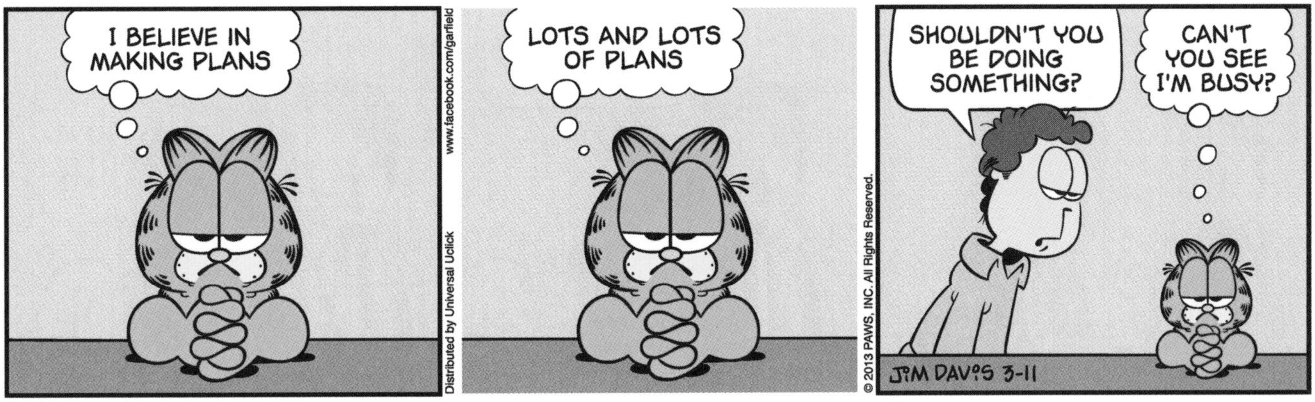
I BELIEVE IN MAKING PLANS
LOTS AND LOTS OF PLANS
SHOULDN'T YOU BE DOING SOMETHING?
CAN'T YOU SEE I'M BUSY?
JIM DAVIS 3-11
Distributed by Universal Uclick www.facebook.com/garfield
© 2013 PAWS, INC. All Rights Reserved.

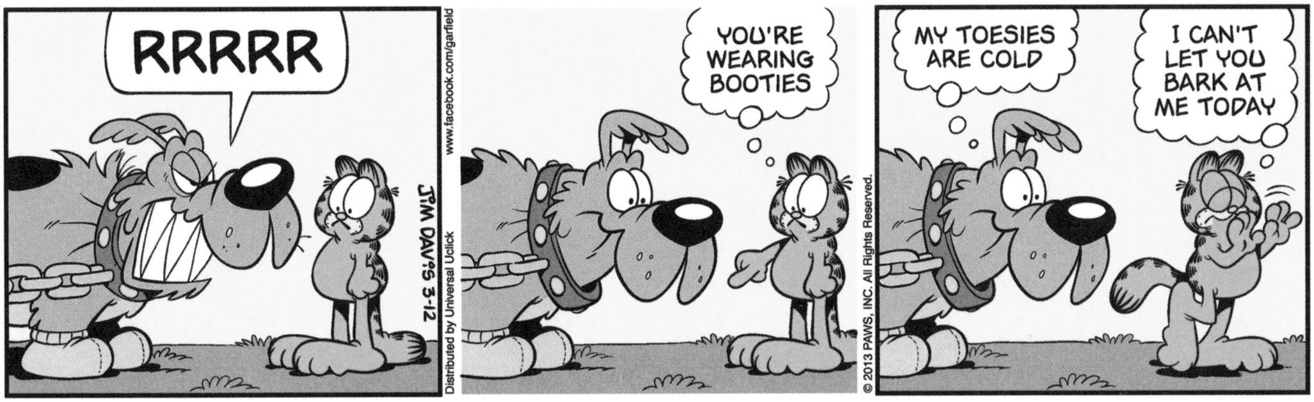
RRRRR
JIM DAVIS 3-12
YOU'RE WEARING BOOTIES
MY TOESIES ARE COLD
I CAN'T LET YOU BARK AT ME TODAY
Distributed by Universal Uclick www.facebook.com/garfield
© 2013 PAWS, INC. All Rights Reserved.

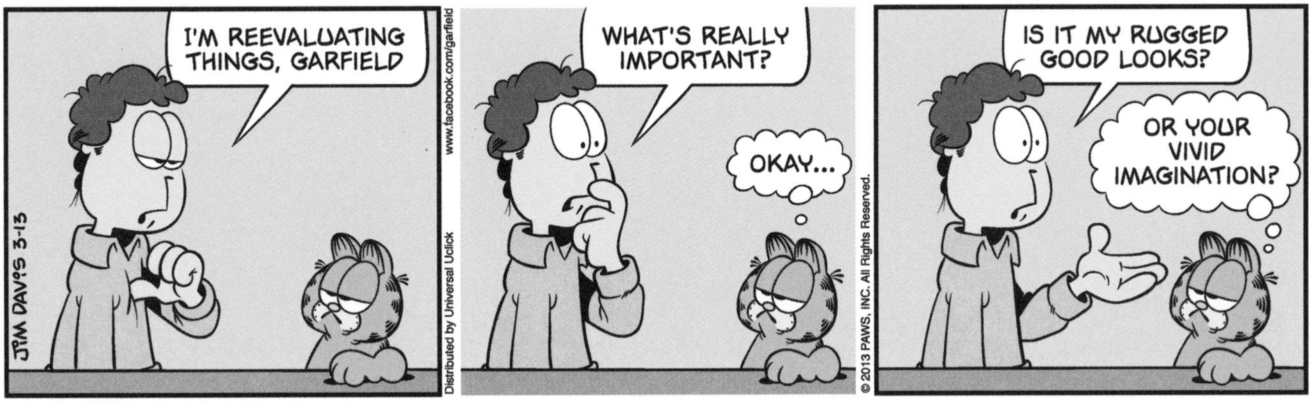
I'M REEVALUATING THINGS, GARFIELD
JIM DAVIS 3-13
WHAT'S REALLY IMPORTANT?
OKAY...
IS IT MY RUGGED GOOD LOOKS?
OR YOUR VIVID IMAGINATION?
Distributed by Universal Uclick www.facebook.com/garfield
© 2013 PAWS, INC. All Rights Reserved.

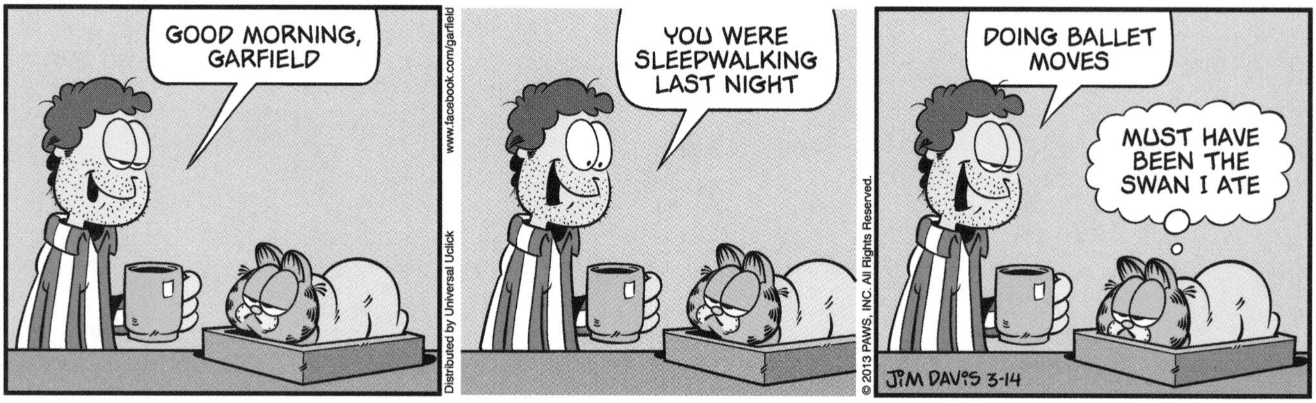
GOOD MORNING, GARFIELD
YOU WERE SLEEPWALKING LAST NIGHT
DOING BALLET MOVES
MUST HAVE BEEN THE SWAN I ATE
Distributed by Universal Uclick www.facebook.com/garfield
© 2013 PAWS, INC. All Rights Reserved.
JIM DAVIS 3-14

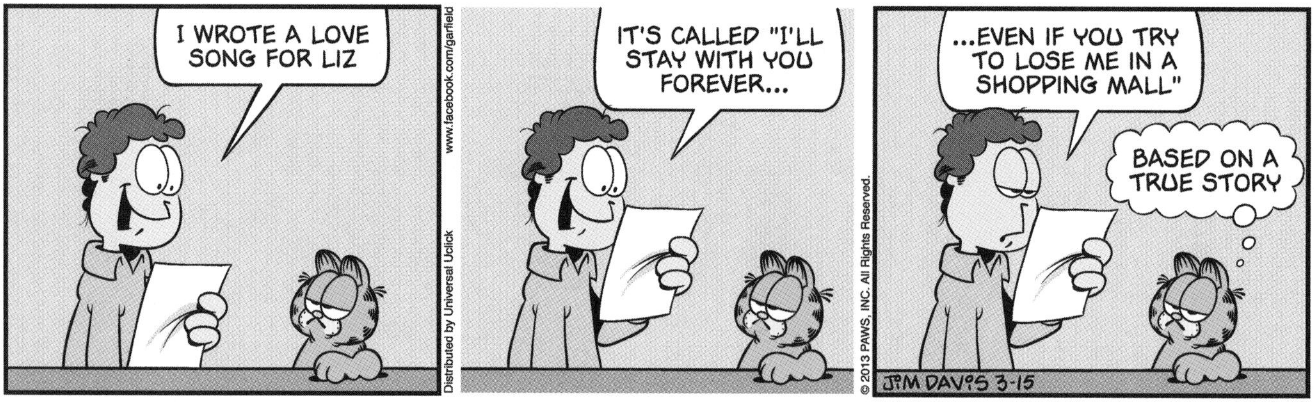
I WROTE A LOVE SONG FOR LIZ
IT'S CALLED "I'LL STAY WITH YOU FOREVER...
...EVEN IF YOU TRY TO LOSE ME IN A SHOPPING MALL"
BASED ON A TRUE STORY
Distributed by Universal Uclick www.facebook.com/garfield
© 2013 PAWS, INC. All Rights Reserved.
JIM DAVIS 3-15

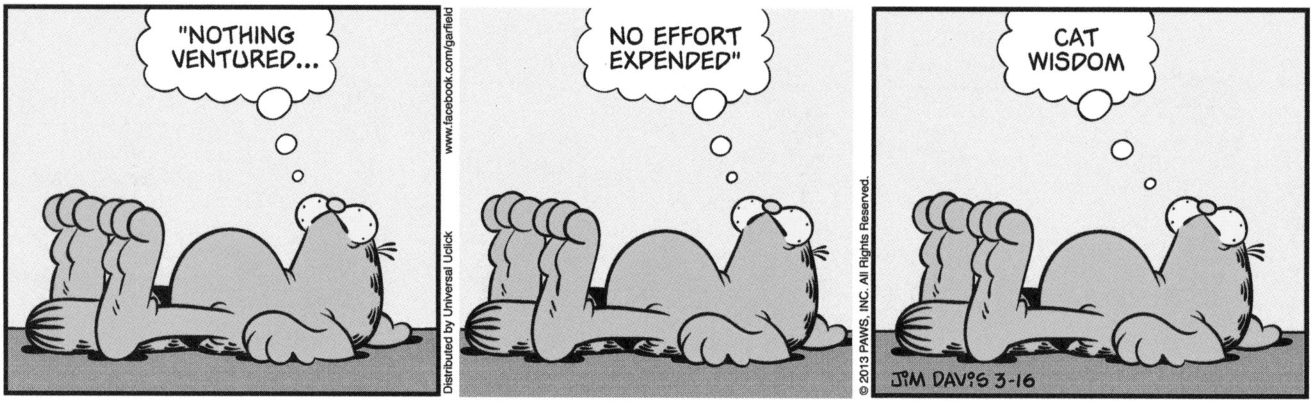
"NOTHING VENTURED...
NO EFFORT EXPENDED"
CAT WISDOM
Distributed by Universal Uclick www.facebook.com/garfield
© 2013 PAWS, INC. All Rights Reserved.
JIM DAVIS 3-16

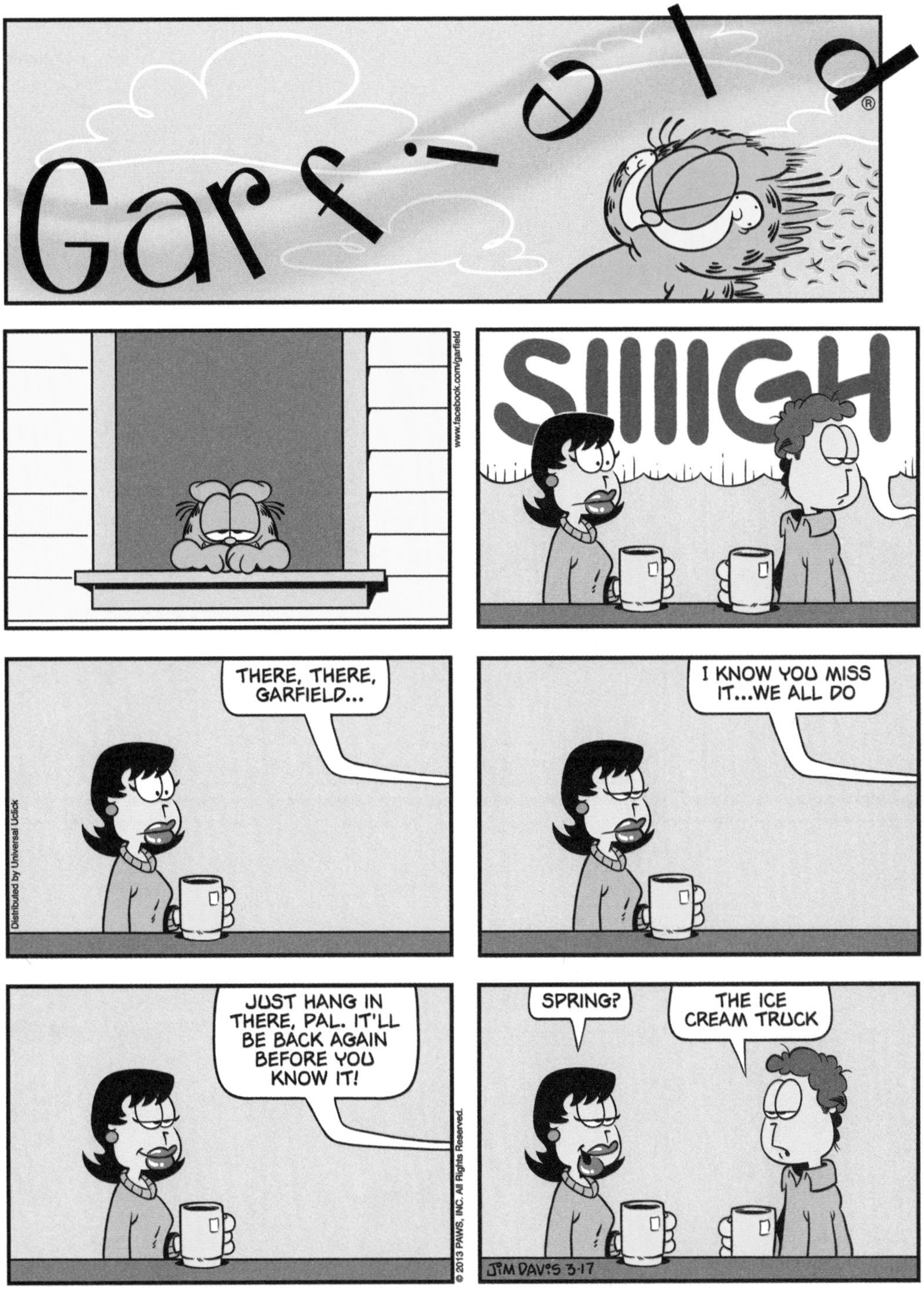
Garfield®
www.facebook.com/garfield
SIIIGH
THERE, THERE, GARFIELD...
Distributed by Universal Uclick
I KNOW YOU MISS IT...WE ALL DO
JUST HANG IN THERE, PAL. IT'LL BE BACK AGAIN BEFORE YOU KNOW IT!
© 2013 PAWS, INC. All Rights Reserved.
SPRING?
THE ICE CREAM TRUCK
JIM DAVIS 3-17

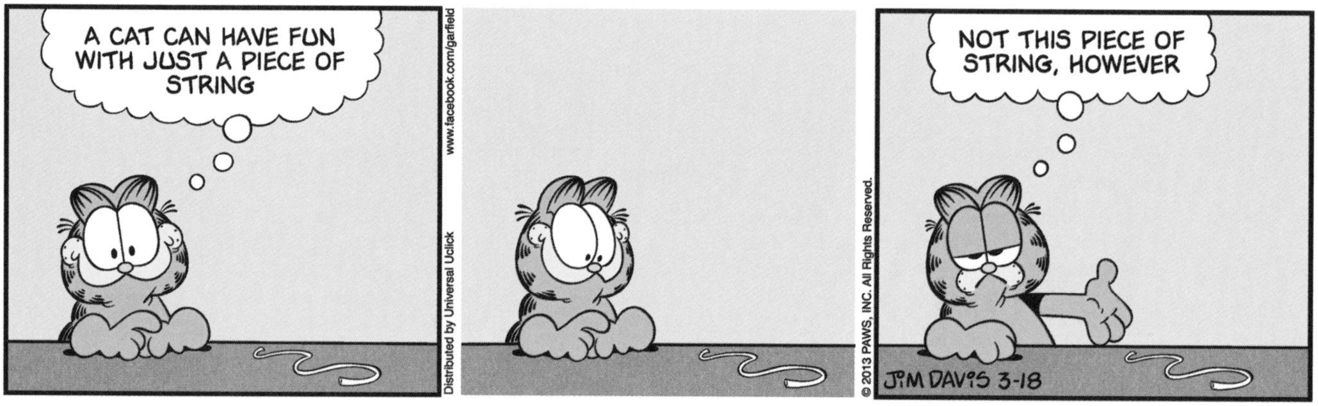
A CAT CAN HAVE FUN WITH JUST A PIECE OF STRING
NOT THIS PIECE OF STRING, HOWEVER
JIM DAVIS 3-18
Distributed by Universal Uclick www.facebook.com/garfield
© 2013 PAWS, INC. All Rights Reserved.

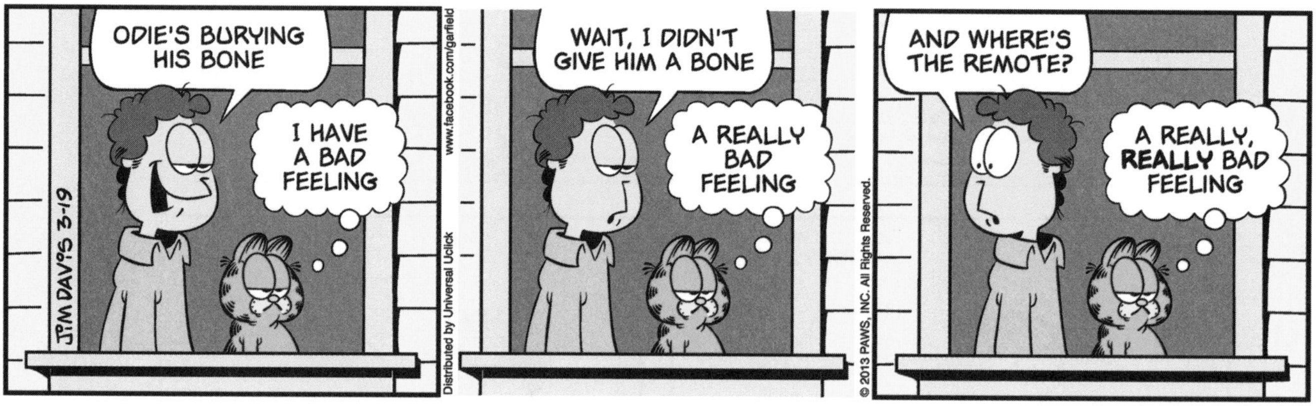
ODIE'S BURYING HIS BONE
I HAVE A BAD FEELING
WAIT, I DIDN'T GIVE HIM A BONE
A REALLY BAD FEELING
AND WHERE'S THE REMOTE?
A REALLY, **REALLY** BAD FEELING
JIM DAVIS 3-19
Distributed by Universal Uclick www.facebook.com/garfield
© 2013 PAWS, INC. All Rights Reserved.

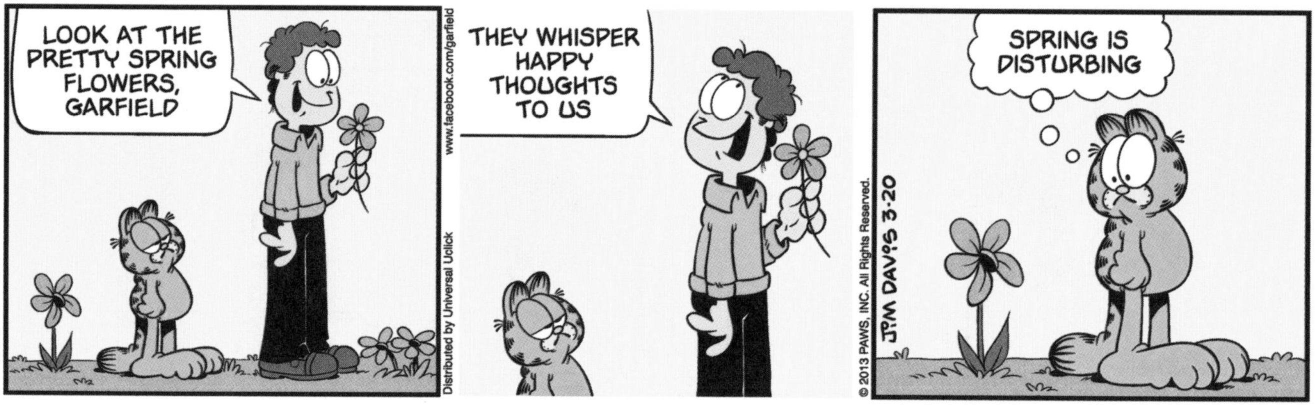
LOOK AT THE PRETTY SPRING FLOWERS, GARFIELD
THEY WHISPER HAPPY THOUGHTS TO US
SPRING IS DISTURBING
JIM DAVIS 3-20
Distributed by Universal Uclick www.facebook.com/garfield
© 2013 PAWS, INC. All Rights Reserved.

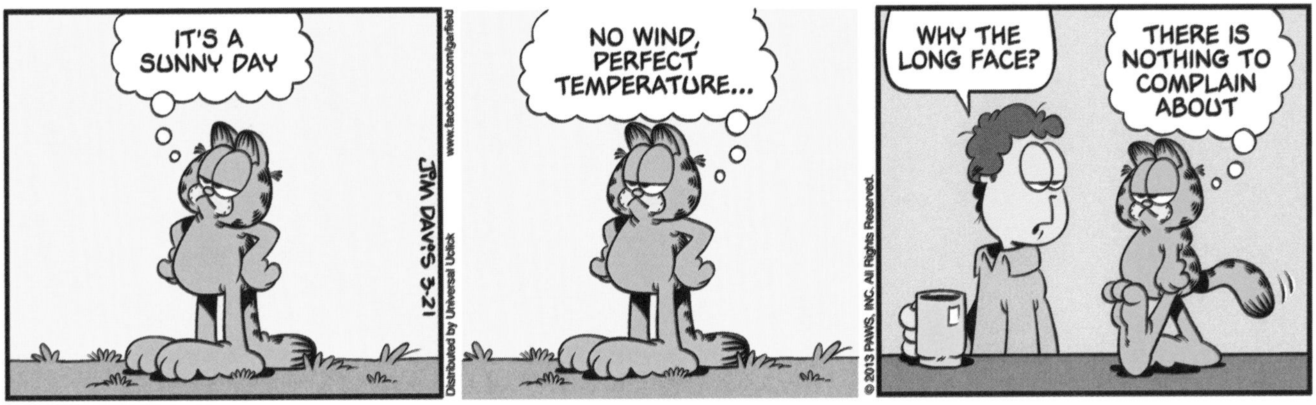
IT'S A SUNNY DAY
JIM DAVIS 3-21
www.facebook.com/garfield
Distributed by Universal Uclick
NO WIND, PERFECT TEMPERATURE...
© 2013 PAWS, INC. All Rights Reserved.
WHY THE LONG FACE?
THERE IS NOTHING TO COMPLAIN ABOUT

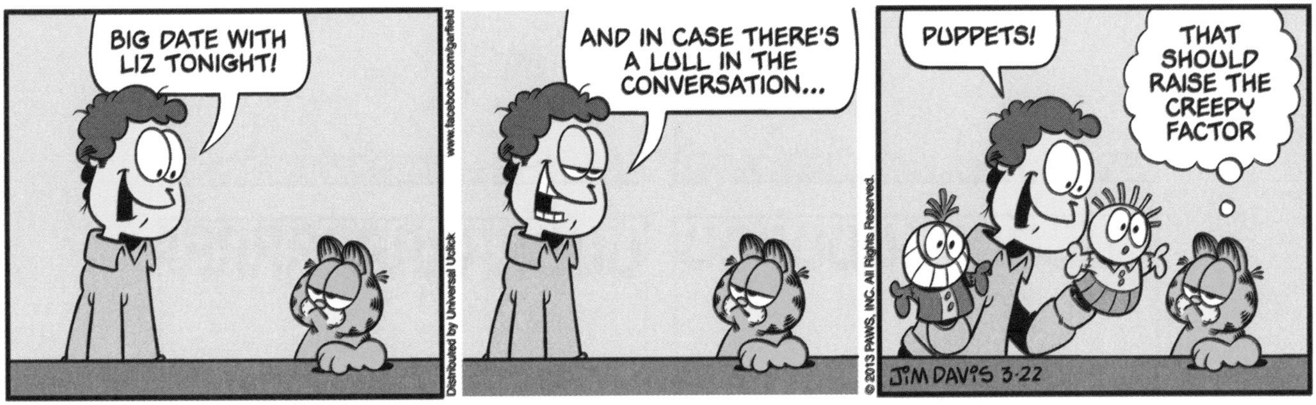
BIG DATE WITH LIZ TONIGHT!
www.facebook.com/garfield
Distributed by Universal Uclick
AND IN CASE THERE'S A LULL IN THE CONVERSATION...
© 2013 PAWS, INC. All Rights Reserved.
PUPPETS!
THAT SHOULD RAISE THE CREEPY FACTOR
JIM DAVIS 3-22

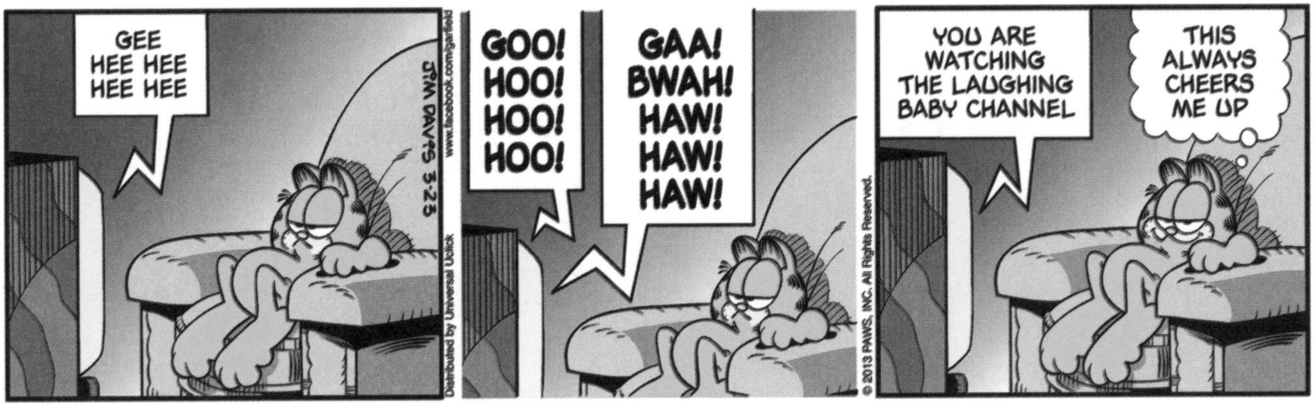
GEE HEE HEE HEE HEE
JIM DAVIS 3-23
www.facebook.com/garfield
Distributed by Universal Uclick
GOO! HOO! HOO! HOO!
GAA! BWAH! HAW! HAW! HAW!
© 2013 PAWS, INC. All Rights Reserved.
YOU ARE WATCHING THE LAUGHING BABY CHANNEL
THIS ALWAYS CHEERS ME UP

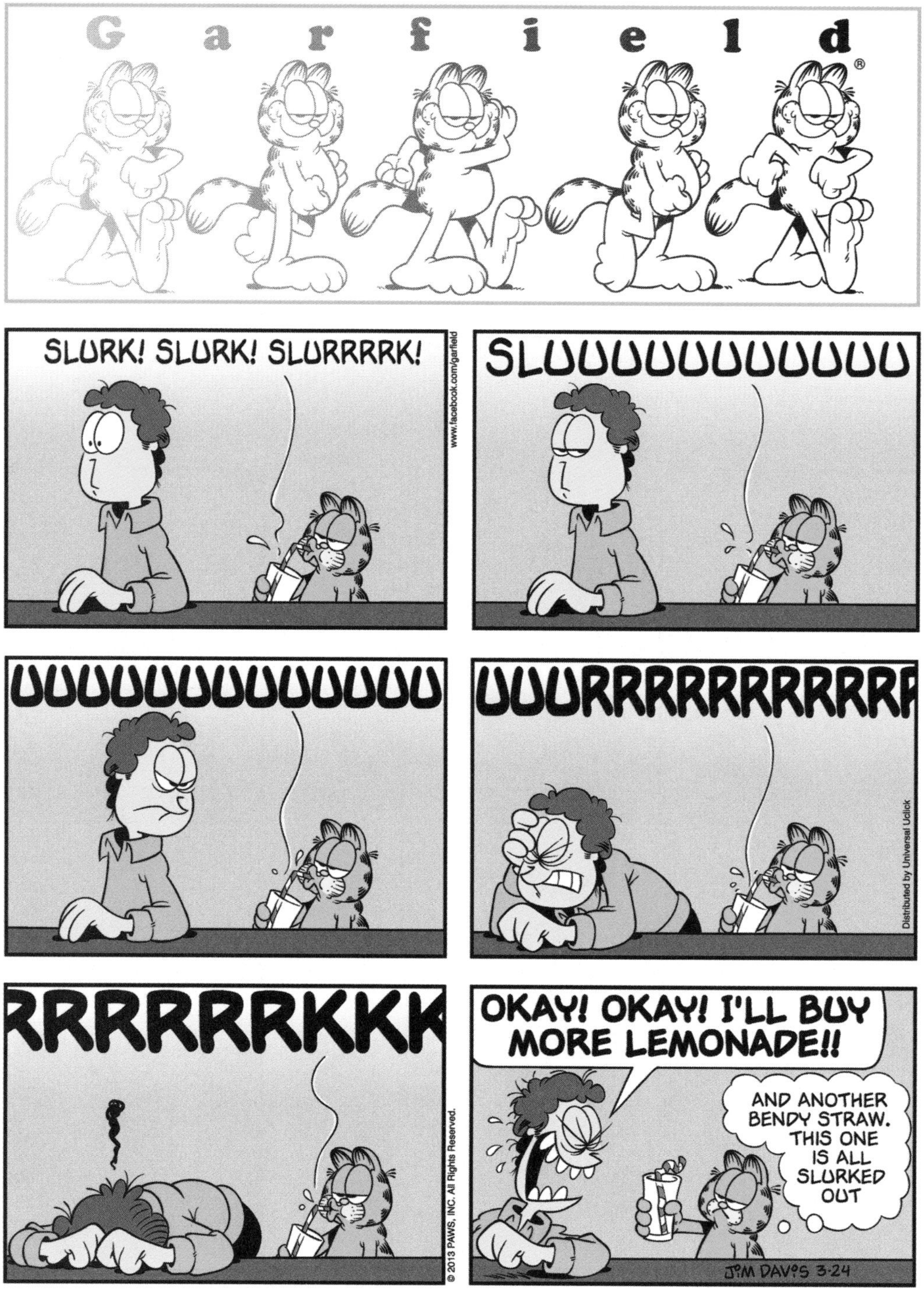
Garfield®
SLURK! SLURK! SLURRRRK!
www.facebook.com/garfield
SLUUUUUUUUUUUU
UUUUUUUUUUUUUU
UUURRRRRRRRRRRR
Distributed by Universal Uclick
RRRRRRRKKK
© 2013 PAWS, INC. All Rights Reserved.
OKAY! OKAY! I'LL BUY MORE LEMONADE!!
AND ANOTHER BENDY STRAW. THIS ONE IS ALL SLURKED OUT
JIM DAVIS 3-24

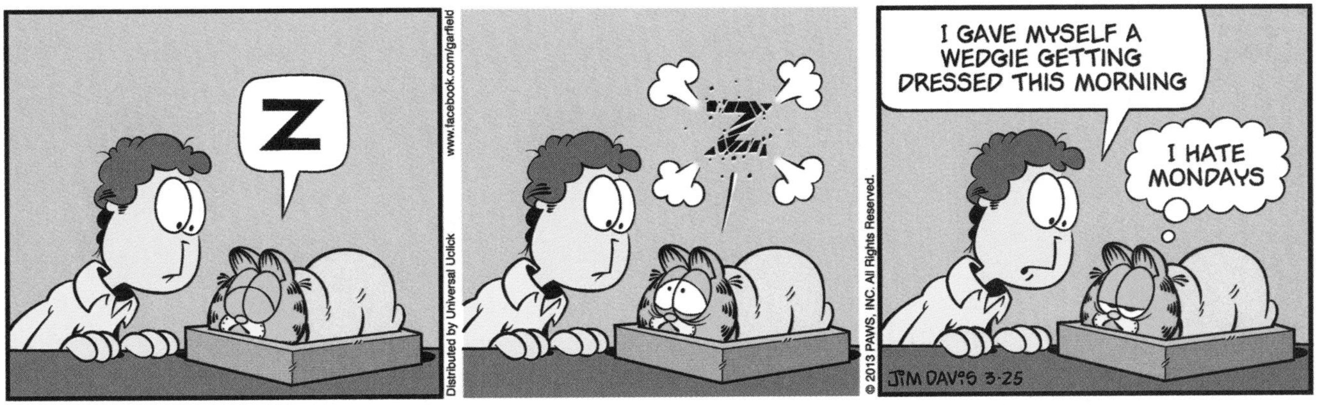
Z
Distributed by Universal Uclick www.facebook.com/garfield
I GAVE MYSELF A WEDGIE GETTING DRESSED THIS MORNING
I HATE MONDAYS
© 2013 PAWS, INC. All Rights Reserved.
JIM DAVIS 3-25

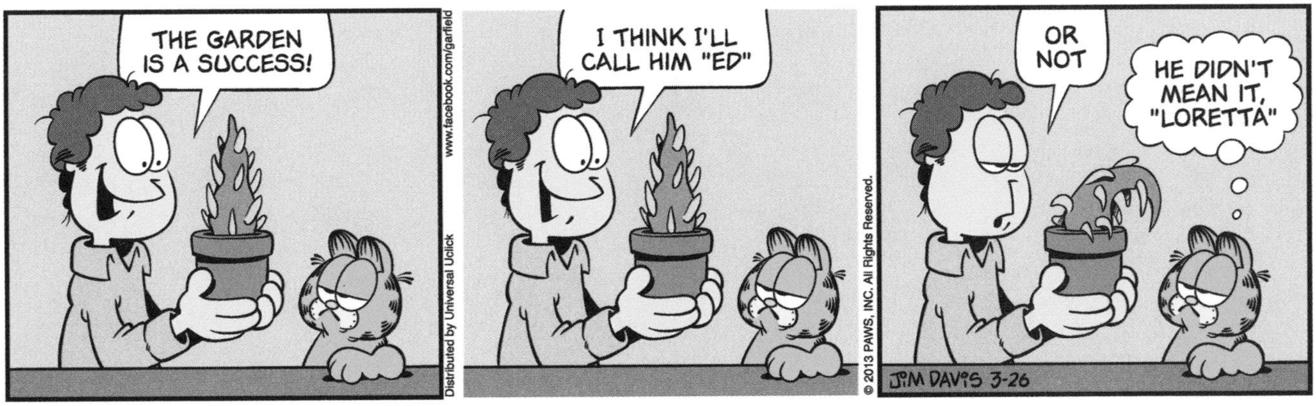
THE GARDEN IS A SUCCESS!
Distributed by Universal Uclick www.facebook.com/garfield
I THINK I'LL CALL HIM "ED"
OR NOT
HE DIDN'T MEAN IT, "LORETTA"
© 2013 PAWS, INC. All Rights Reserved.
JIM DAVIS 3-26

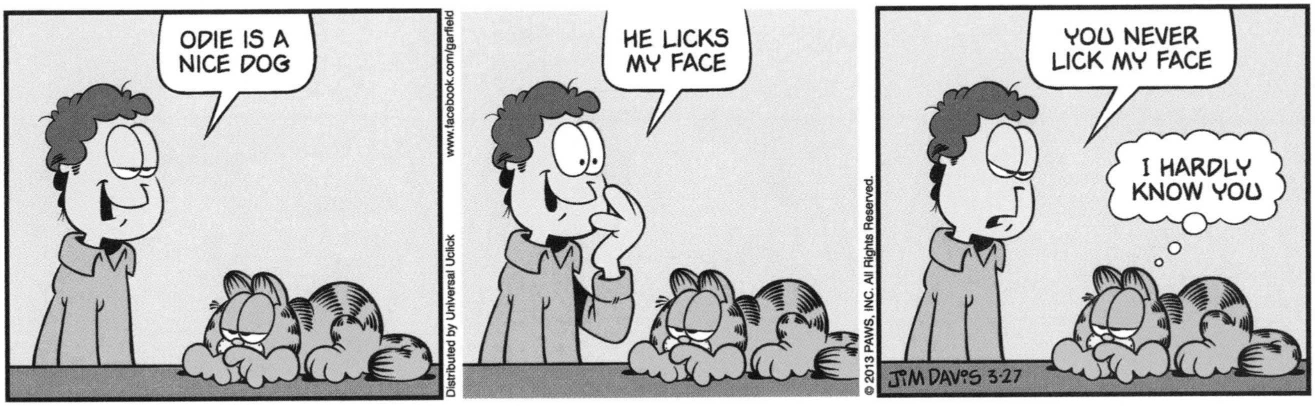
ODIE IS A NICE DOG
Distributed by Universal Uclick www.facebook.com/garfield
HE LICKS MY FACE
YOU NEVER LICK MY FACE
I HARDLY KNOW YOU
© 2013 PAWS, INC. All Rights Reserved.
JIM DAVIS 3-27

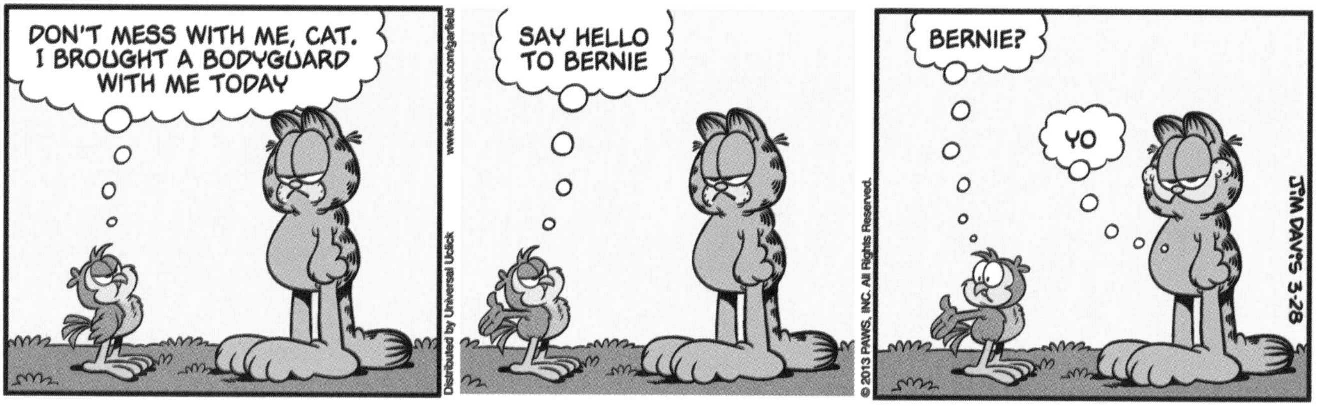
DON'T MESS WITH ME, CAT. I BROUGHT A BODYGUARD WITH ME TODAY
SAY HELLO TO BERNIE
BERNIE?
YO
JIM DAVIS 3-28
Distributed by Universal Uclick
www.facebook.com/garfield
© 2013 PAWS, INC. All Rights Reserved.

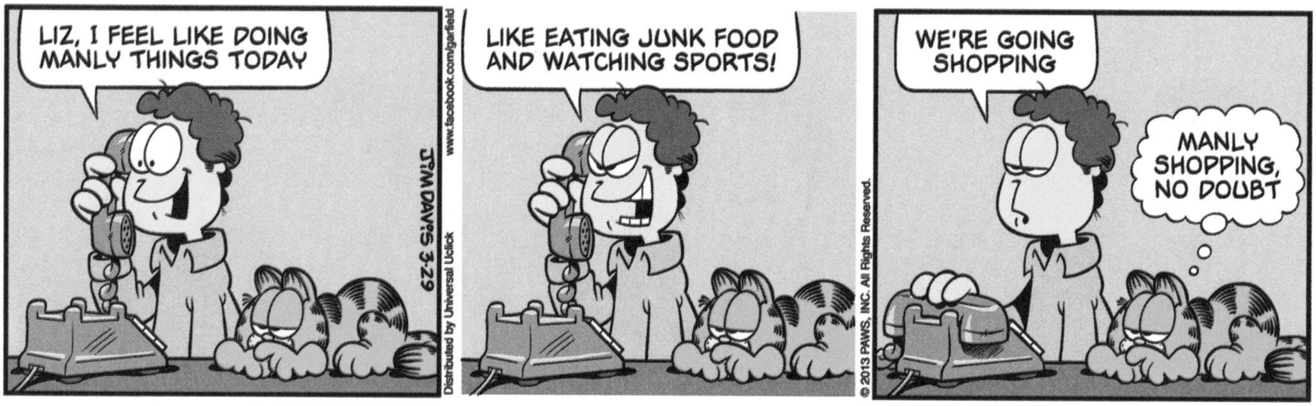
LIZ, I FEEL LIKE DOING MANLY THINGS TODAY
JIM DAVIS 3-29
LIKE EATING JUNK FOOD AND WATCHING SPORTS!
WE'RE GOING SHOPPING
MANLY SHOPPING, NO DOUBT
Distributed by Universal Uclick
www.facebook.com/garfield
© 2013 PAWS, INC. All Rights Reserved.

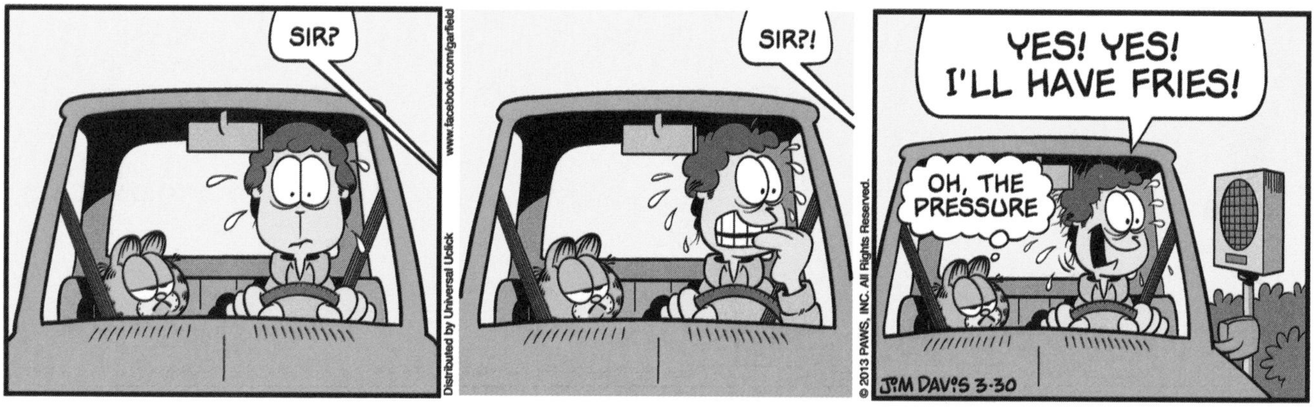
SIR?
SIR?!
YES! YES! I'LL HAVE FRIES!
OH, THE PRESSURE
JIM DAVIS 3-30
Distributed by Universal Uclick
www.facebook.com/garfield
© 2013 PAWS, INC. All Rights Reserved.

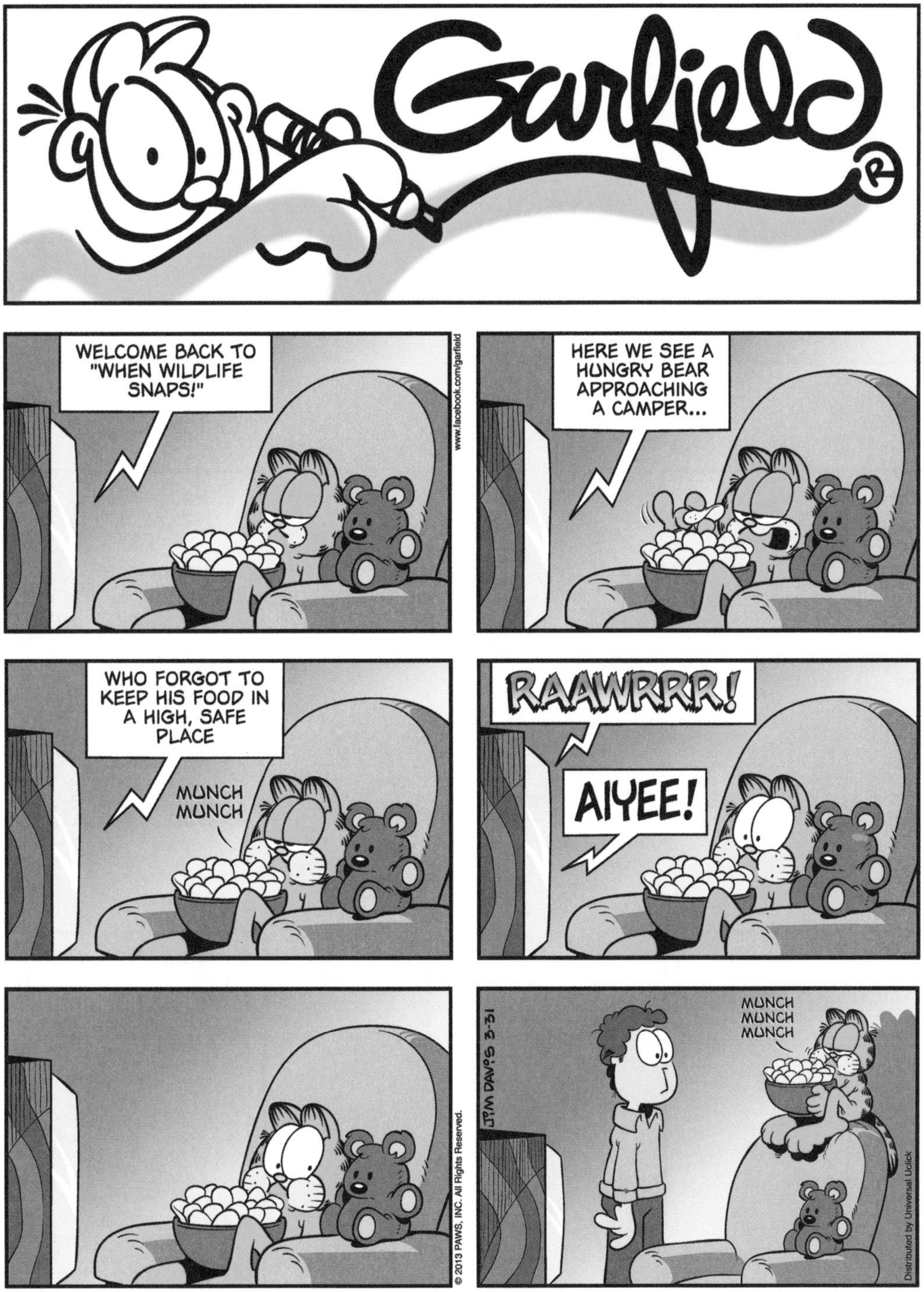
Garfield
WELCOME BACK TO "WHEN WILDLIFE SNAPS!"
www.facebook.com/garfield
HERE WE SEE A HUNGRY BEAR APPROACHING A CAMPER...
WHO FORGOT TO KEEP HIS FOOD IN A HIGH, SAFE PLACE
MUNCH MUNCH
RAAWRRR!
AIYEE!
© 2013 PAWS, INC. All Rights Reserved.
JIM DAVIS 3-31
MUNCH MUNCH MUNCH
Distributed by Universal Uclick

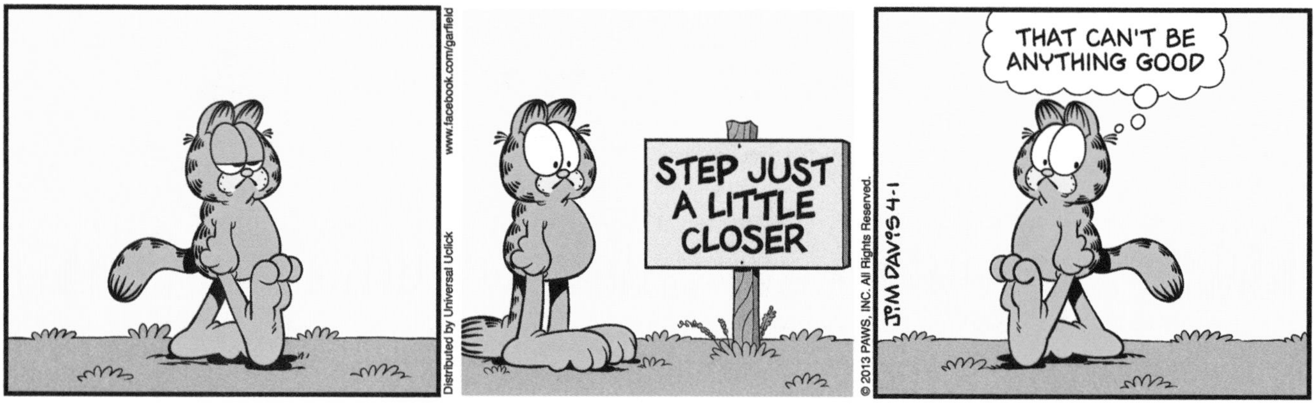
www.facebook.com/garfield
Distributed by Universal Uclick
STEP JUST A LITTLE CLOSER
© 2013 PAWS, INC. All Rights Reserved.
JIM DAVIS 4-1
THAT CAN'T BE ANYTHING GOOD

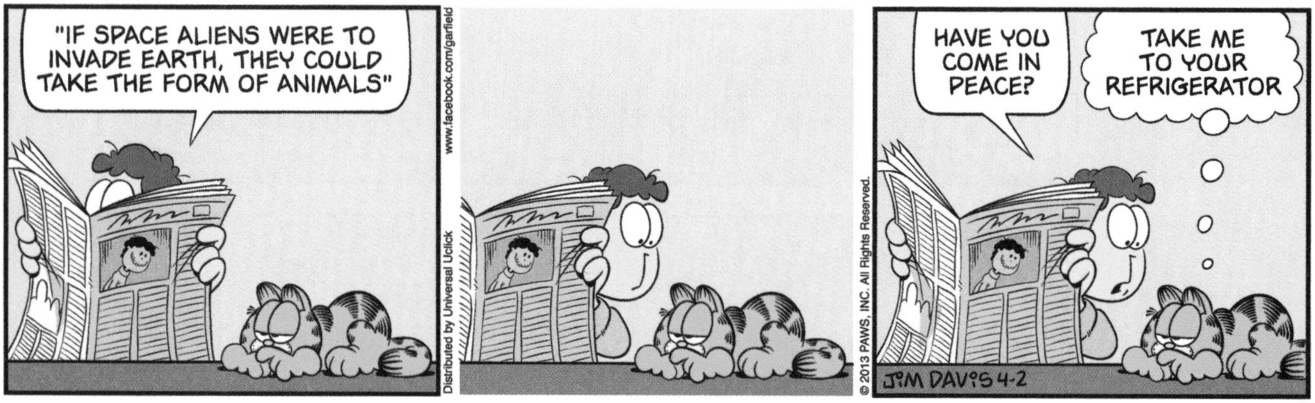
"IF SPACE ALIENS WERE TO INVADE EARTH, THEY COULD TAKE THE FORM OF ANIMALS"
www.facebook.com/garfield
Distributed by Universal Uclick
© 2013 PAWS, INC. All Rights Reserved.
HAVE YOU COME IN PEACE?
TAKE ME TO YOUR REFRIGERATOR
JIM DAVIS 4-2

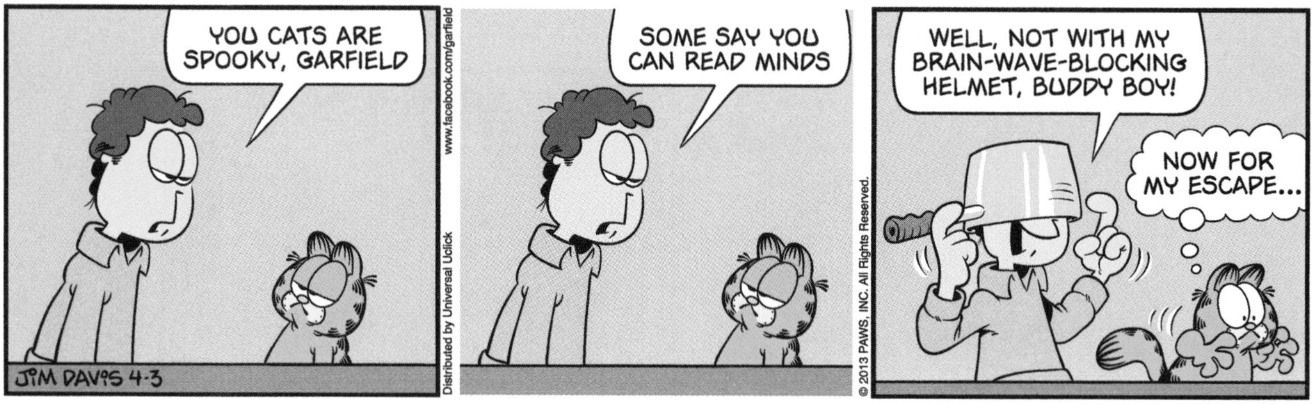
YOU CATS ARE SPOOKY, GARFIELD
JIM DAVIS 4-3
www.facebook.com/garfield
Distributed by Universal Uclick
SOME SAY YOU CAN READ MINDS
© 2013 PAWS, INC. All Rights Reserved.
WELL, NOT WITH MY BRAIN-WAVE-BLOCKING HELMET, BUDDY BOY!
NOW FOR MY ESCAPE...

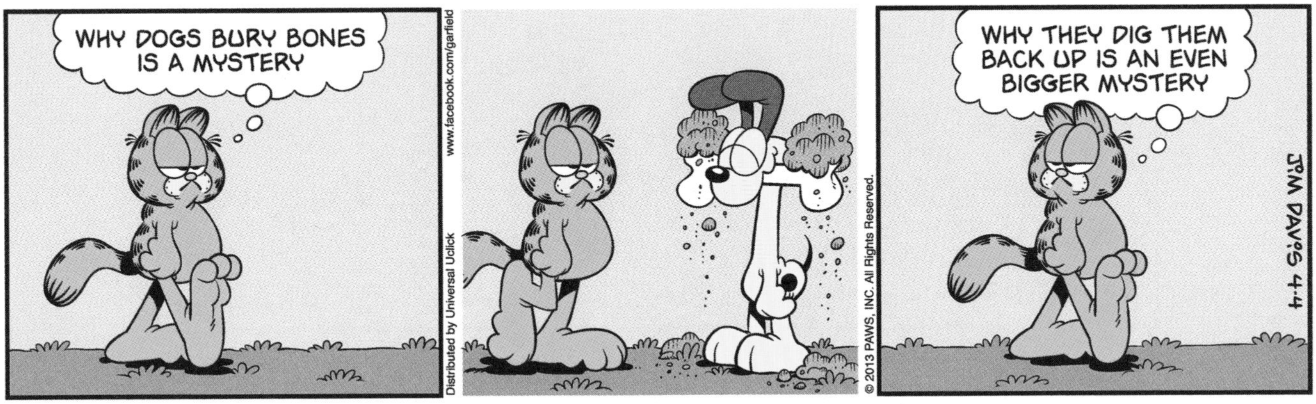
WHY DOGS BURY BONES IS A MYSTERY
WHY THEY DIG THEM BACK UP IS AN EVEN BIGGER MYSTERY
JIM DAVIS 4-4
www.facebook.com/garfield
Distributed by Universal Uclick
© 2013 PAWS, INC. All Rights Reserved.

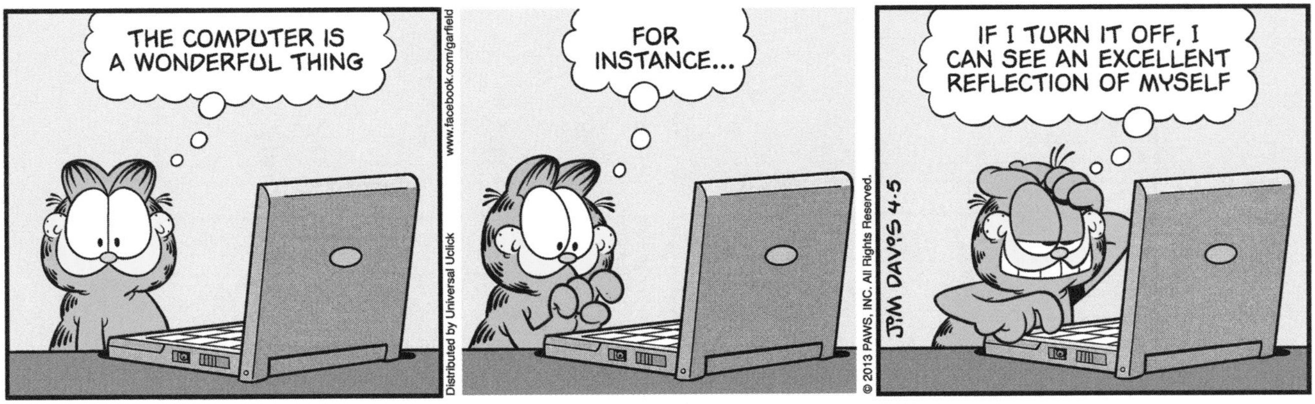
THE COMPUTER IS A WONDERFUL THING
FOR INSTANCE...
IF I TURN IT OFF, I CAN SEE AN EXCELLENT REFLECTION OF MYSELF
JIM DAVIS 4-5
www.facebook.com/garfield
Distributed by Universal Uclick
© 2013 PAWS, INC. All Rights Reserved.

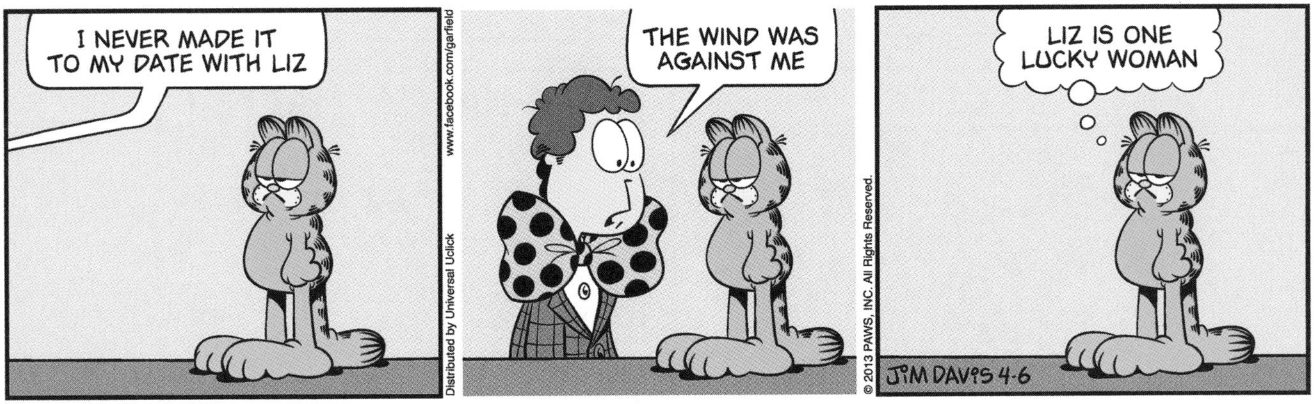
I NEVER MADE IT TO MY DATE WITH LIZ
THE WIND WAS AGAINST ME
LIZ IS ONE LUCKY WOMAN
JIM DAVIS 4-6
www.facebook.com/garfield
Distributed by Universal Uclick
© 2013 PAWS, INC. All Rights Reserved.

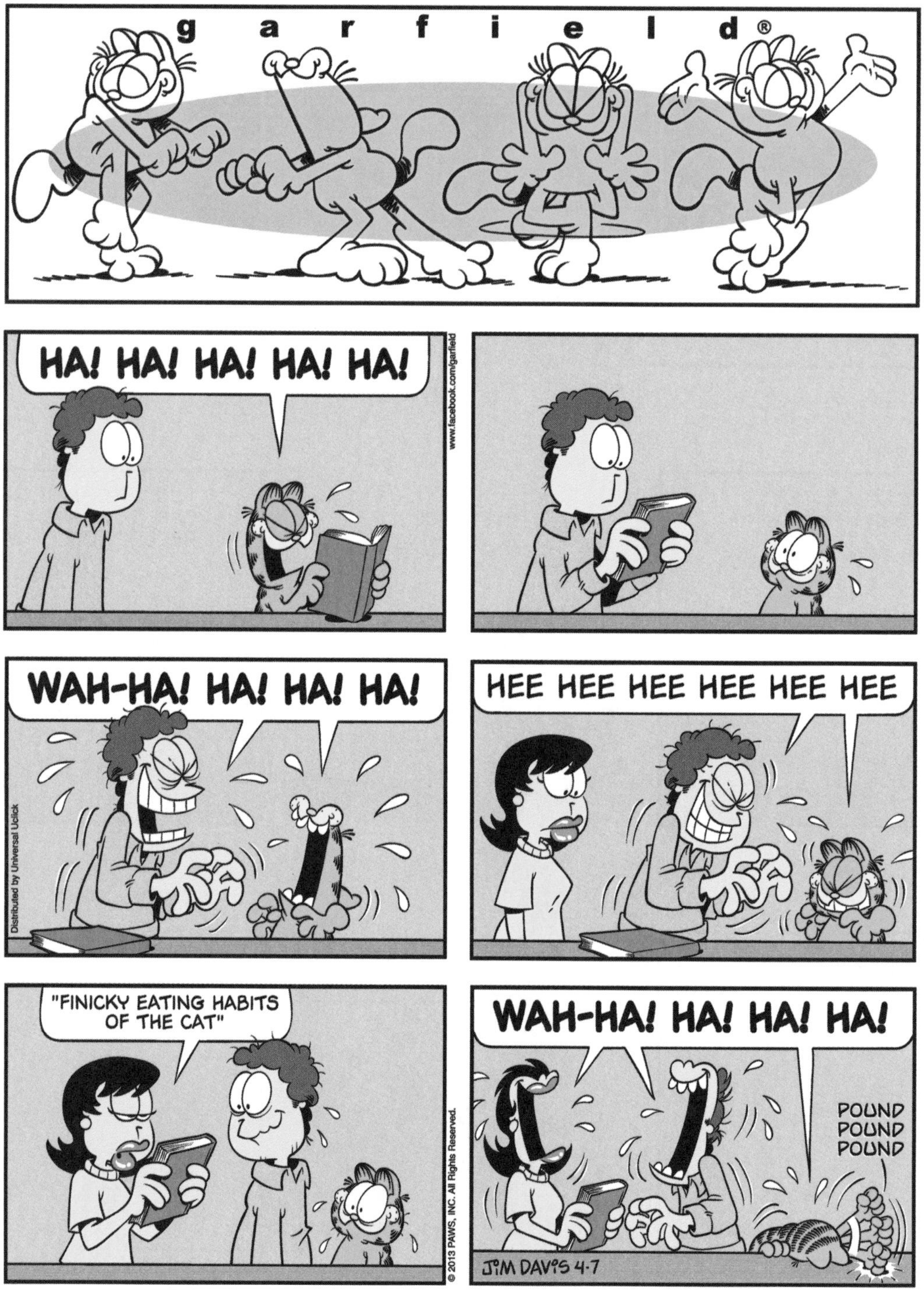
garfield®
HA! HA! HA! HA! HA!
www.facebook.com/garfield
Distributed by Universal Uclick
WAH-HA! HA! HA! HA!
HEE HEE HEE HEE HEE HEE
"FINICKY EATING HABITS OF THE CAT"
© 2013 PAWS, INC. All Rights Reserved.
WAH-HA! HA! HA! HA!
POUND
POUND
POUND
JIM DAVIS 4·7

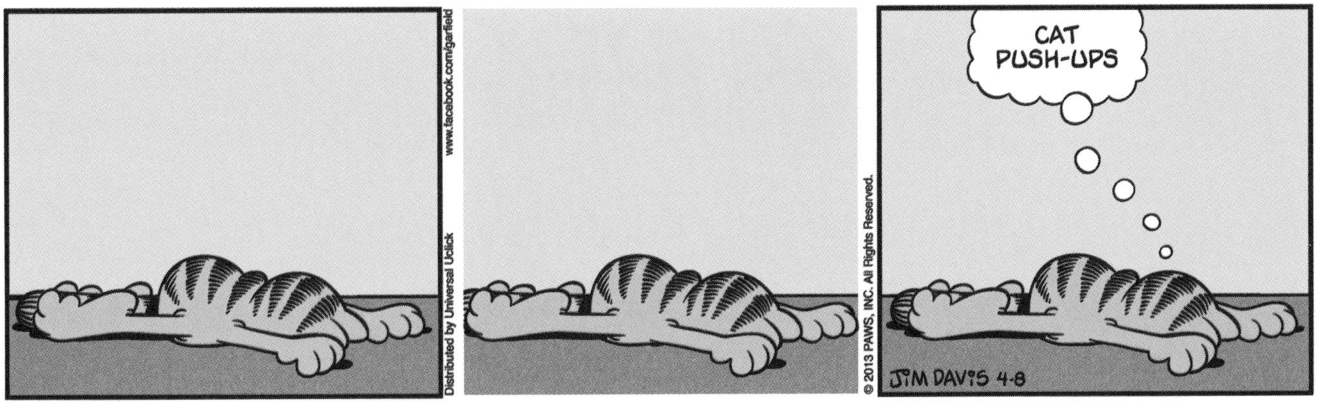
Distributed by Universal Uclick
www.facebook.com/garfield
© 2013 PAWS, INC. All Rights Reserved.
CAT PUSH-UPS
JIM DAVIS 4-8

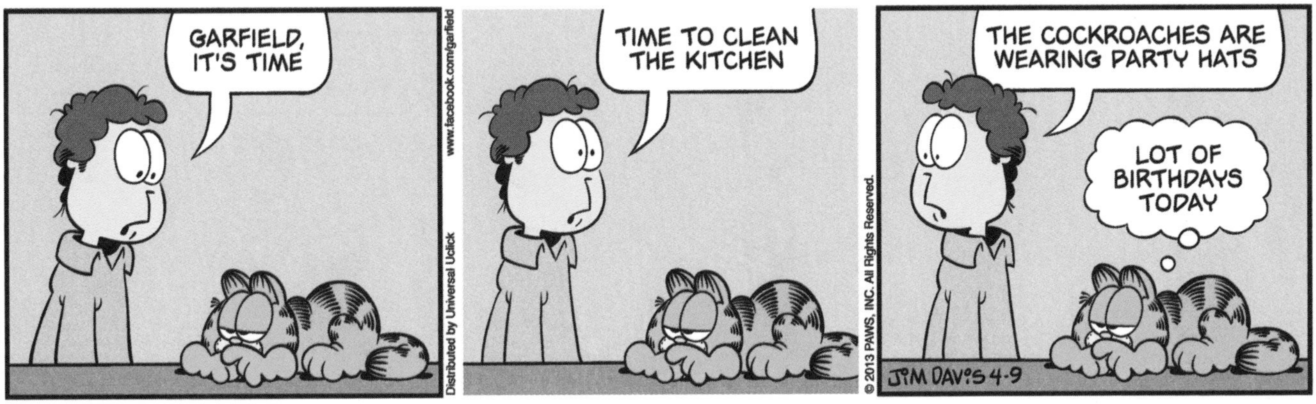
GARFIELD, IT'S TIME
Distributed by Universal Uclick
www.facebook.com/garfield
TIME TO CLEAN THE KITCHEN
© 2013 PAWS, INC. All Rights Reserved.
THE COCKROACHES ARE WEARING PARTY HATS
LOT OF BIRTHDAYS TODAY
JIM DAVIS 4-9

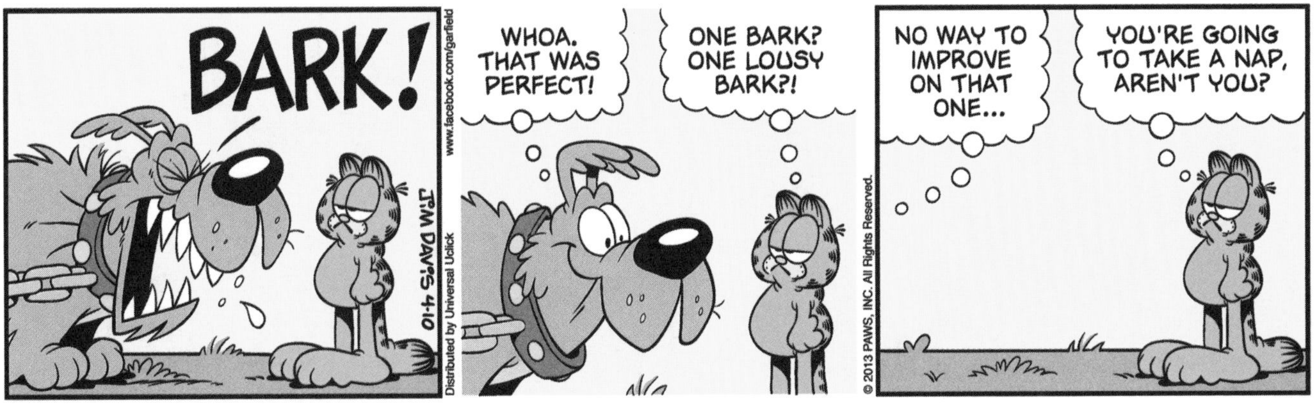
BARK!
JIM DAVIS 4-10
Distributed by Universal Uclick
www.facebook.com/garfield
WHOA. THAT WAS PERFECT!
ONE BARK? ONE LOUSY BARK?!
© 2013 PAWS, INC. All Rights Reserved.
NO WAY TO IMPROVE ON THAT ONE...
YOU'RE GOING TO TAKE A NAP, AREN'T YOU?

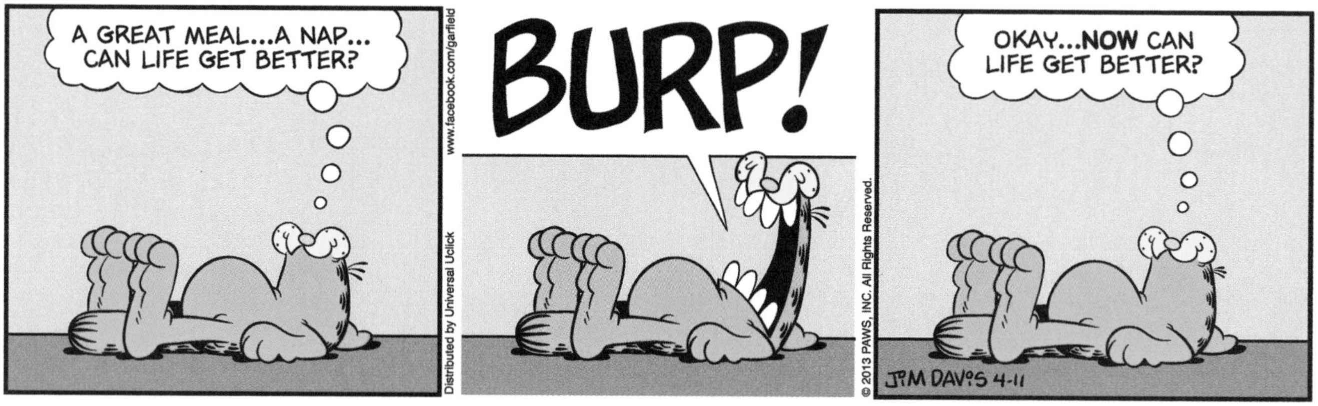
A GREAT MEAL...A NAP... CAN LIFE GET BETTER?
Distributed by Universal Uclick www.facebook.com/garfield
BURP!
© 2013 PAWS, INC. All Rights Reserved.
OKAY...**NOW** CAN LIFE GET BETTER?
JIM DAVIS 4-11

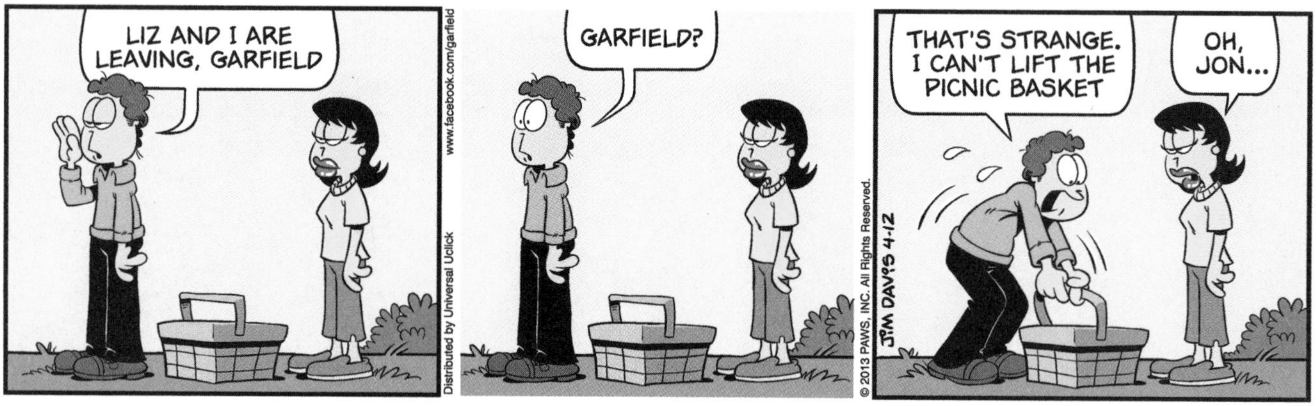
LIZ AND I ARE LEAVING, GARFIELD
Distributed by Universal Uclick www.facebook.com/garfield
GARFIELD?
© 2013 PAWS, INC. All Rights Reserved.
JIM DAVIS 4-12
THAT'S STRANGE. I CAN'T LIFT THE PICNIC BASKET
OH, JON...

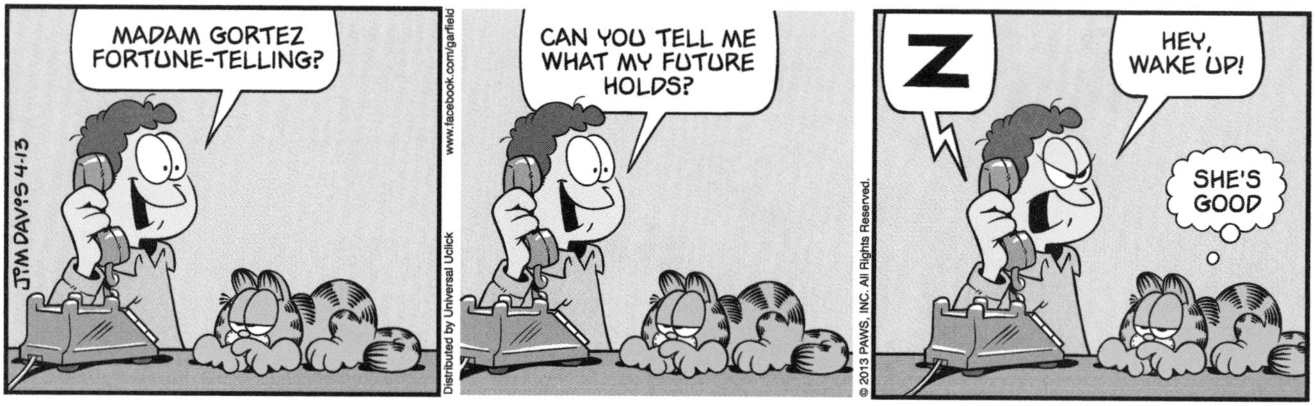
JIM DAVIS 4-13
MADAM GORTEZ FORTUNE-TELLING?
Distributed by Universal Uclick www.facebook.com/garfield
CAN YOU TELL ME WHAT MY FUTURE HOLDS?
© 2013 PAWS, INC. All Rights Reserved.
Z
HEY, WAKE UP!
SHE'S GOOD

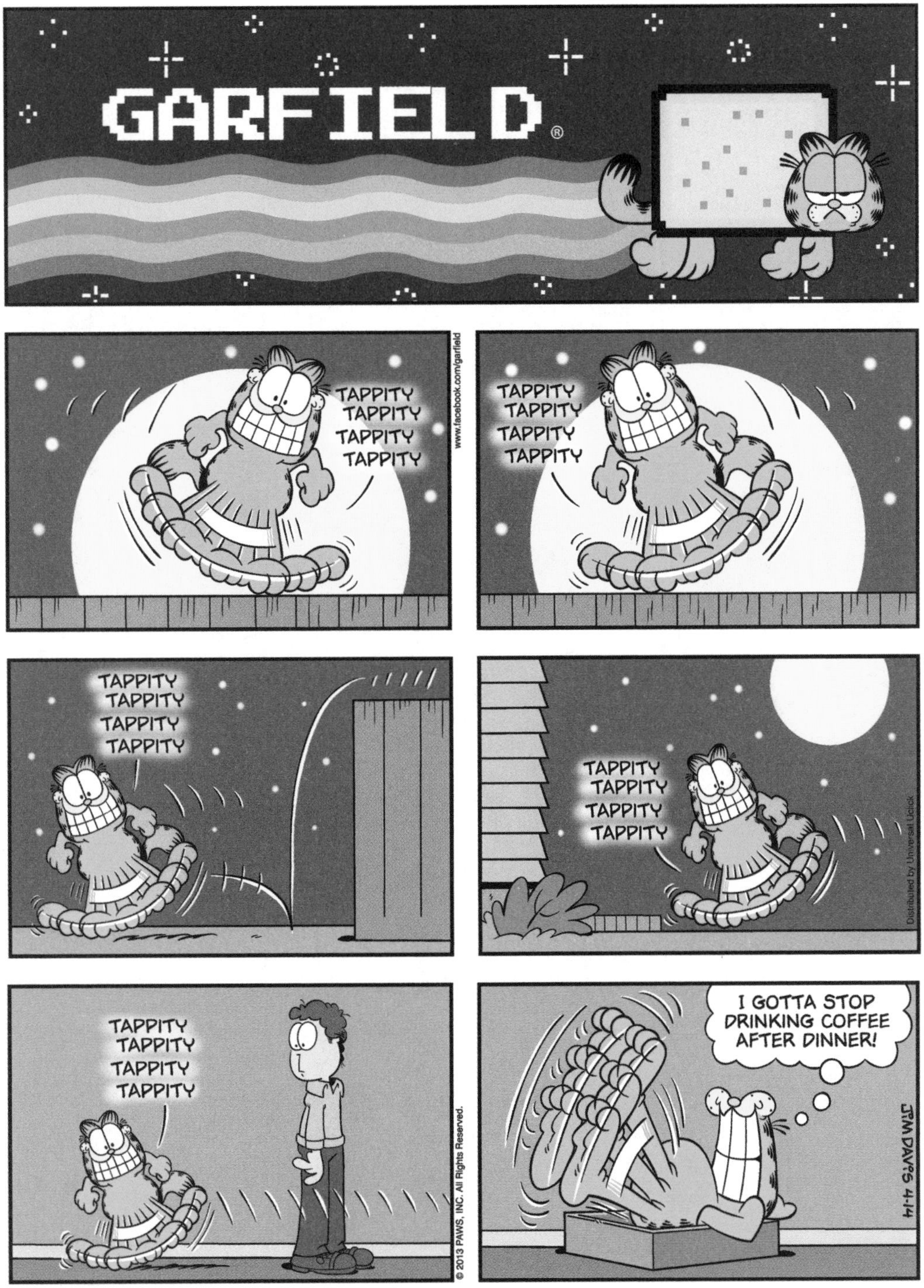
GARFIELD®
www.facebook.com/garfield
TAPPITY TAPPITY TAPPITY TAPPITY
TAPPITY TAPPITY TAPPITY TAPPITY
TAPPITY TAPPITY TAPPITY TAPPITY
TAPPITY TAPPITY TAPPITY TAPPITY
Distributed by Universal Uclick
TAPPITY TAPPITY TAPPITY TAPPITY
© 2013 PAWS, INC. All Rights Reserved.
I GOTTA STOP DRINKING COFFEE AFTER DINNER!
JIM DAVIS 4-14

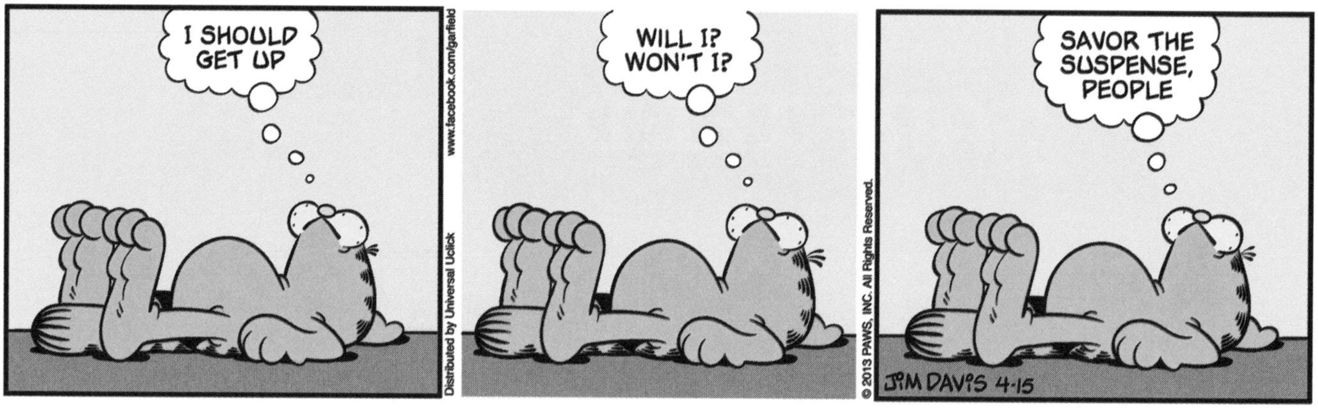
I SHOULD GET UP
WILL I? WON'T I?
SAVOR THE SUSPENSE, PEOPLE
JIM DAVIS 4-15
www.facebook.com/garfield
Distributed by Universal Uclick
© 2013 PAWS, INC. All Rights Reserved.

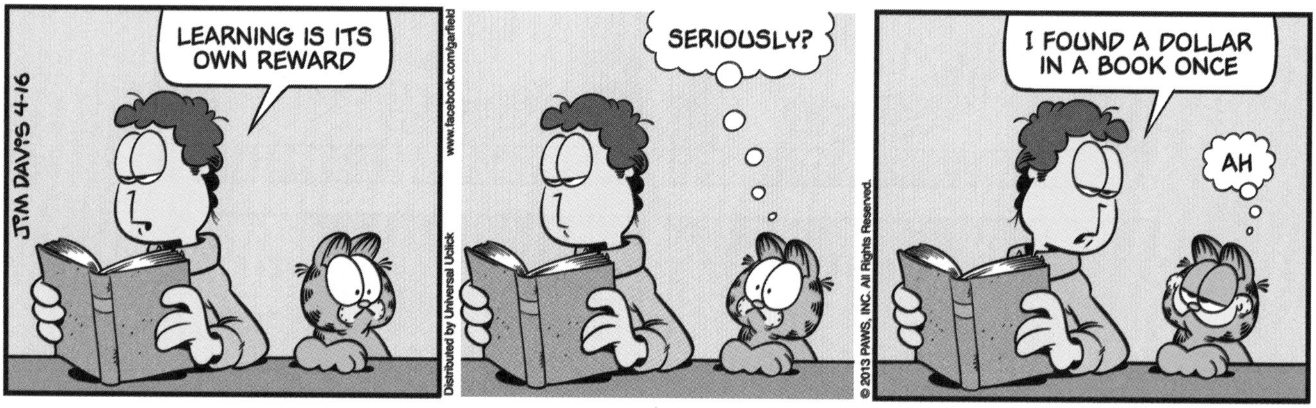
LEARNING IS ITS OWN REWARD
SERIOUSLY?
I FOUND A DOLLAR IN A BOOK ONCE
AH
JIM DAVIS 4-16
www.facebook.com/garfield
Distributed by Universal Uclick
© 2013 PAWS, INC. All Rights Reserved.

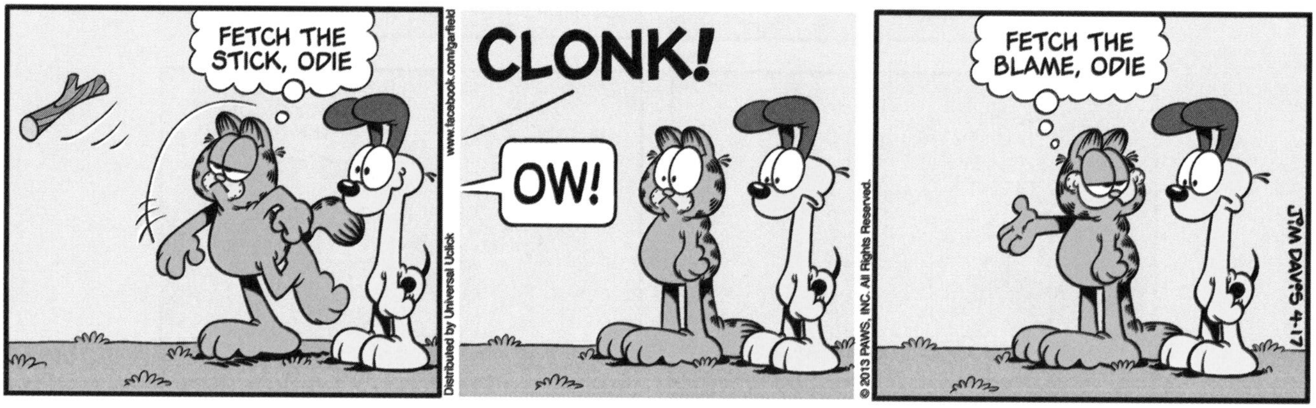
FETCH THE STICK, ODIE
CLONK!
OW!
FETCH THE BLAME, ODIE
JIM DAVIS 4-17
www.facebook.com/garfield
Distributed by Universal Uclick
© 2013 PAWS, INC. All Rights Reserved.

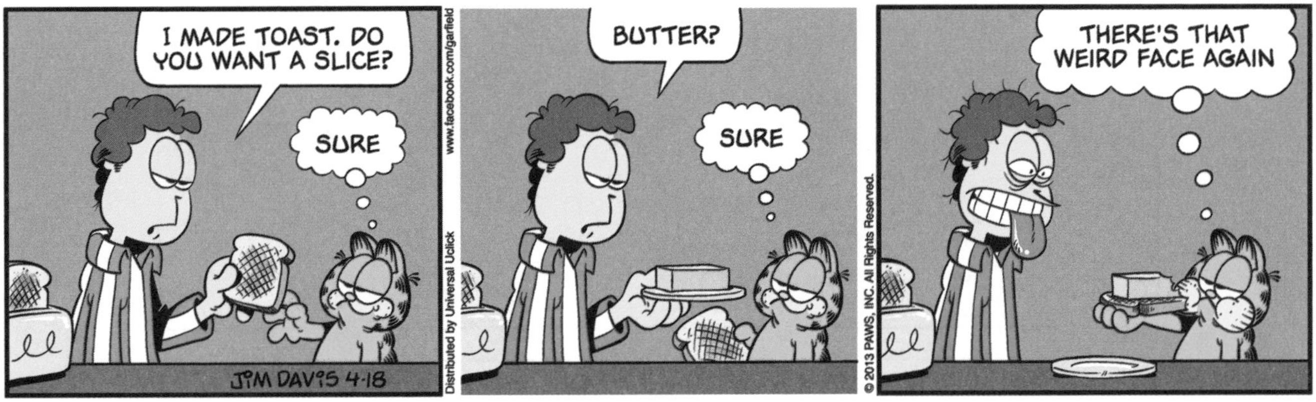
I MADE TOAST. DO YOU WANT A SLICE?
SURE
BUTTER?
SURE
THERE'S THAT WEIRD FACE AGAIN
JIM DAVIS 4-18
Distributed by Universal Uclick www.facebook.com/garfield
© 2013 PAWS, INC. All Rights Reserved.

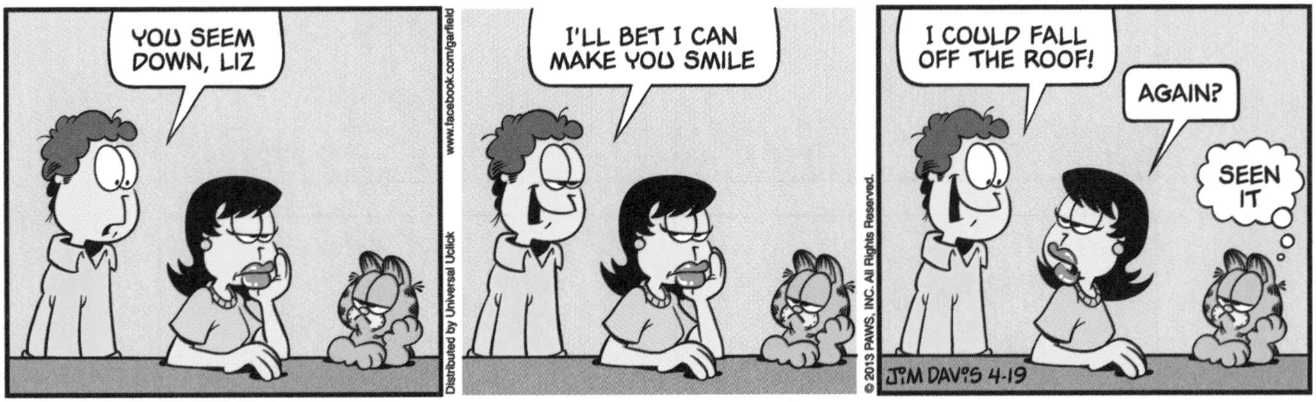
YOU SEEM DOWN, LIZ
I'LL BET I CAN MAKE YOU SMILE
I COULD FALL OFF THE ROOF!
AGAIN?
SEEN IT
JIM DAVIS 4-19
Distributed by Universal Uclick www.facebook.com/garfield
© 2013 PAWS, INC. All Rights Reserved.

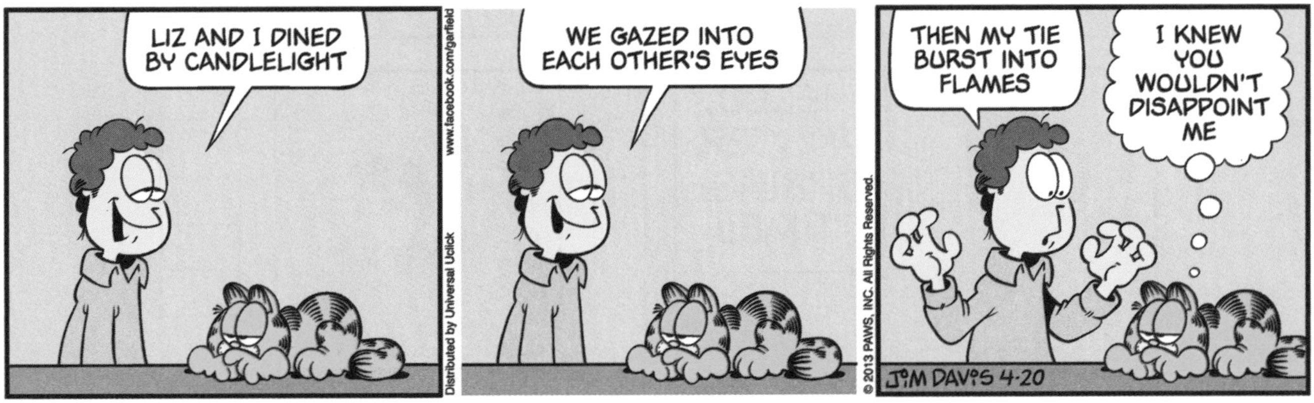
LIZ AND I DINED BY CANDLELIGHT
WE GAZED INTO EACH OTHER'S EYES
THEN MY TIE BURST INTO FLAMES
I KNEW YOU WOULDN'T DISAPPOINT ME
JIM DAVIS 4-20
Distributed by Universal Uclick www.facebook.com/garfield
© 2013 PAWS, INC. All Rights Reserved.

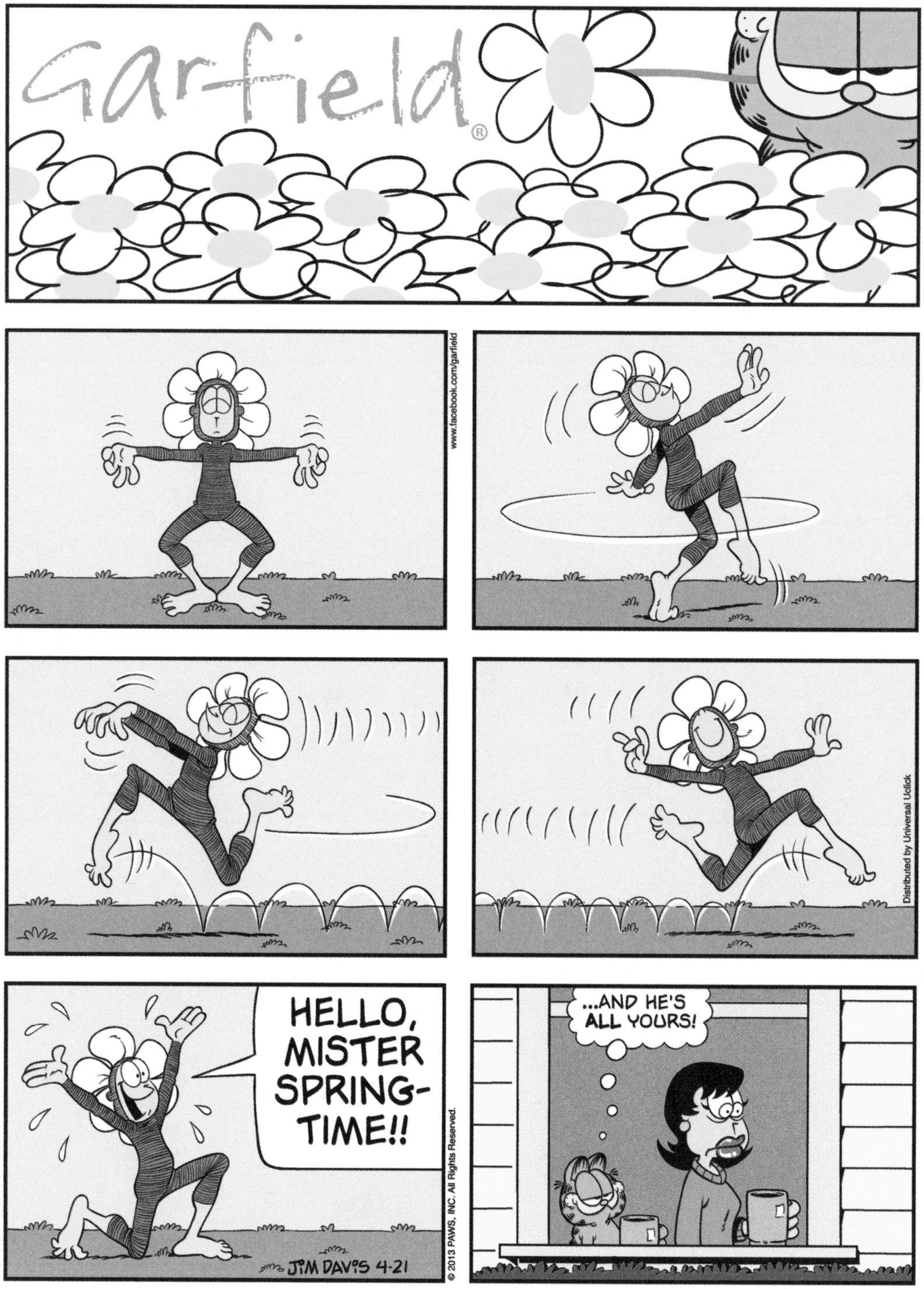

Garfield®
www.facebook.com/garfield
Distributed by Universal Uclick
HELLO, MISTER SPRING-TIME!!
JIM DAVIS 4-21
© 2013 PAWS, INC. All Rights Reserved.
...AND HE'S ALL YOURS!

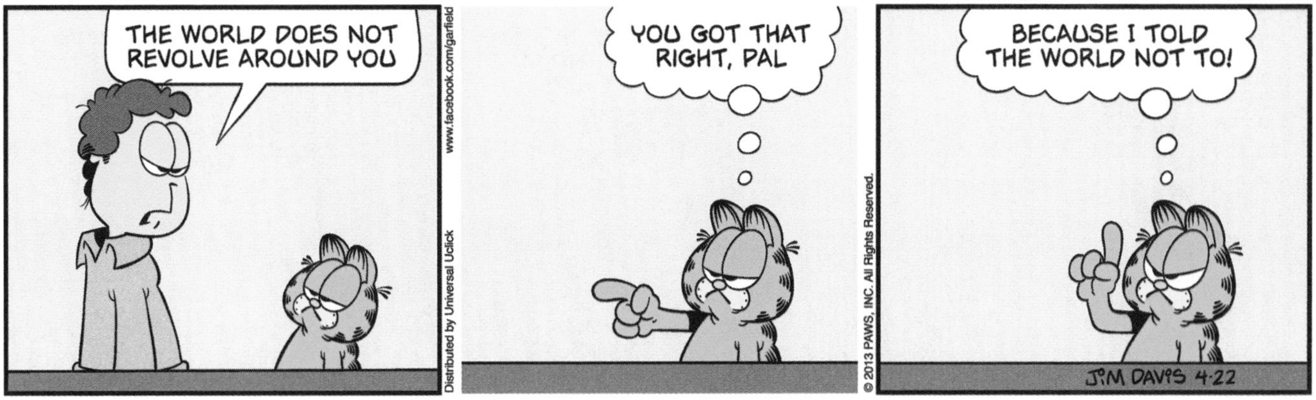
THE WORLD DOES NOT REVOLVE AROUND YOU
YOU GOT THAT RIGHT, PAL
BECAUSE I TOLD THE WORLD NOT TO!
JIM DAVIS 4-22
www.facebook.com/garfield
Distributed by Universal Uclick
© 2013 PAWS, INC. All Rights Reserved.

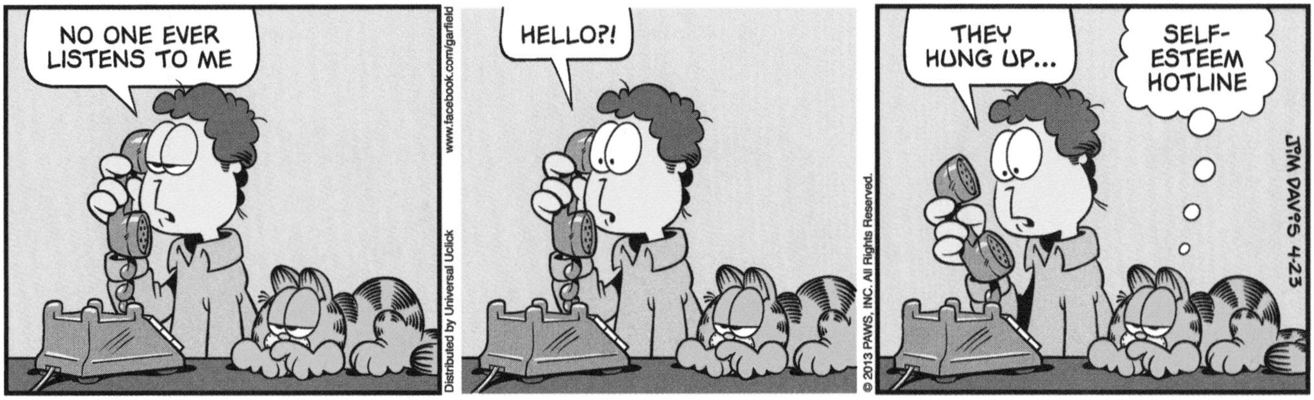
NO ONE EVER LISTENS TO ME
HELLO?!
THEY HUNG UP...
SELF-ESTEEM HOTLINE
JIM DAVIS 4-23
www.facebook.com/garfield
Distributed by Universal Uclick
© 2013 PAWS, INC. All Rights Reserved.

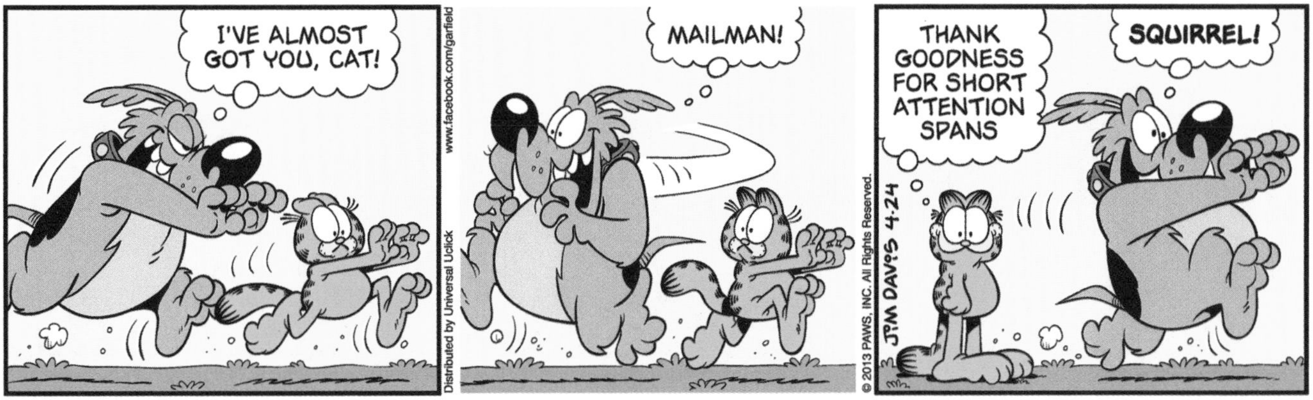
I'VE ALMOST GOT YOU, CAT!
MAILMAN!
THANK GOODNESS FOR SHORT ATTENTION SPANS
SQUIRREL!
JIM DAVIS 4-24
www.facebook.com/garfield
Distributed by Universal Uclick
© 2013 PAWS, INC. All Rights Reserved.

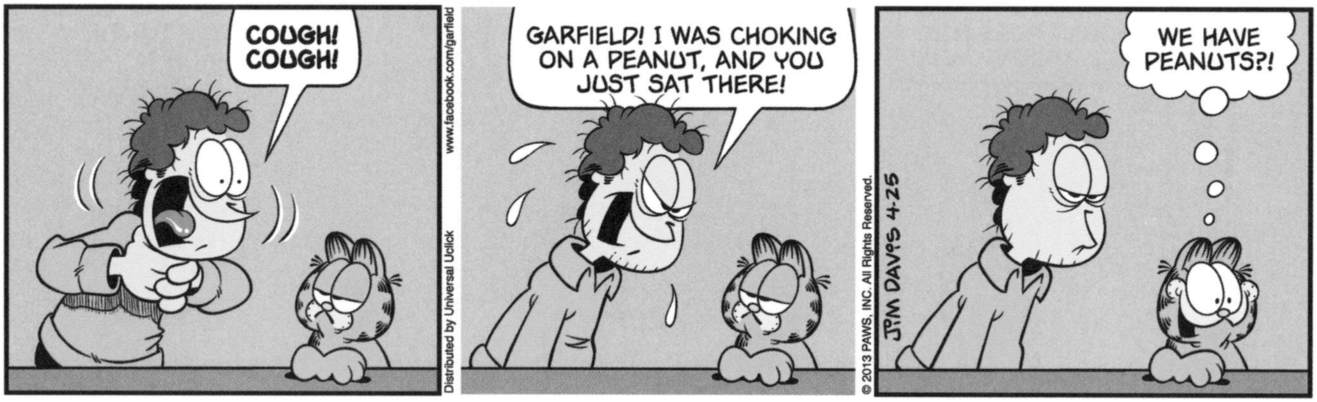
COUGH! COUGH!
www.facebook.com/garfield
Distributed by Universal Uclick
GARFIELD! I WAS CHOKING ON A PEANUT, AND YOU JUST SAT THERE!
© 2013 PAWS, INC. All Rights Reserved.
JIM DAVIS 4-25
WE HAVE PEANUTS?!

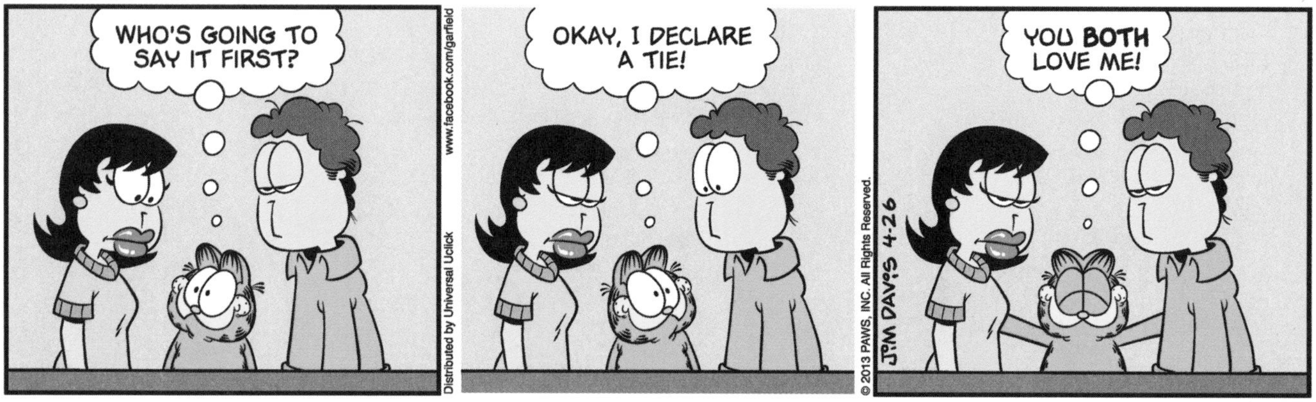
WHO'S GOING TO SAY IT FIRST?
www.facebook.com/garfield
Distributed by Universal Uclick
OKAY, I DECLARE A TIE!
© 2013 PAWS, INC. All Rights Reserved.
JIM DAVIS 4-26
YOU **BOTH** LOVE ME!

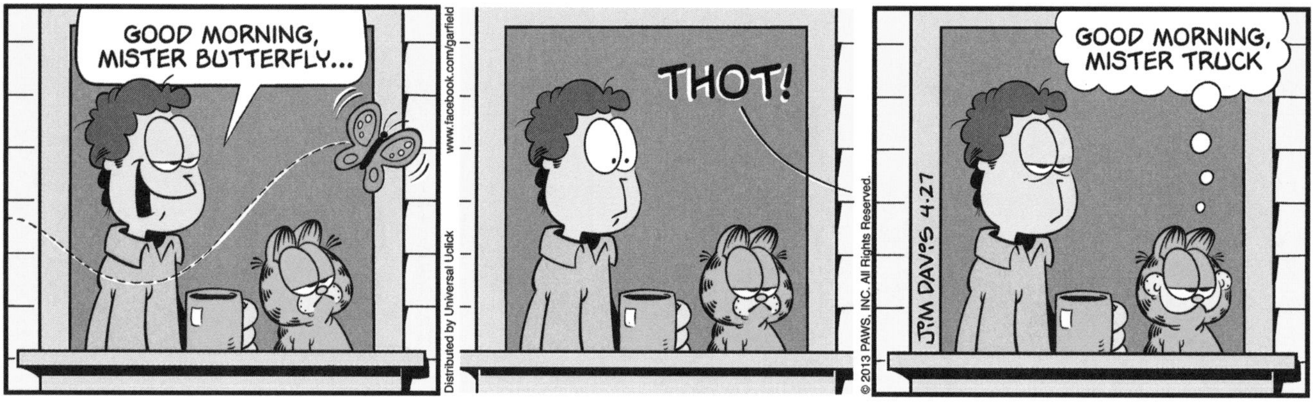
GOOD MORNING, MISTER BUTTERFLY...
www.facebook.com/garfield
Distributed by Universal Uclick
THOT!
© 2013 PAWS, INC. All Rights Reserved.
JIM DAVIS 4-27
GOOD MORNING, MISTER TRUCK

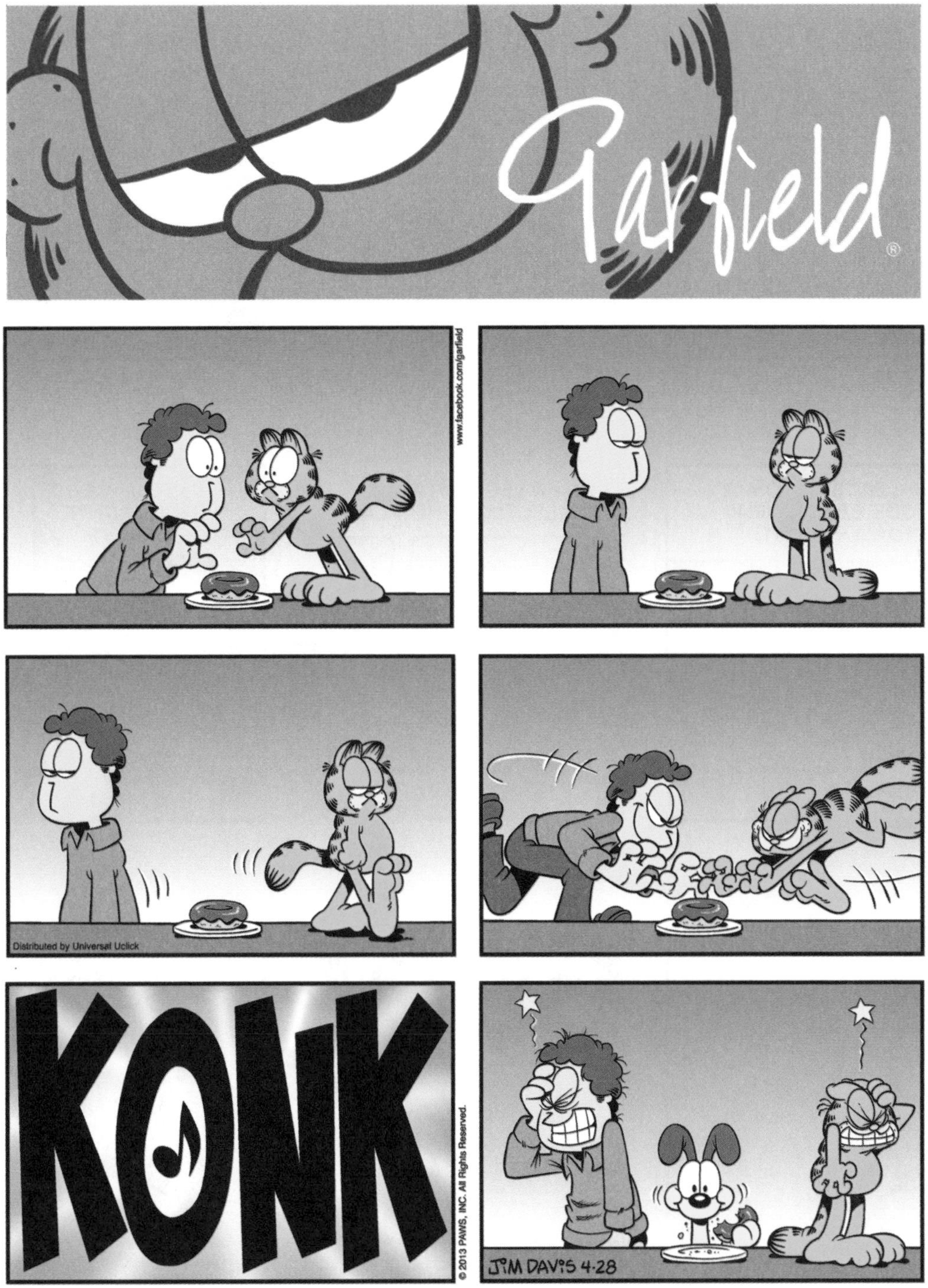
Garfield®
www.facebook.com/garfield
Distributed by Universal Uclick
KONK
© 2013 PAWS, INC. All Rights Reserved.
JIM DAVIS 4-28

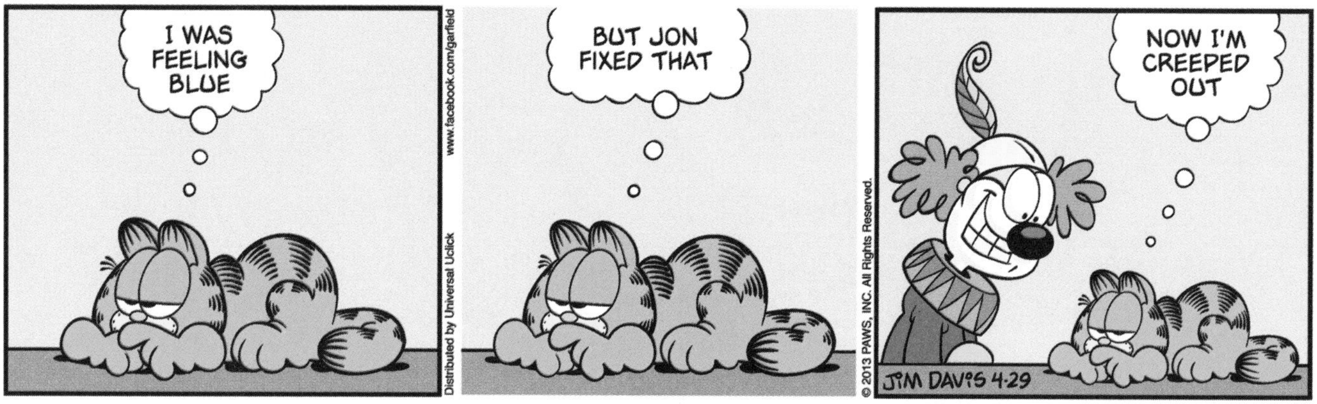
I WAS FEELING BLUE
BUT JON FIXED THAT
NOW I'M CREEPED OUT
JIM DAVIS 4-29
Distributed by Universal Uclick
www.facebook.com/garfield
© 2013 PAWS, INC. All Rights Reserved.

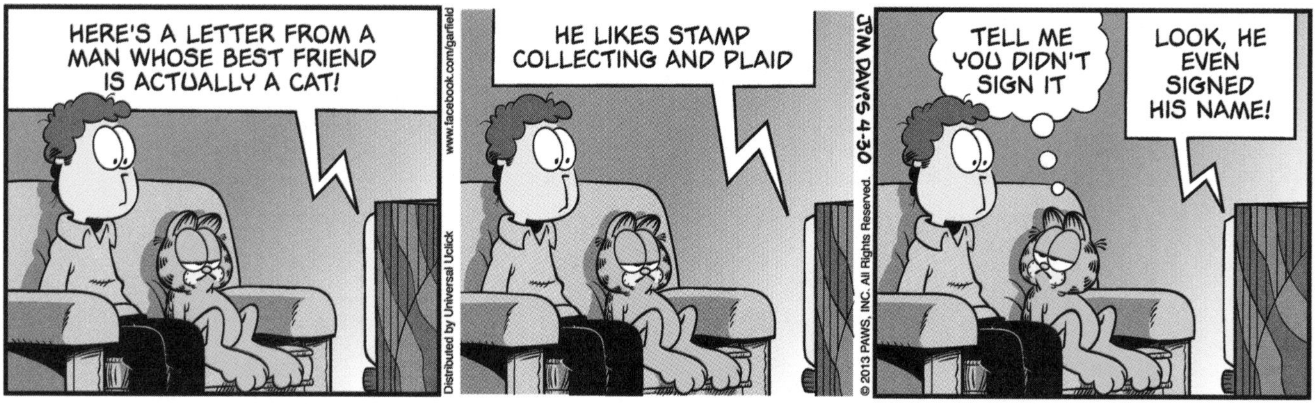
HERE'S A LETTER FROM A MAN WHOSE BEST FRIEND IS ACTUALLY A CAT!
HE LIKES STAMP COLLECTING AND PLAID
TELL ME YOU DIDN'T SIGN IT
LOOK, HE EVEN SIGNED HIS NAME!
JIM DAVIS 4-30
Distributed by Universal Uclick
www.facebook.com/garfield
© 2013 PAWS, INC. All Rights Reserved.

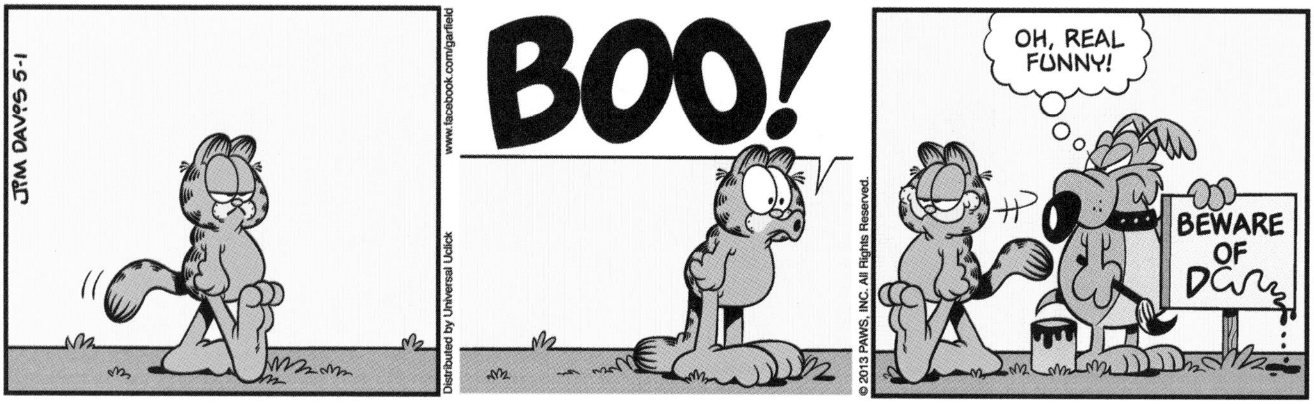
JIM DAVIS 5-1
BOO!
OH, REAL FUNNY!
BEWARE OF
Distributed by Universal Uclick
www.facebook.com/garfield
© 2013 PAWS, INC. All Rights Reserved.

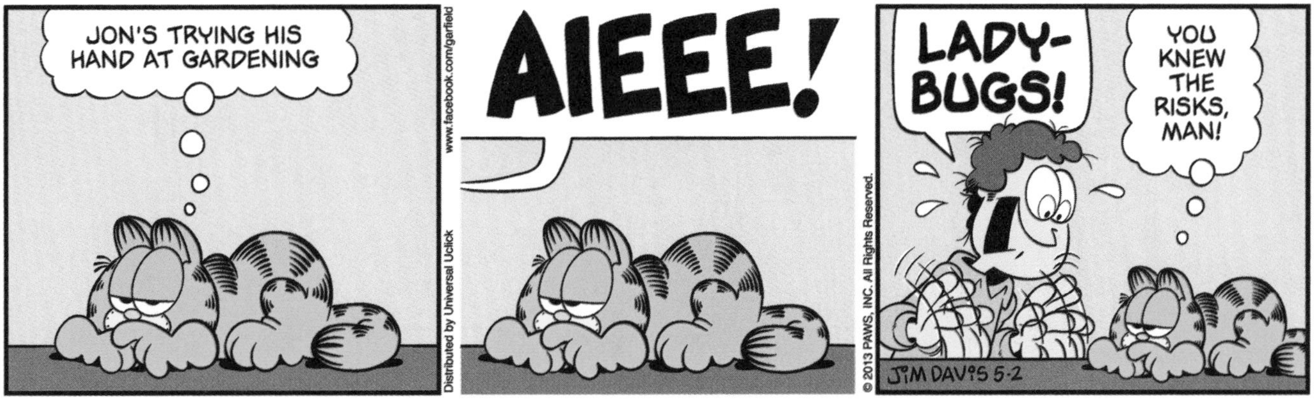
JON'S TRYING HIS HAND AT GARDENING
AIEEE!
LADY-BUGS!
YOU KNEW THE RISKS, MAN!
JIM DAVIS 5-2
www.facebook.com/garfield
Distributed by Universal Uclick
© 2013 PAWS, INC. All Rights Reserved.

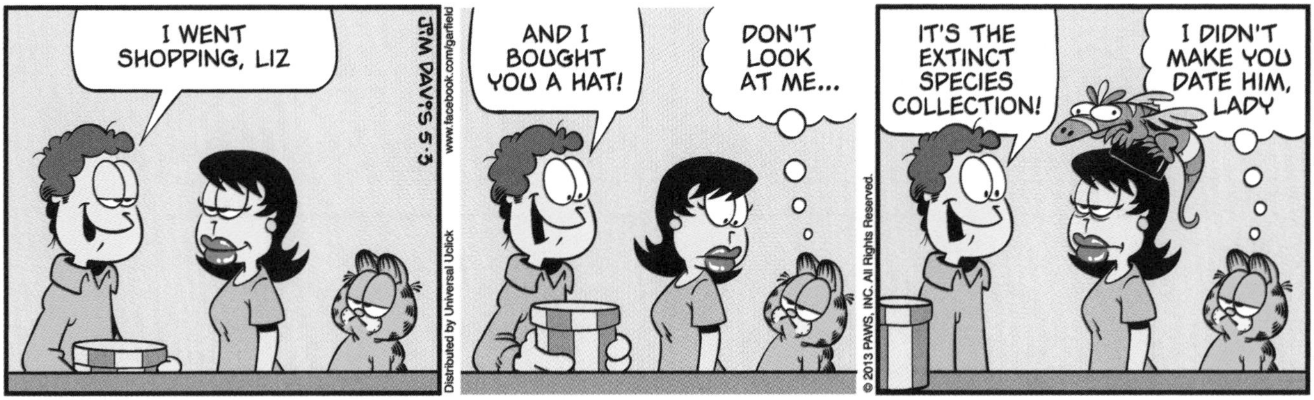
I WENT SHOPPING, LIZ
JIM DAVIS 5-3
AND I BOUGHT YOU A HAT!
DON'T LOOK AT ME...
IT'S THE EXTINCT SPECIES COLLECTION!
I DIDN'T MAKE YOU DATE HIM, LADY
www.facebook.com/garfield
Distributed by Universal Uclick
© 2013 PAWS, INC. All Rights Reserved.

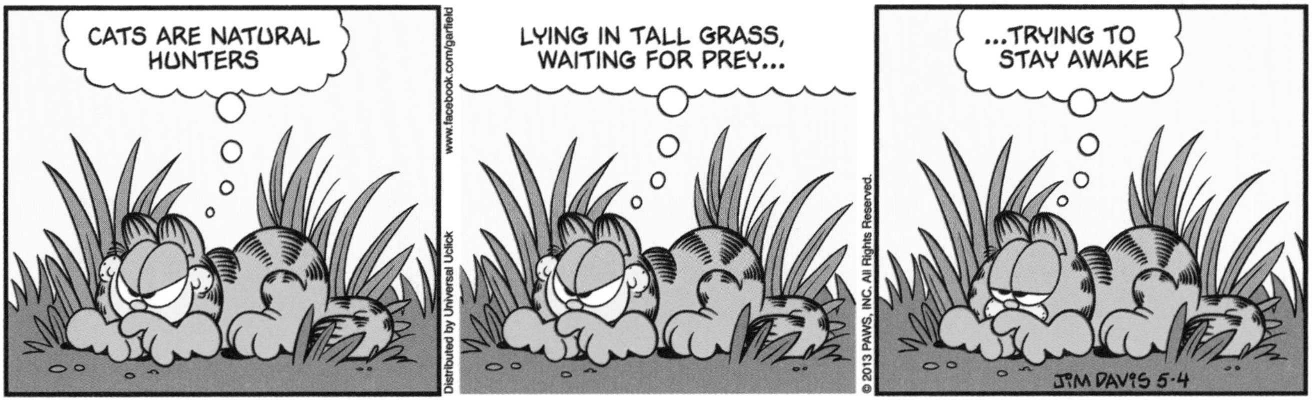
CATS ARE NATURAL HUNTERS
LYING IN TALL GRASS, WAITING FOR PREY...
...TRYING TO STAY AWAKE
JIM DAVIS 5-4
www.facebook.com/garfield
Distributed by Universal Uclick
© 2013 PAWS, INC. All Rights Reserved.

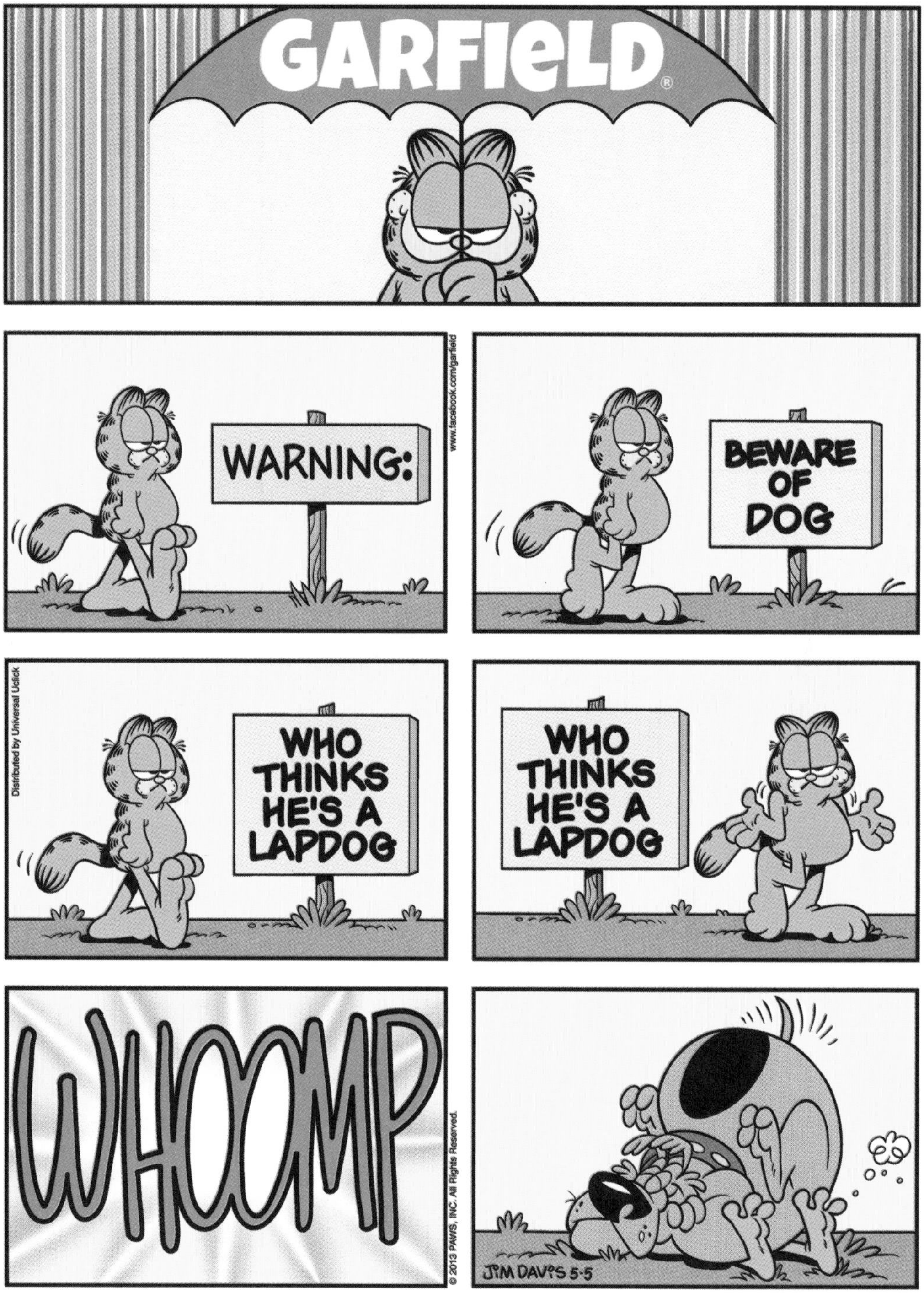
GARFIELD
www.facebook.com/garfield
WARNING:
BEWARE OF DOG
Distributed by Universal Uclick
WHO THINKS HE'S A LAPDOG
WHO THINKS HE'S A LAPDOG
WHOOMP
© 2013 PAWS, INC. All Rights Reserved.
JIM DAVIS 5-5

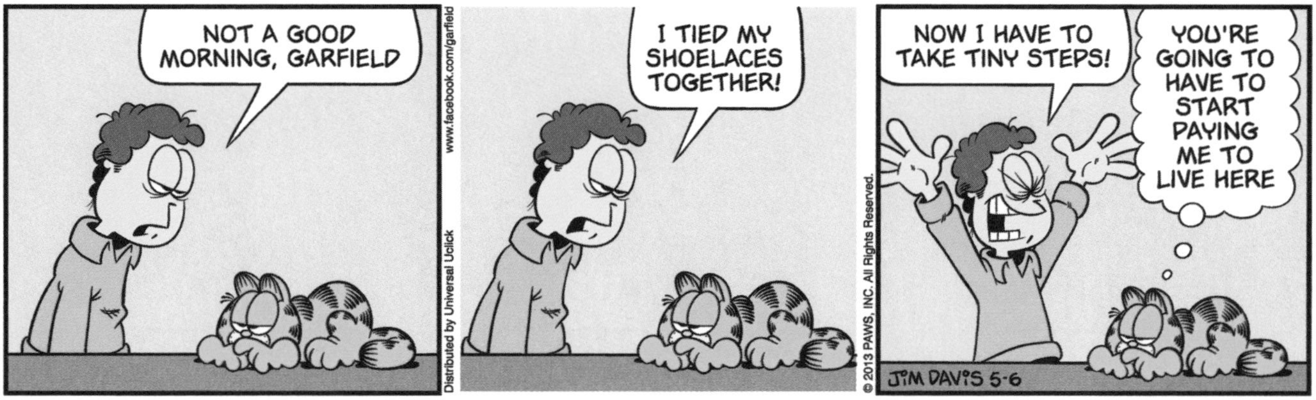
NOT A GOOD MORNING, GARFIELD
I TIED MY SHOELACES TOGETHER!
NOW I HAVE TO TAKE TINY STEPS!
YOU'RE GOING TO HAVE TO START PAYING ME TO LIVE HERE
www.facebook.com/garfield
Distributed by Universal Uclick
© 2013 PAWS, INC. All Rights Reserved.
JIM DAVIS 5-6

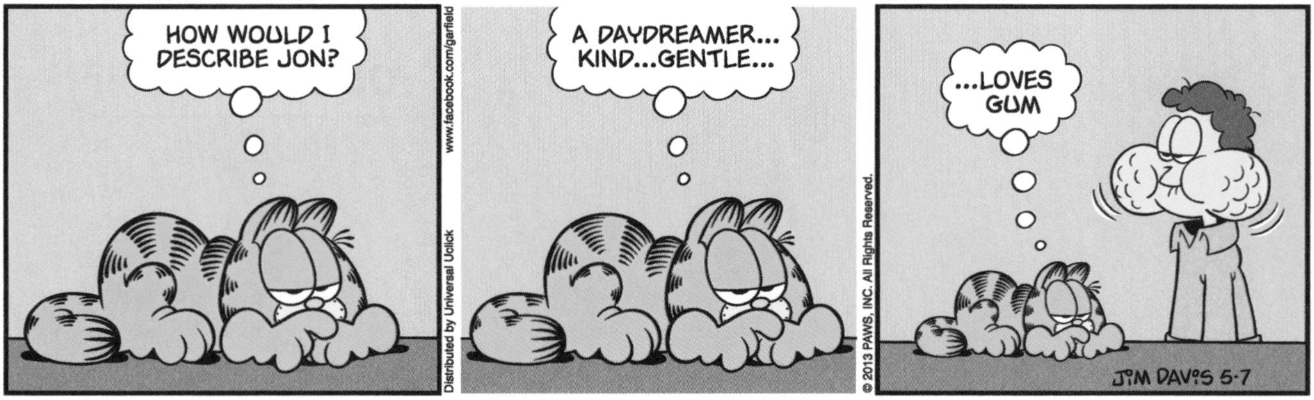
HOW WOULD I DESCRIBE JON?
A DAYDREAMER... KIND...GENTLE...
...LOVES GUM
www.facebook.com/garfield
Distributed by Universal Uclick
© 2013 PAWS, INC. All Rights Reserved.
JIM DAVIS 5-7

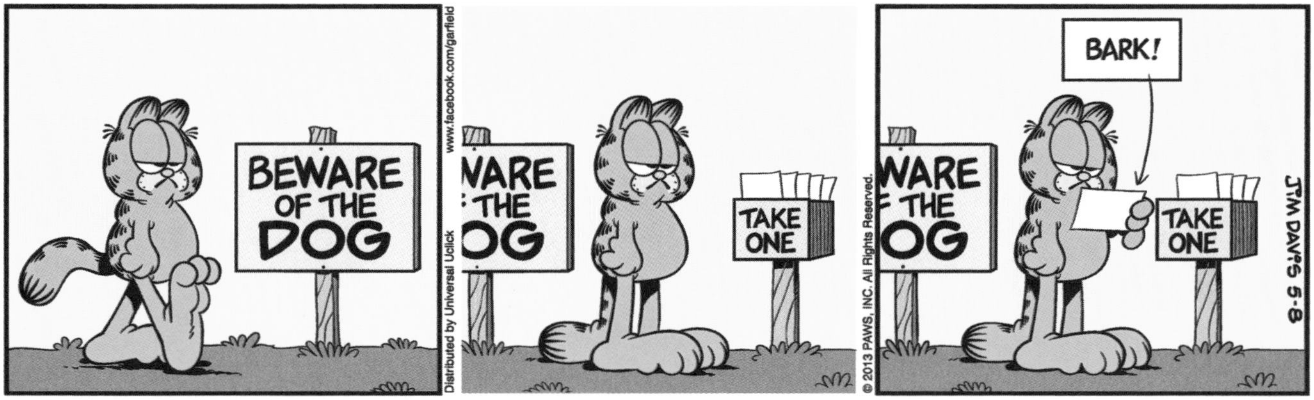
BEWARE OF THE DOG
www.facebook.com/garfield
Distributed by Universal Uclick
WARE THE OG
TAKE ONE
© 2013 PAWS, INC. All Rights Reserved.
WARE THE OG
BARK!
TAKE ONE
JIM DAVIS 5-8

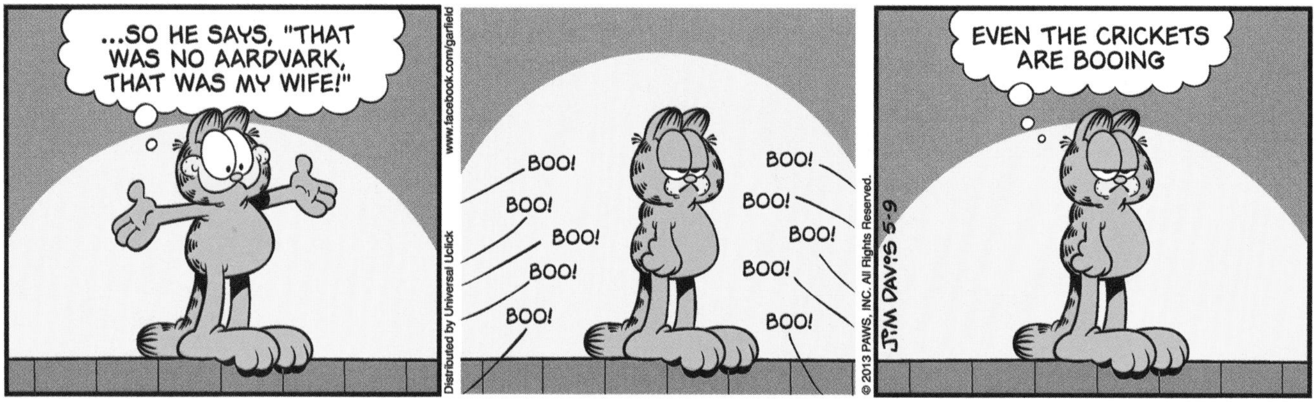
...SO HE SAYS, "THAT WAS NO AARDVARK, THAT WAS MY WIFE!"
Distributed by Universal Uclick
www.facebook.com/garfield
BOO!
BOO!
BOO!
BOO!
BOO!
BOO!
BOO!
BOO!
BOO!
BOO!
© 2013 PAWS, INC. All Rights Reserved.
JIM DAVIS 5-9
EVEN THE CRICKETS ARE BOOING

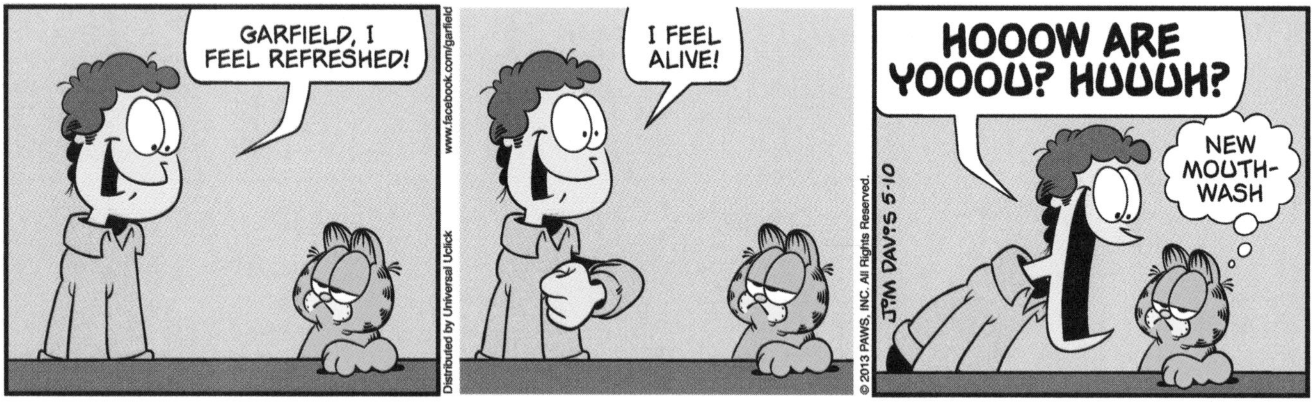
GARFIELD, I FEEL REFRESHED!
Distributed by Universal Uclick
www.facebook.com/garfield
I FEEL ALIVE!
© 2013 PAWS, INC. All Rights Reserved.
JIM DAVIS 5-10
HOOOW ARE YOOOU? HUUUH?
NEW MOUTH-WASH

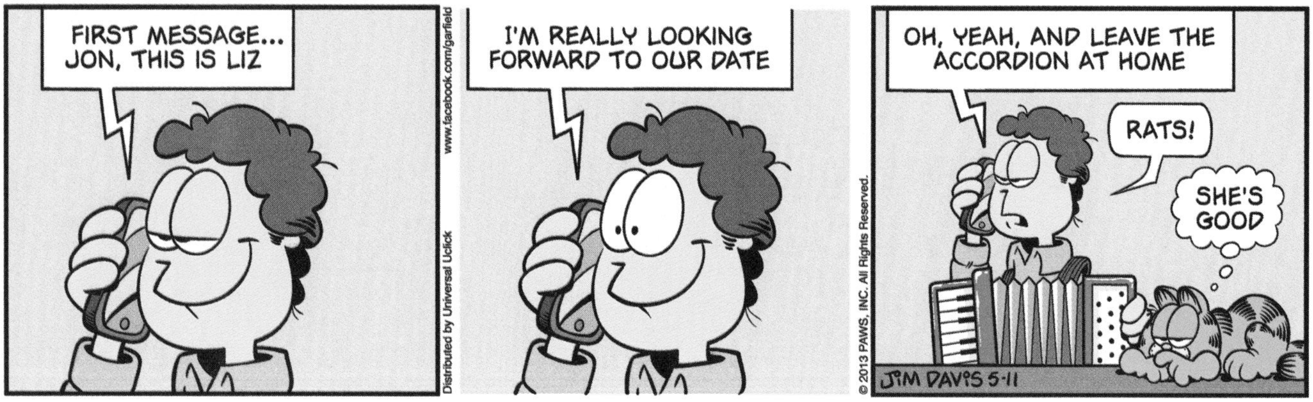
FIRST MESSAGE... JON, THIS IS LIZ
Distributed by Universal Uclick
www.facebook.com/garfield
I'M REALLY LOOKING FORWARD TO OUR DATE
© 2013 PAWS, INC. All Rights Reserved.
OH, YEAH, AND LEAVE THE ACCORDION AT HOME
RATS!
SHE'S GOOD
JIM DAVIS 5-11

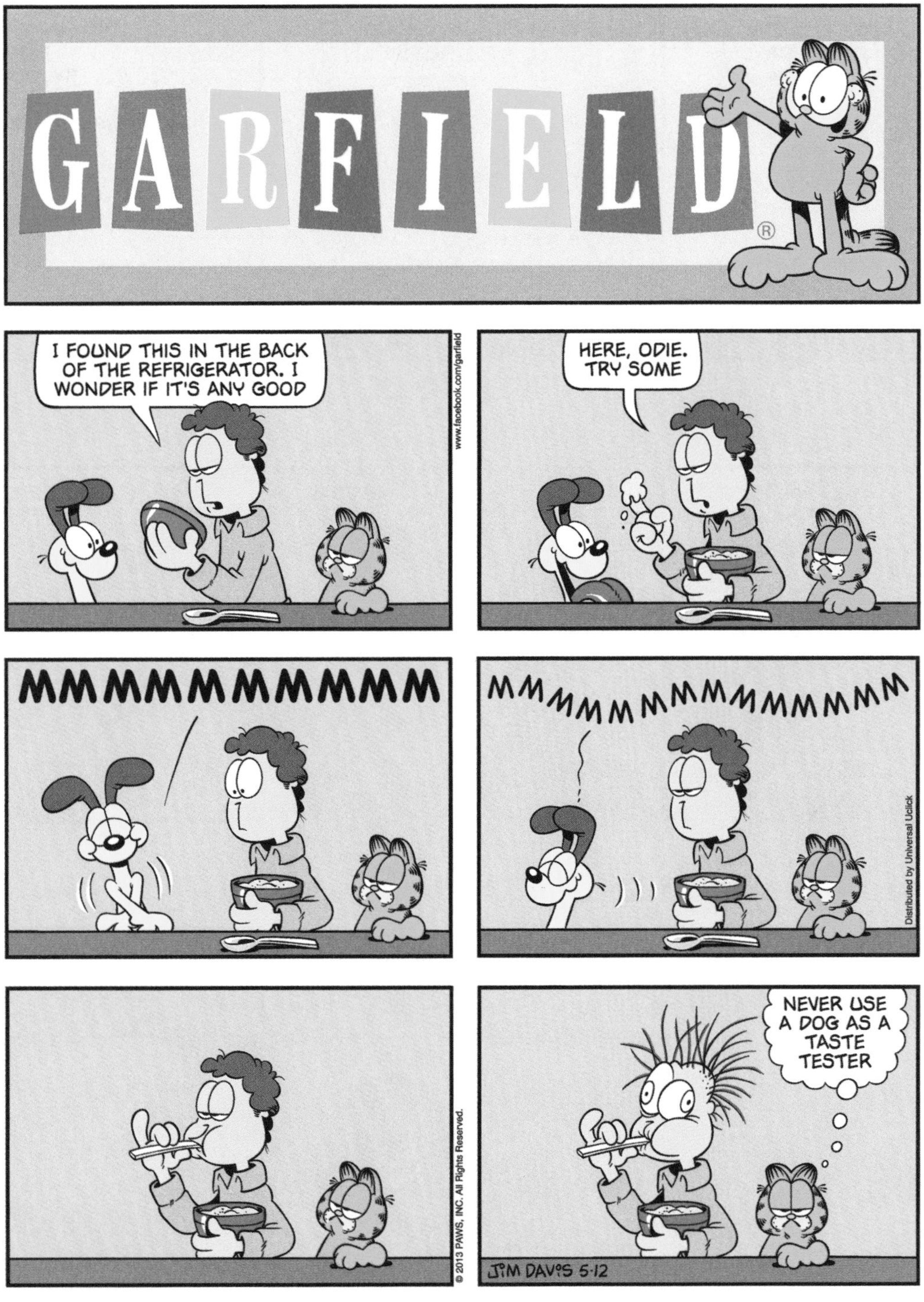
GARFIELD®
I FOUND THIS IN THE BACK OF THE REFRIGERATOR. I WONDER IF IT'S ANY GOOD
www.facebook.com/garfield
HERE, ODIE. TRY SOME
MMMMMMMMMM
MMMMMMMMMMMMMMM
Distributed by Universal Uclick
© 2013 PAWS, INC. All Rights Reserved.
NEVER USE A DOG AS A TASTE TESTER
JIM DAVIS 5-12

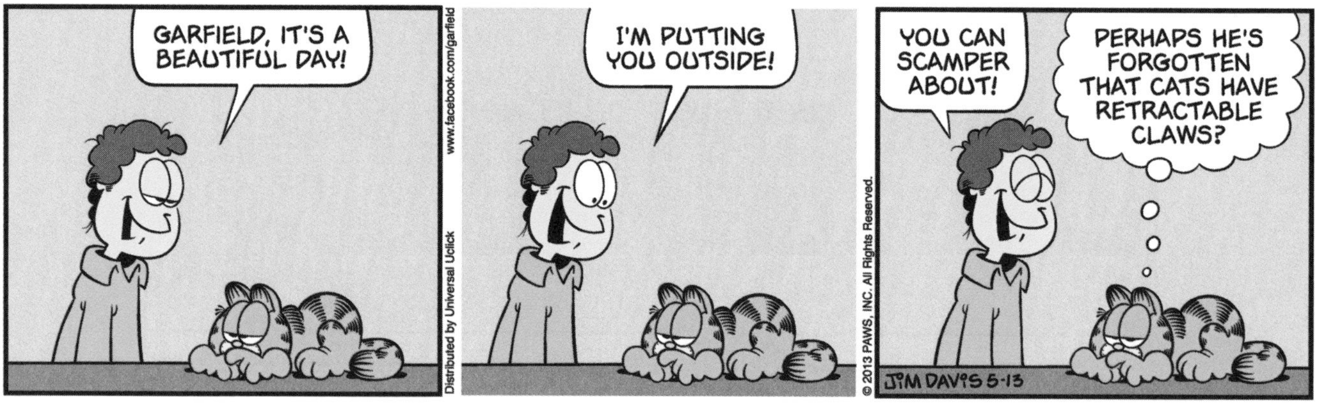
GARFIELD, IT'S A BEAUTIFUL DAY!
www.facebook.com/garfield
Distributed by Universal Uclick
I'M PUTTING YOU OUTSIDE!
YOU CAN SCAMPER ABOUT!
PERHAPS HE'S FORGOTTEN THAT CATS HAVE RETRACTABLE CLAWS?
© 2013 PAWS, INC. All Rights Reserved.
JIM DAVIS 5-13

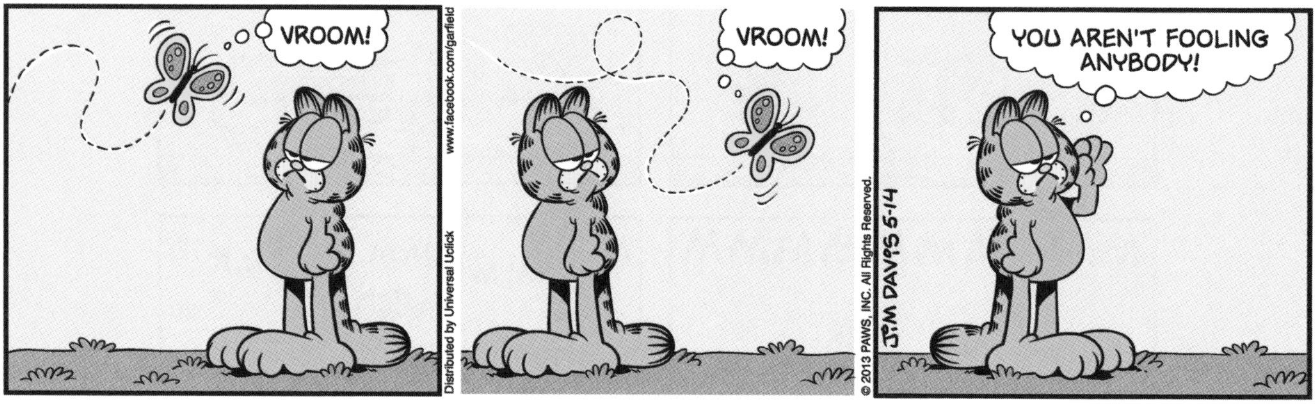
VROOM!
www.facebook.com/garfield
Distributed by Universal Uclick
VROOM!
YOU AREN'T FOOLING ANYBODY!
© 2013 PAWS, INC. All Rights Reserved.
JIM DAVIS 5-14

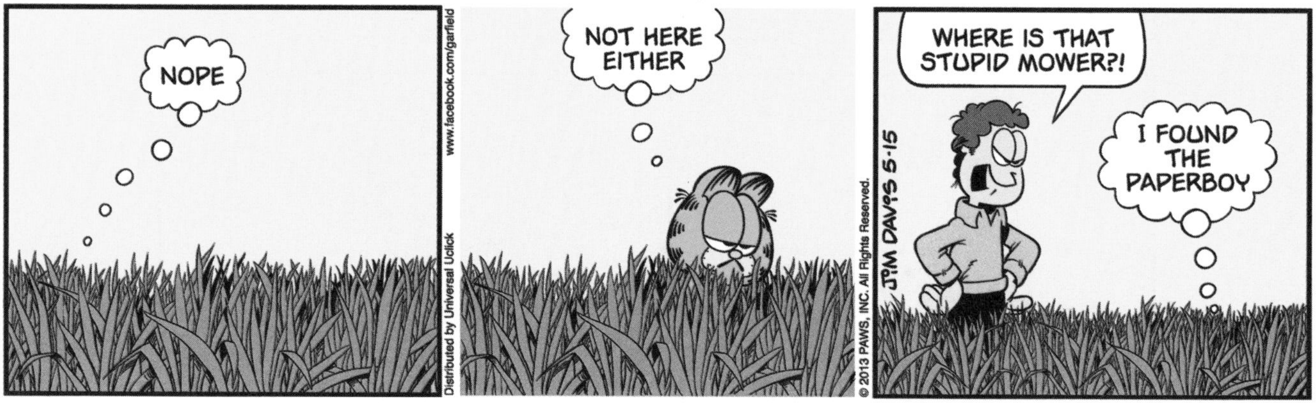
NOPE
www.facebook.com/garfield
Distributed by Universal Uclick
NOT HERE EITHER
WHERE IS THAT STUPID MOWER?!
I FOUND THE PAPERBOY
© 2013 PAWS, INC. All Rights Reserved.
JIM DAVIS 5-15

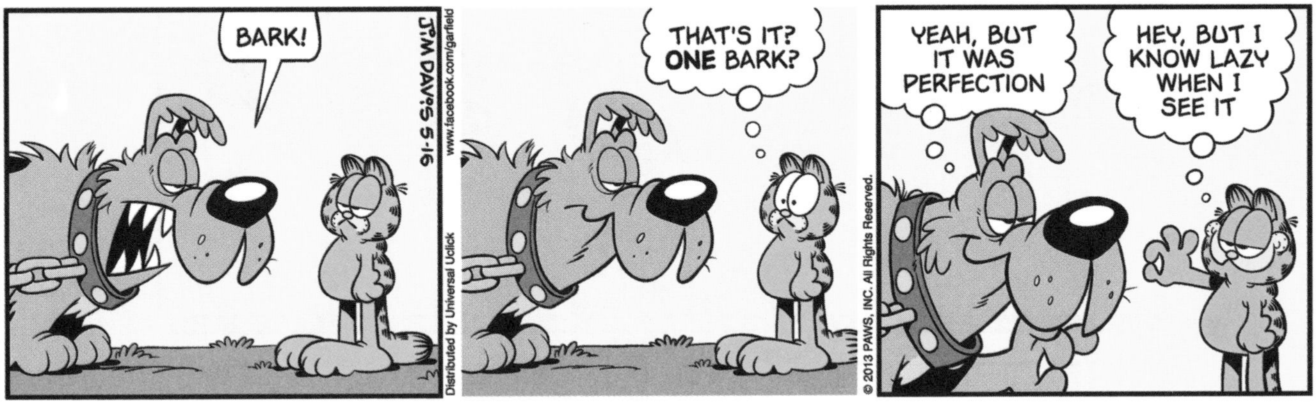
BARK!
JIM DAVIS 5-16
www.facebook.com/garfield
Distributed by Universal Uclick
THAT'S IT? **ONE** BARK?
© 2013 PAWS, INC. All Rights Reserved.
YEAH, BUT IT WAS PERFECTION
HEY, BUT I KNOW LAZY WHEN I SEE IT

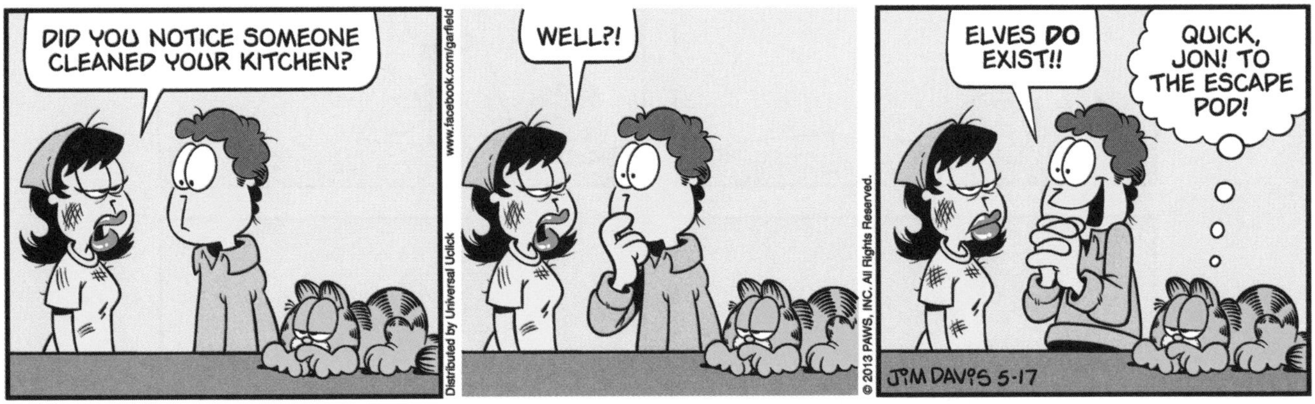
DID YOU NOTICE SOMEONE CLEANED YOUR KITCHEN?
www.facebook.com/garfield
Distributed by Universal Uclick
WELL?!
© 2013 PAWS, INC. All Rights Reserved.
ELVES **DO** EXIST!!
QUICK, JON! TO THE ESCAPE POD!
JIM DAVIS 5-17

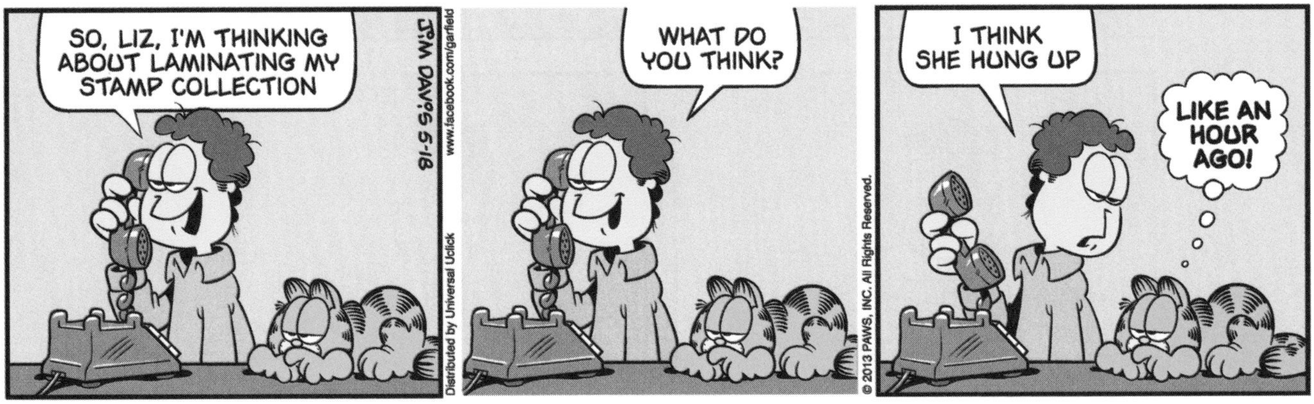
SO, LIZ, I'M THINKING ABOUT LAMINATING MY STAMP COLLECTION
JIM DAVIS 5-18
www.facebook.com/garfield
Distributed by Universal Uclick
WHAT DO YOU THINK?
© 2013 PAWS, INC. All Rights Reserved.
I THINK SHE HUNG UP
LIKE AN HOUR AGO!

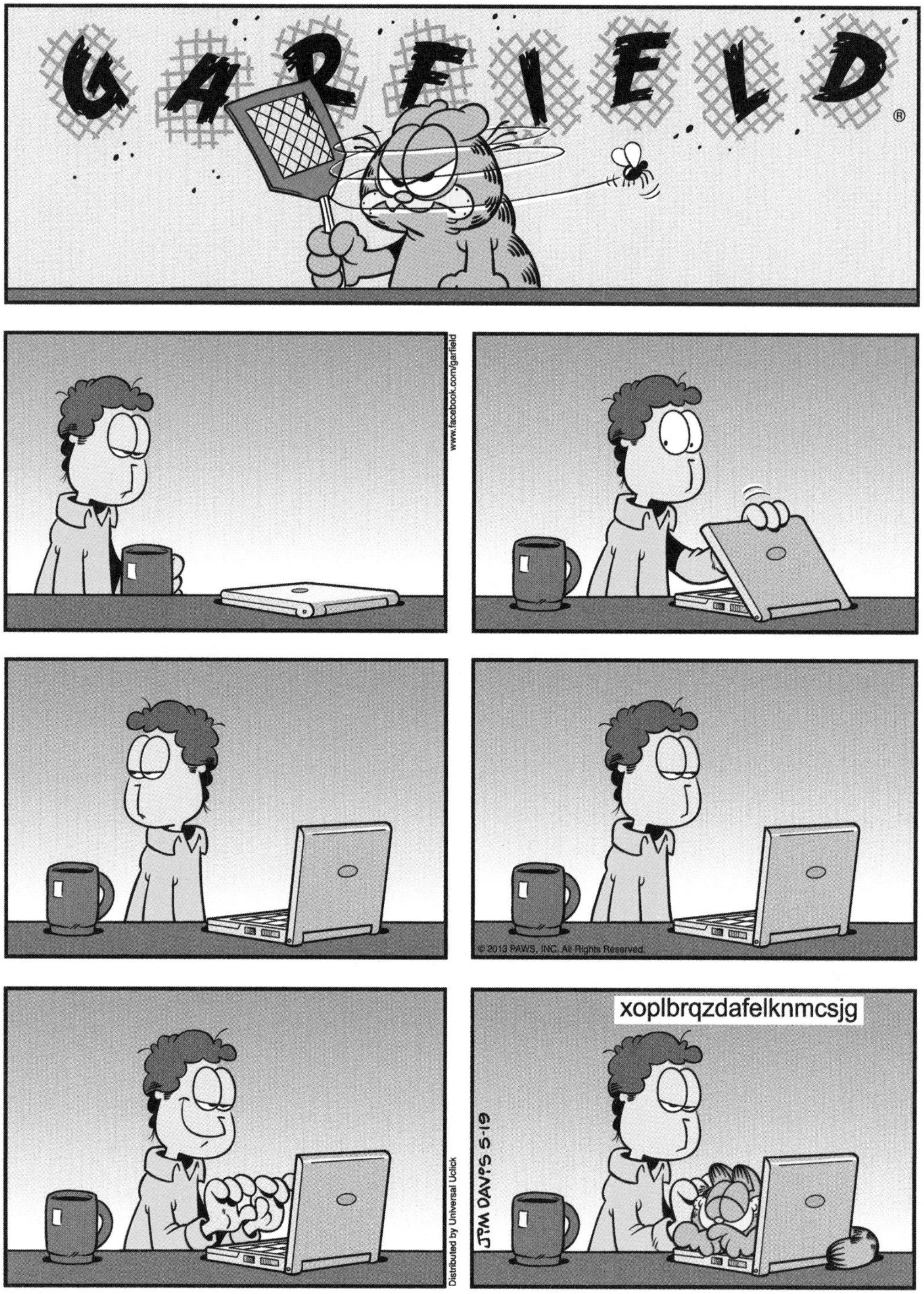
GARFIELD
www.facebook.com/garfield
© 2013 PAWS, INC. All Rights Reserved.
Distributed by Universal Uclick
JIM DAVIS 5-19
xoplbrqzdafelknmcsjg

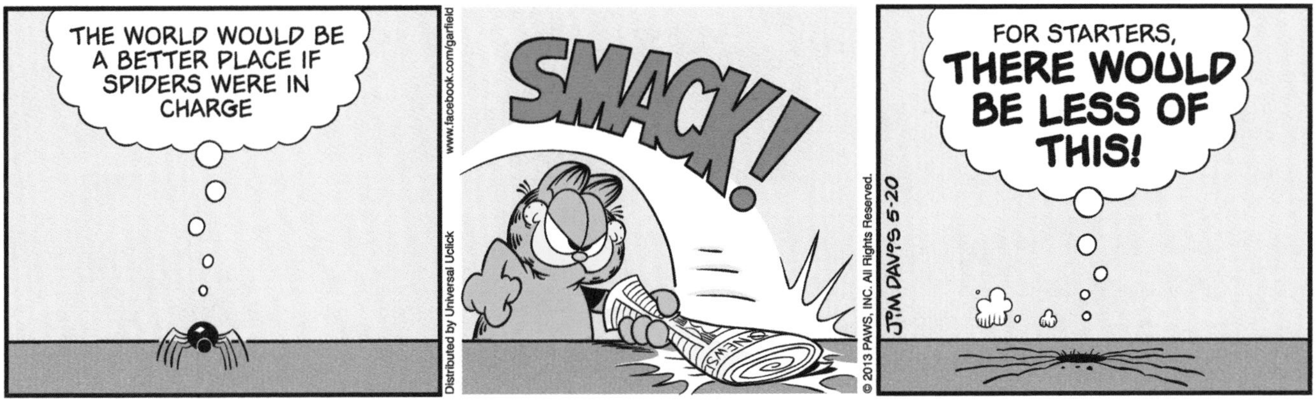
THE WORLD WOULD BE A BETTER PLACE IF SPIDERS WERE IN CHARGE
Distributed by Universal Uclick www.facebook.com/garfield
SMACK!
NEWS
© 2013 PAWS, INC. All Rights Reserved.
JIM DAVIS 5-20
FOR STARTERS, THERE WOULD BE LESS OF THIS!

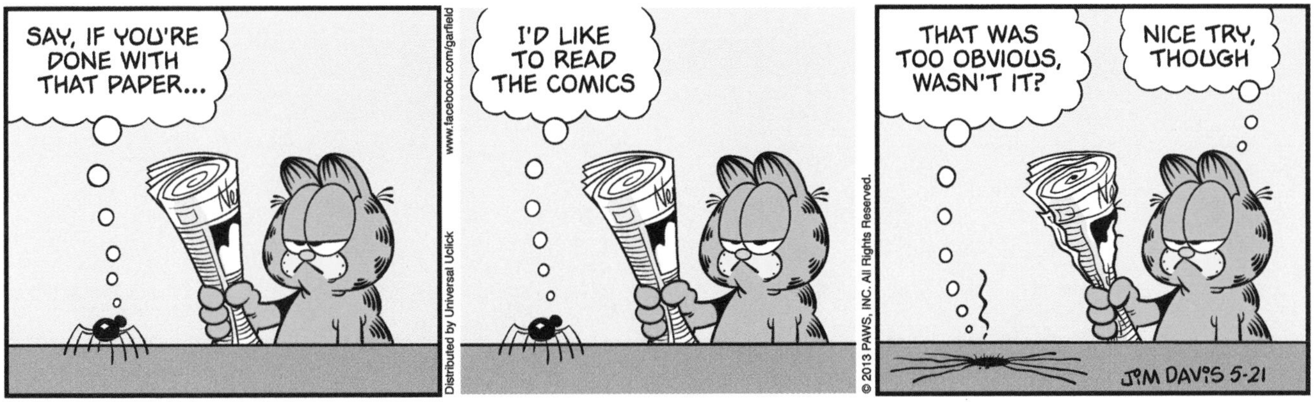
SAY, IF YOU'RE DONE WITH THAT PAPER...
Distributed by Universal Uclick www.facebook.com/garfield
I'D LIKE TO READ THE COMICS
© 2013 PAWS, INC. All Rights Reserved.
THAT WAS TOO OBVIOUS, WASN'T IT?
NICE TRY, THOUGH
JIM DAVIS 5-21

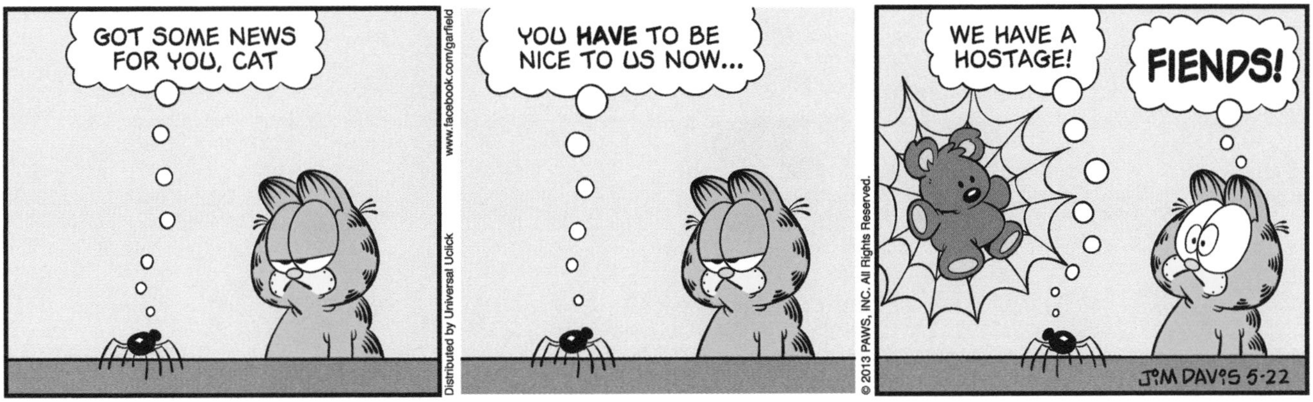
GOT SOME NEWS FOR YOU, CAT
Distributed by Universal Uclick www.facebook.com/garfield
YOU **HAVE** TO BE NICE TO US NOW...
© 2013 PAWS, INC. All Rights Reserved.
WE HAVE A HOSTAGE!
FIENDS!
JIM DAVIS 5-22

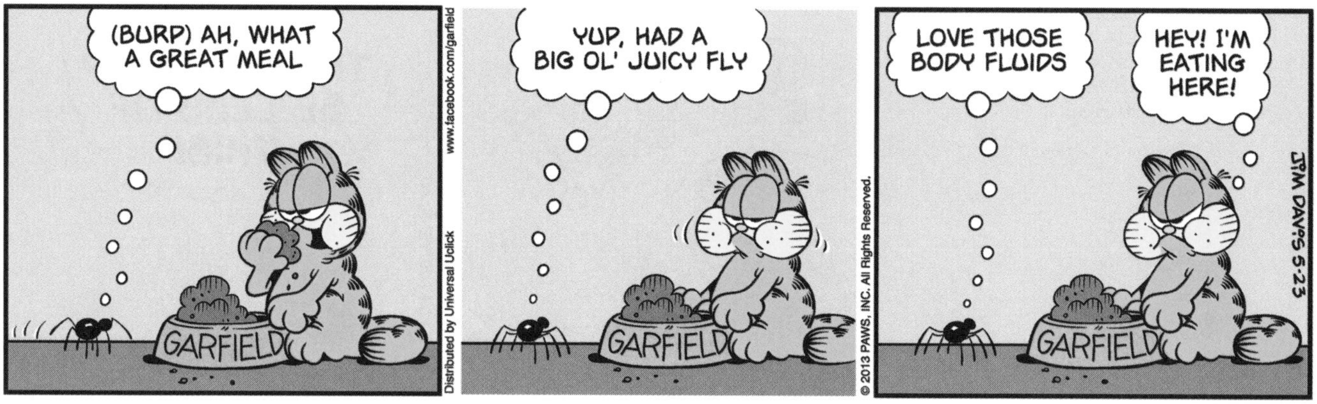
(BURP) AH, WHAT A GREAT MEAL
YUP, HAD A BIG OL' JUICY FLY
LOVE THOSE BODY FLUIDS
HEY! I'M EATING HERE!
GARFIELD
JIM DAVIS 5-23
Distributed by Universal Uclick www.facebook.com/garfield
© 2013 PAWS, INC. All Rights Reserved.

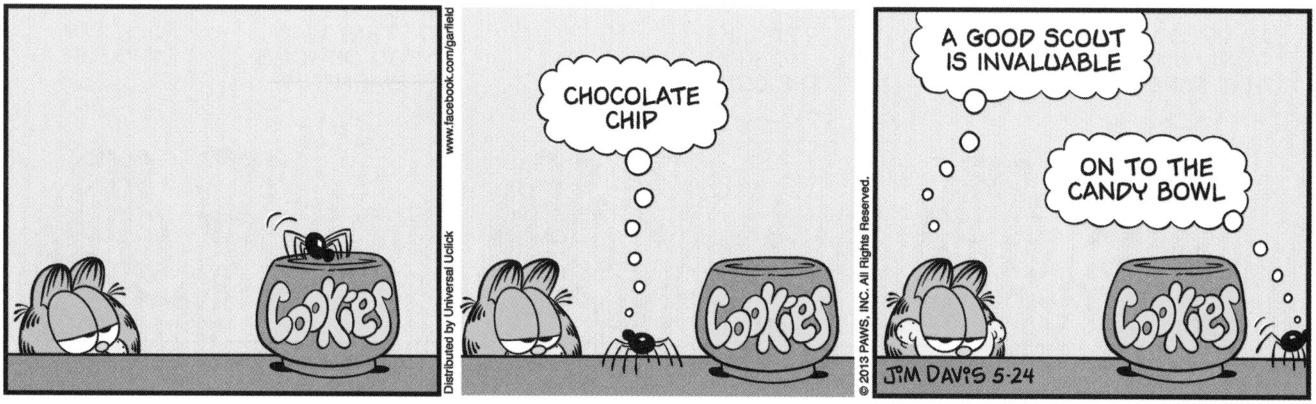
COOKIES
CHOCOLATE CHIP
A GOOD SCOUT IS INVALUABLE
ON TO THE CANDY BOWL
JIM DAVIS 5-24
Distributed by Universal Uclick www.facebook.com/garfield
© 2013 PAWS, INC. All Rights Reserved.

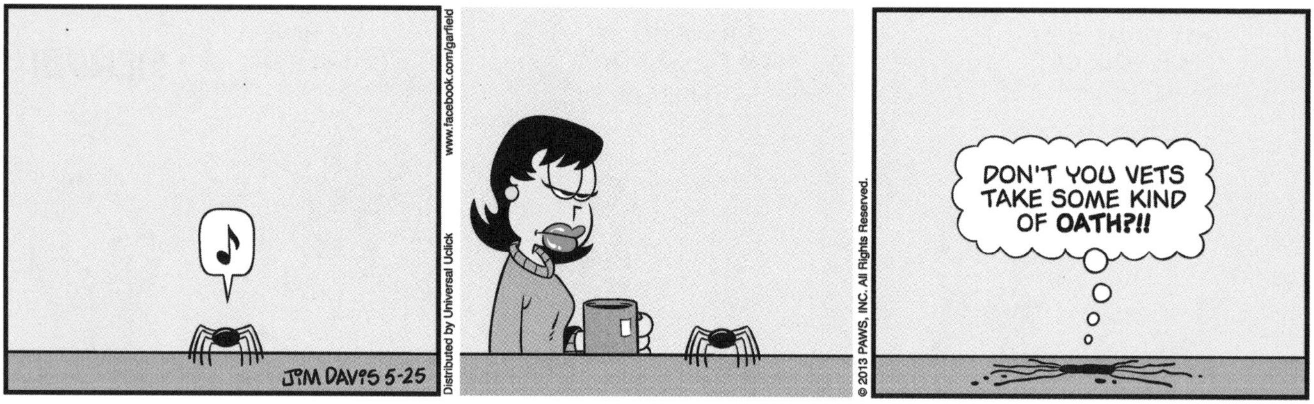
♪
JIM DAVIS 5-25
DON'T YOU VETS TAKE SOME KIND OF **OATH?!!**
Distributed by Universal Uclick www.facebook.com/garfield
© 2013 PAWS, INC. All Rights Reserved.

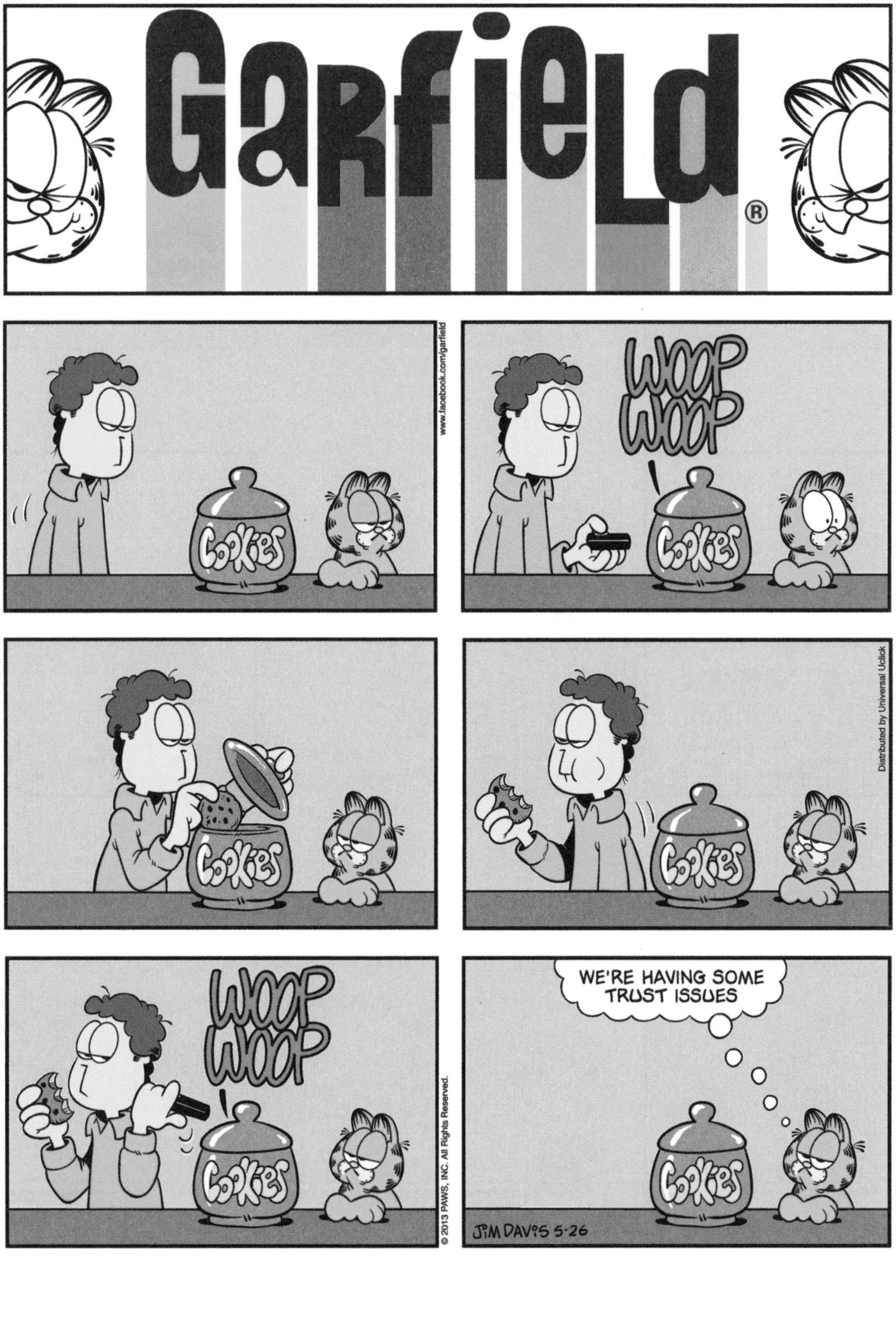
GARFIELD®
www.facebook.com/garfield
WOOP WOOP
COOKIES
Distributed by Universal Uclick
WOOP WOOP
© 2013 PAWS, INC. All Rights Reserved.
WE'RE HAVING SOME TRUST ISSUES
JIM DAVIS 5-26

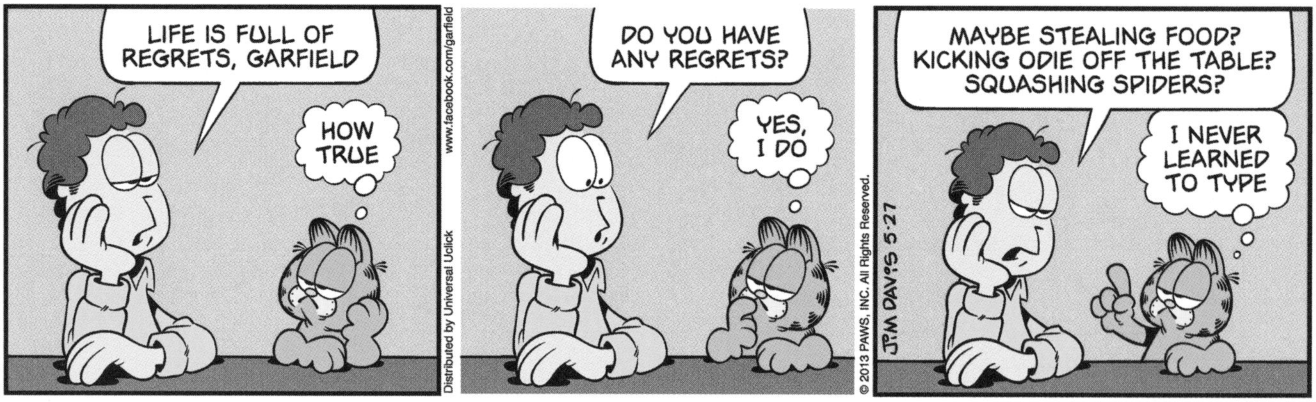
LIFE IS FULL OF REGRETS, GARFIELD
HOW TRUE
DO YOU HAVE ANY REGRETS?
YES, I DO
MAYBE STEALING FOOD? KICKING ODIE OFF THE TABLE? SQUASHING SPIDERS?
I NEVER LEARNED TO TYPE
JIM DAVIS 5-27
Distributed by Universal Uclick www.facebook.com/garfield
© 2013 PAWS, INC. All Rights Reserved.

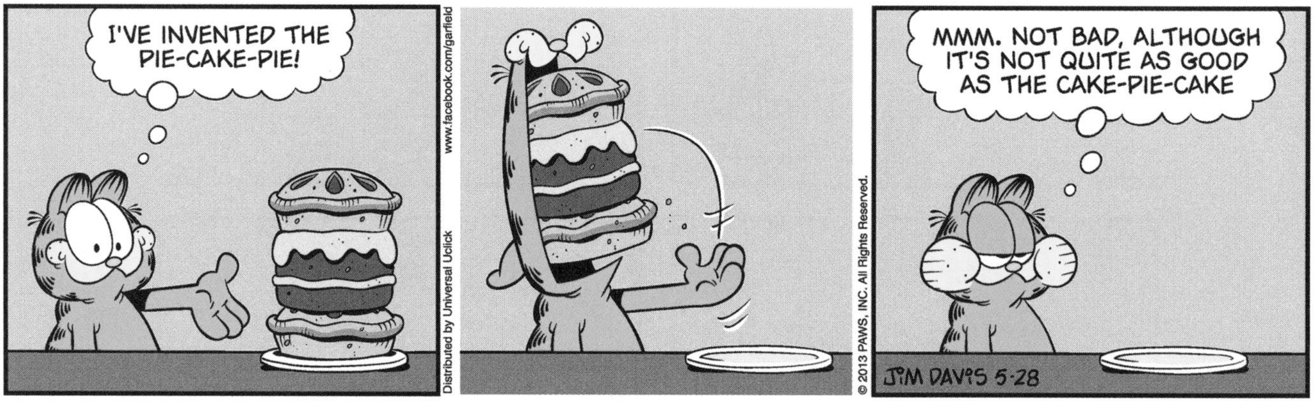
I'VE INVENTED THE PIE-CAKE-PIE!
MMM. NOT BAD, ALTHOUGH IT'S NOT QUITE AS GOOD AS THE CAKE-PIE-CAKE
JIM DAVIS 5-28
Distributed by Universal Uclick www.facebook.com/garfield
© 2013 PAWS, INC. All Rights Reserved.

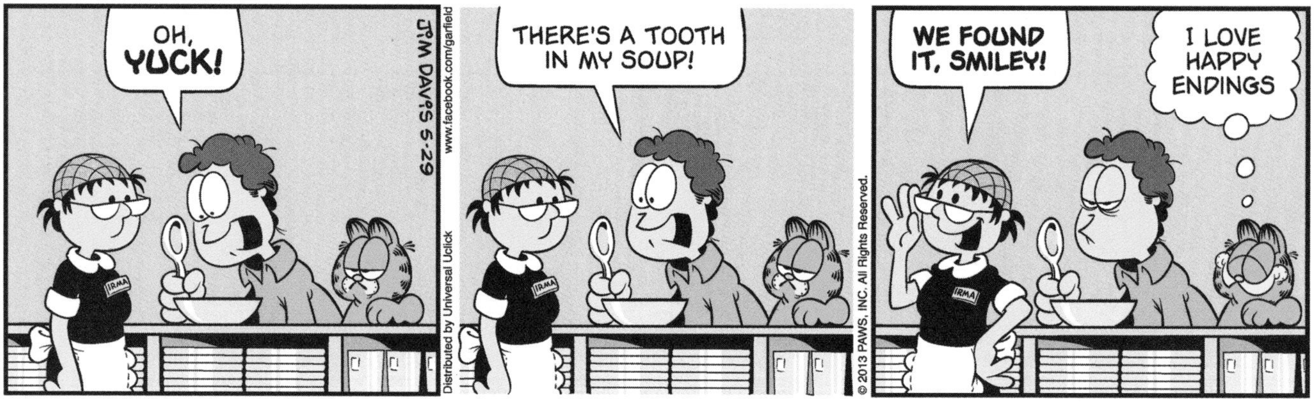
OH, **YUCK!**
THERE'S A TOOTH IN MY SOUP!
WE FOUND IT, SMILEY!
I LOVE HAPPY ENDINGS
IRMA
JIM DAVIS 5-29
Distributed by Universal Uclick www.facebook.com/garfield
© 2013 PAWS, INC. All Rights Reserved.

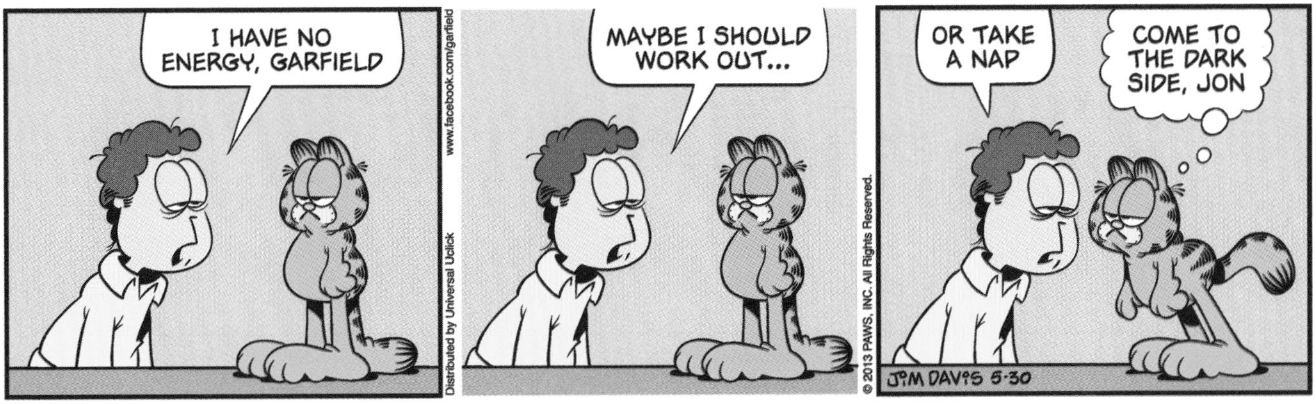
I HAVE NO ENERGY, GARFIELD
MAYBE I SHOULD WORK OUT...
OR TAKE A NAP
COME TO THE DARK SIDE, JON
JIM DAVIS 5-30

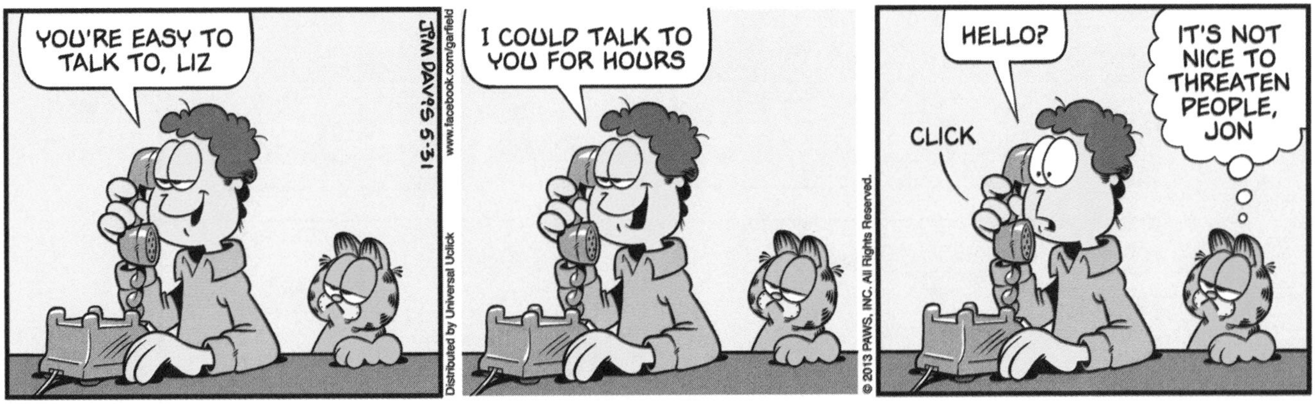
YOU'RE EASY TO TALK TO, LIZ
JIM DAVIS 5-31
I COULD TALK TO YOU FOR HOURS
HELLO?
CLICK
IT'S NOT NICE TO THREATEN PEOPLE, JON

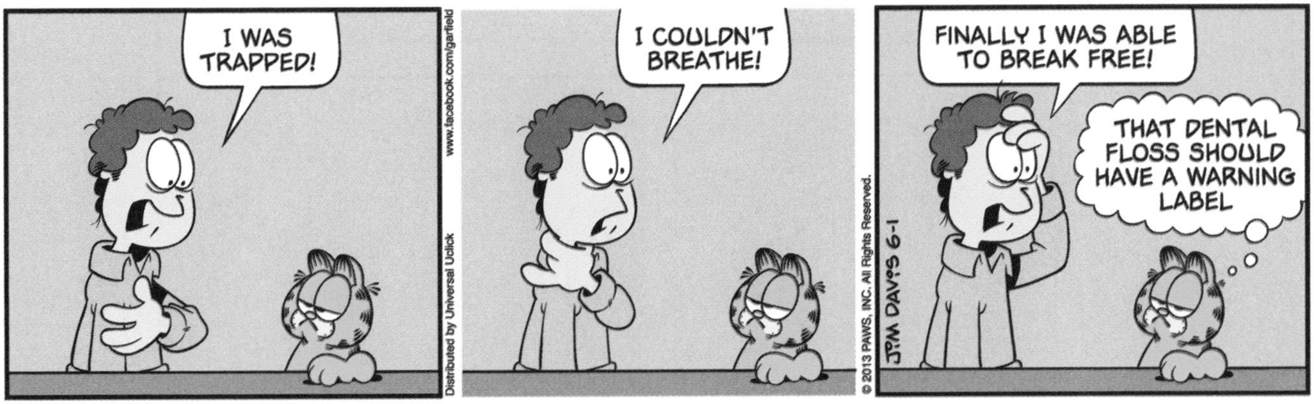
I WAS TRAPPED!
I COULDN'T BREATHE!
JIM DAVIS 6-1
FINALLY I WAS ABLE TO BREAK FREE!
THAT DENTAL FLOSS SHOULD HAVE A WARNING LABEL

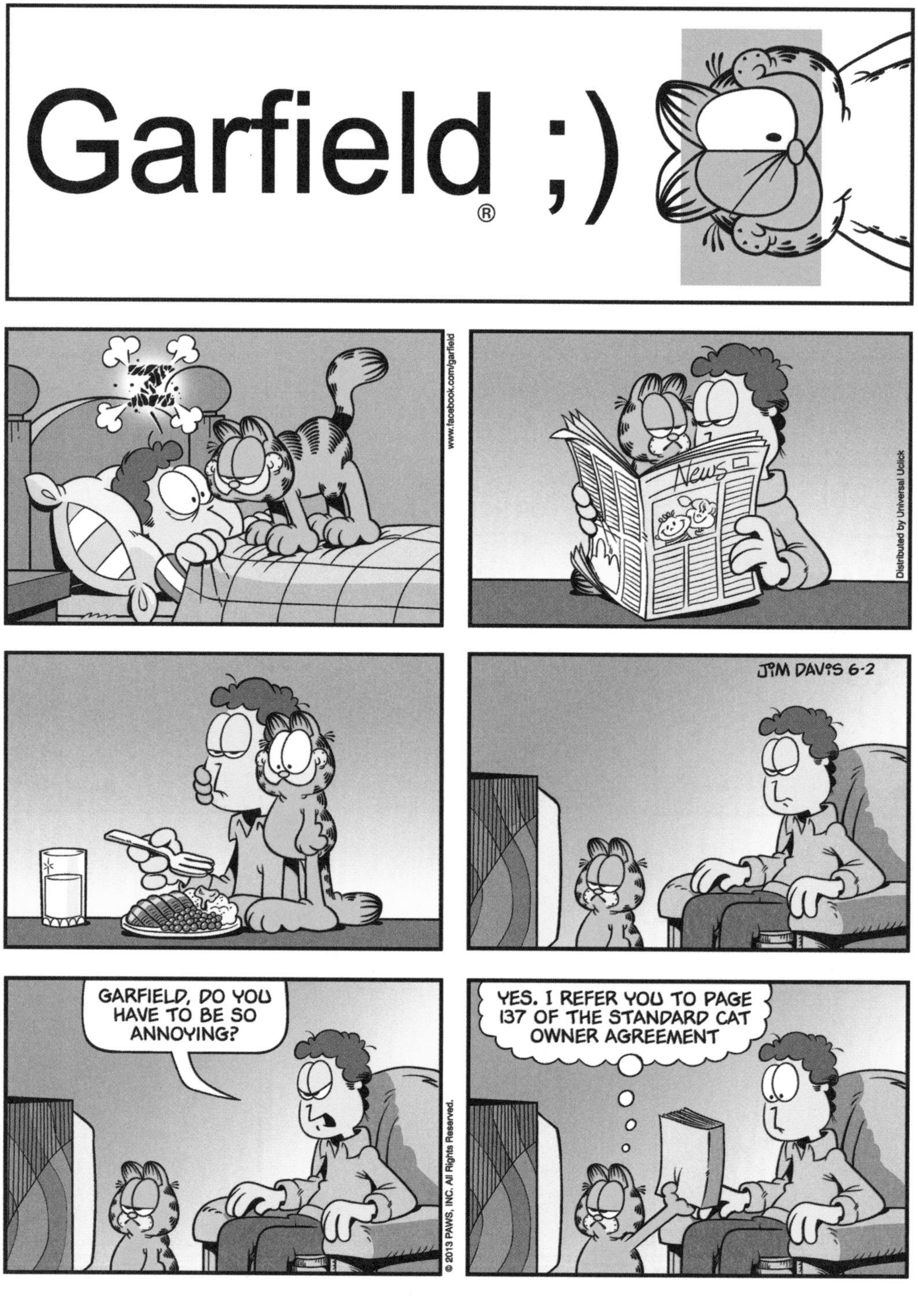
Garfield ;)
www.facebook.com/garfield
News
Distributed by Universal Uclick
JIM DAVIS 6-2
GARFIELD, DO YOU HAVE TO BE SO ANNOYING?
© 2013 PAWS, INC. All Rights Reserved.
YES. I REFER YOU TO PAGE 137 OF THE STANDARD CAT OWNER AGREEMENT

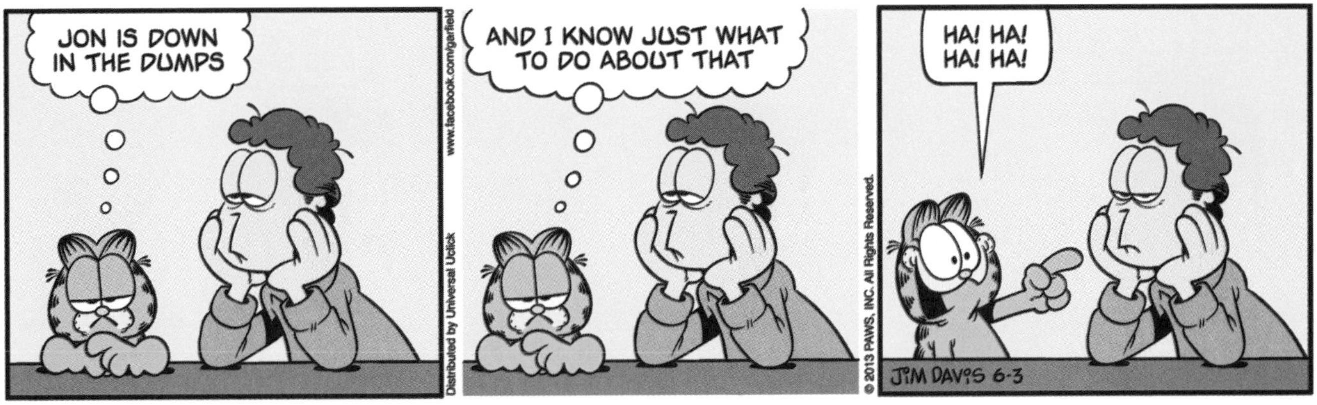
JON IS DOWN IN THE DUMPS
www.facebook.com/garfield
Distributed by Universal Uclick
AND I KNOW JUST WHAT TO DO ABOUT THAT
HA! HA! HA! HA!
© 2013 PAWS, INC. All Rights Reserved.
JIM DAVIS 6-3

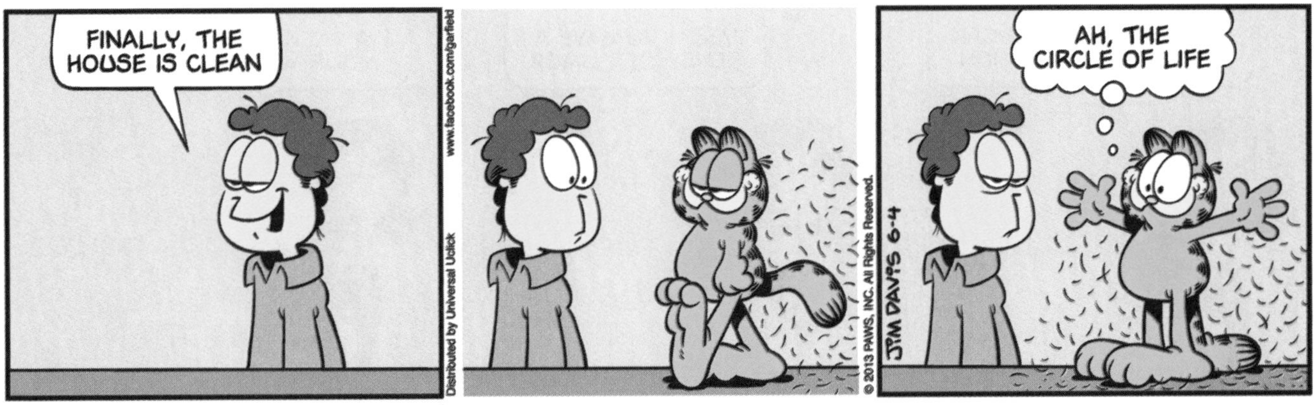
FINALLY, THE HOUSE IS CLEAN
www.facebook.com/garfield
Distributed by Universal Uclick
© 2013 PAWS, INC. All Rights Reserved.
JIM DAVIS 6-4
AH, THE CIRCLE OF LIFE

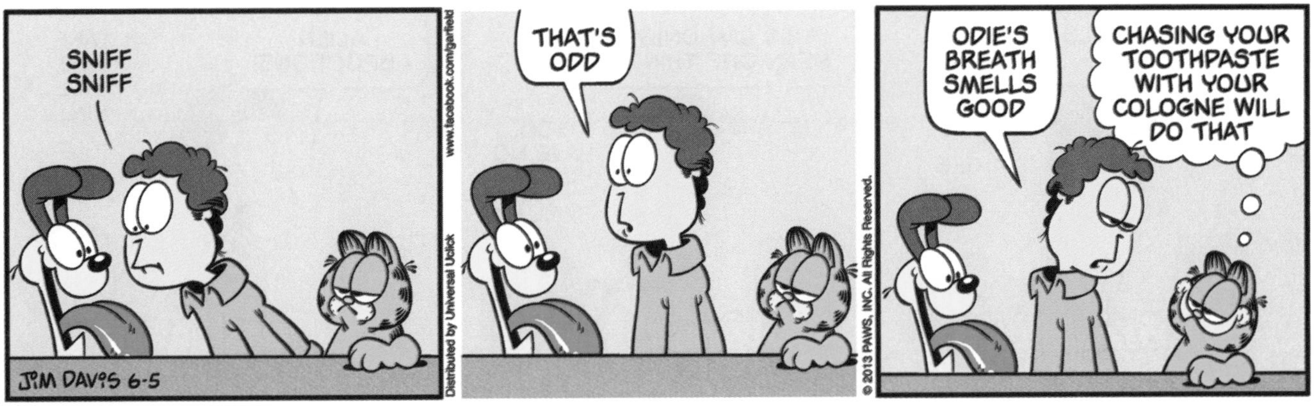
SNIFF SNIFF
JIM DAVIS 6-5
www.facebook.com/garfield
Distributed by Universal Uclick
THAT'S ODD
© 2013 PAWS, INC. All Rights Reserved.
ODIE'S BREATH SMELLS GOOD
CHASING YOUR TOOTHPASTE WITH YOUR COLOGNE WILL DO THAT

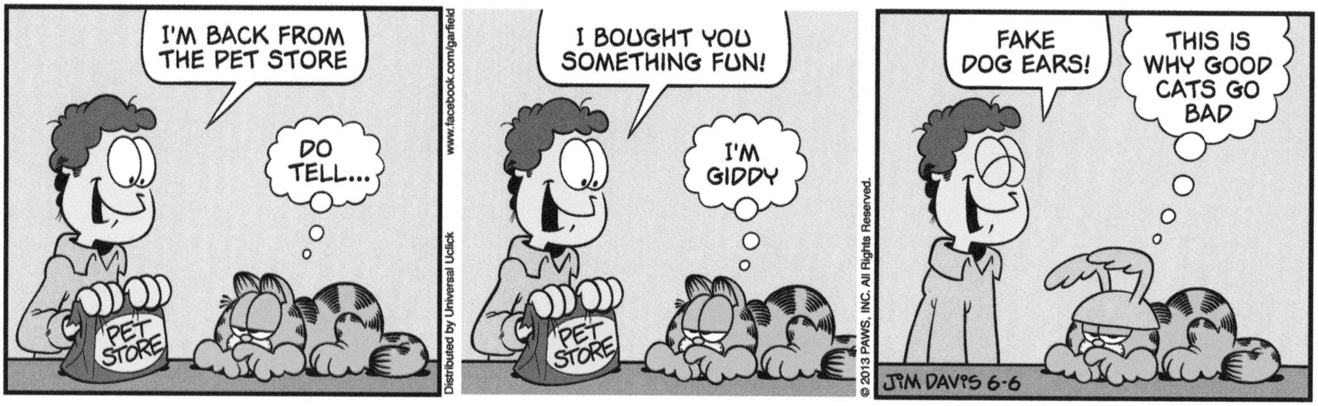
I'M BACK FROM THE PET STORE
DO TELL...
PET STORE
www.facebook.com/garfield
Distributed by Universal Uclick
I BOUGHT YOU SOMETHING FUN!
I'M GIDDY
PET STORE
© 2013 PAWS, INC. All Rights Reserved.
FAKE DOG EARS!
THIS IS WHY GOOD CATS GO BAD
JIM DAVIS 6-6

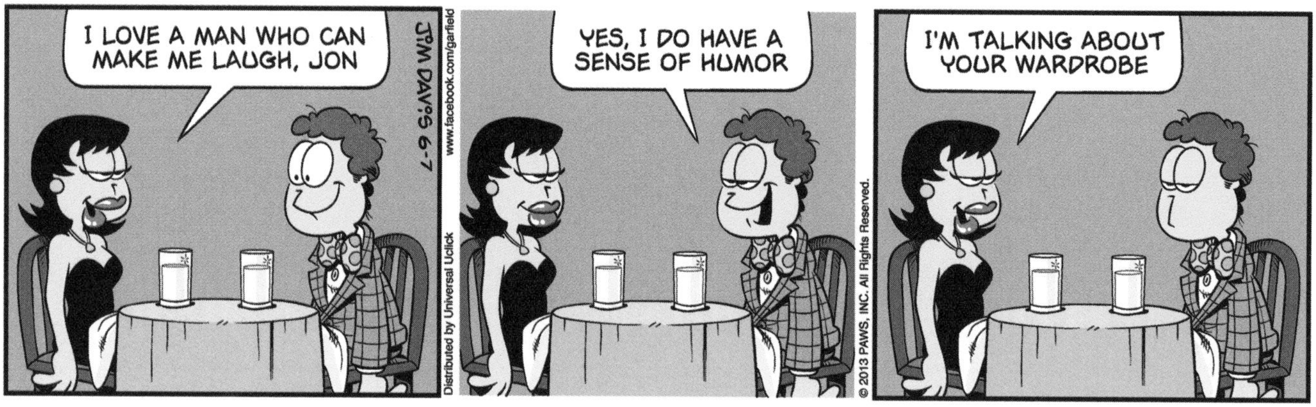
I LOVE A MAN WHO CAN MAKE ME LAUGH, JON
JIM DAVIS 6-7
www.facebook.com/garfield
Distributed by Universal Uclick
YES, I DO HAVE A SENSE OF HUMOR
© 2013 PAWS, INC. All Rights Reserved.
I'M TALKING ABOUT YOUR WARDROBE

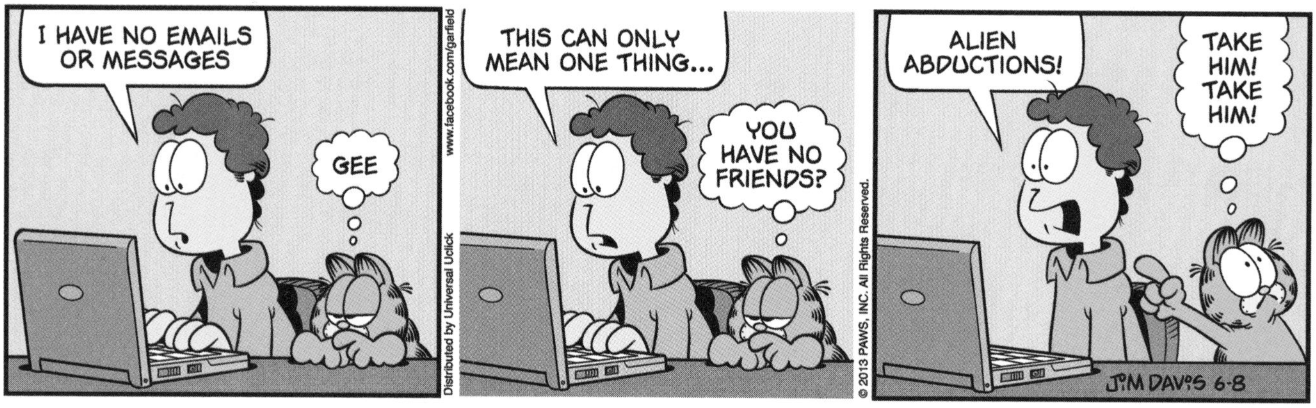
I HAVE NO EMAILS OR MESSAGES
GEE
www.facebook.com/garfield
Distributed by Universal Uclick
THIS CAN ONLY MEAN ONE THING...
YOU HAVE NO FRIENDS?
© 2013 PAWS, INC. All Rights Reserved.
ALIEN ABDUCTIONS!
TAKE HIM! TAKE HIM!
JIM DAVIS 6-8

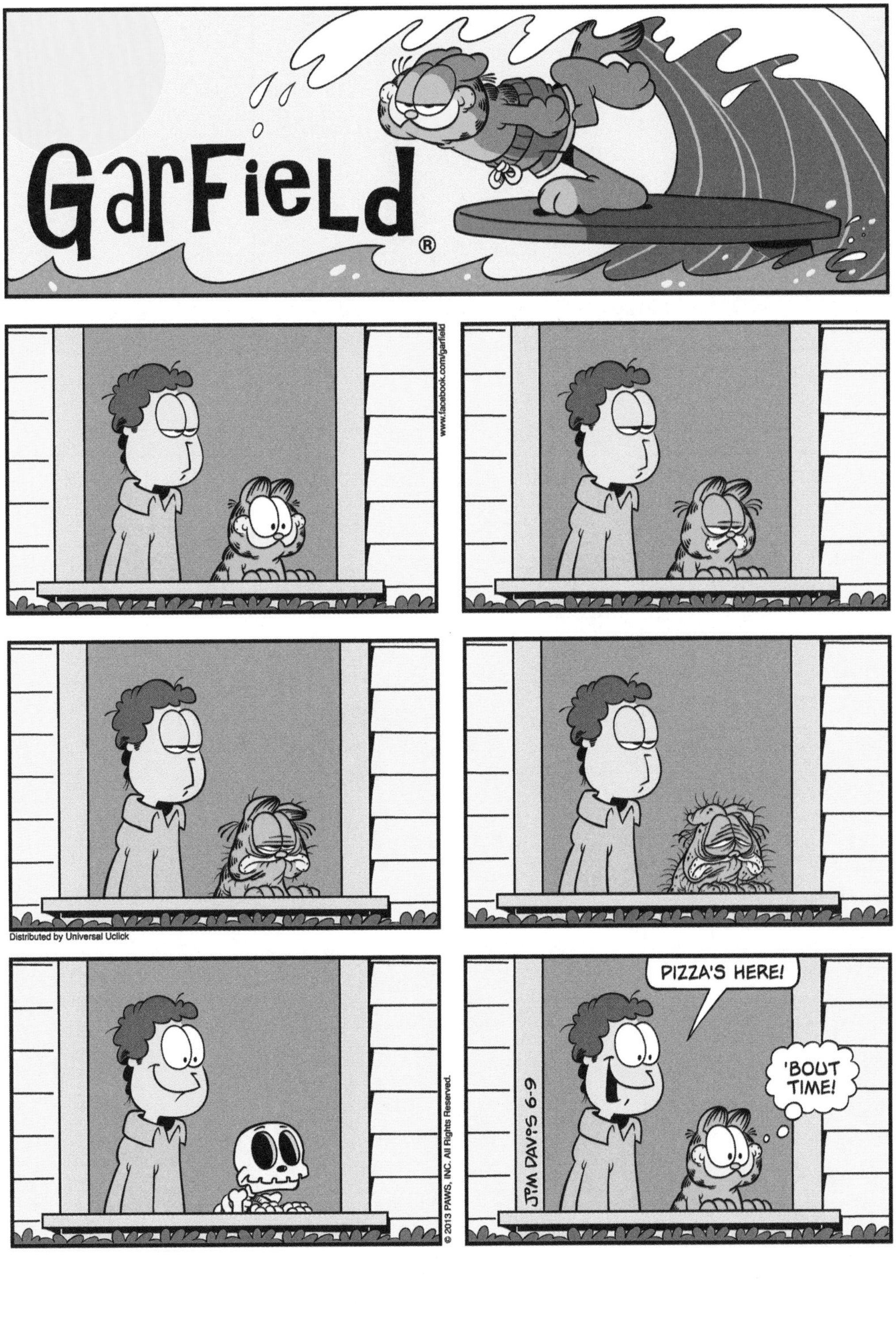
GARFIELD ®
www.facebook.com/garfield
Distributed by Universal Uclick
© 2013 PAWS, INC. All Rights Reserved.
JIM DAVIS 6-9
PIZZA'S HERE!
'BOUT TIME!

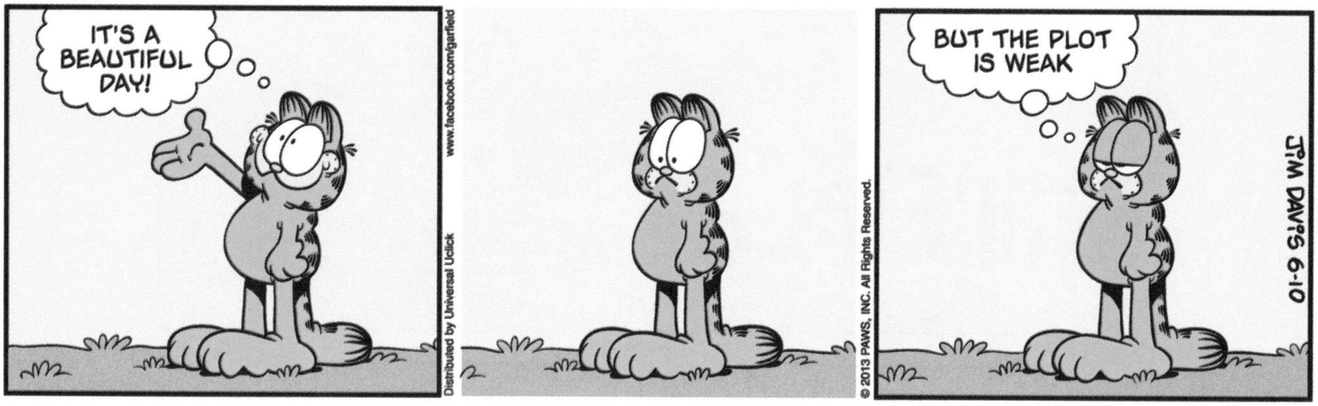
IT'S A BEAUTIFUL DAY!
BUT THE PLOT IS WEAK
JIM DAVIS 6-10
Distributed by Universal Uclick
www.facebook.com/garfield
© 2013 PAWS, INC. All Rights Reserved.

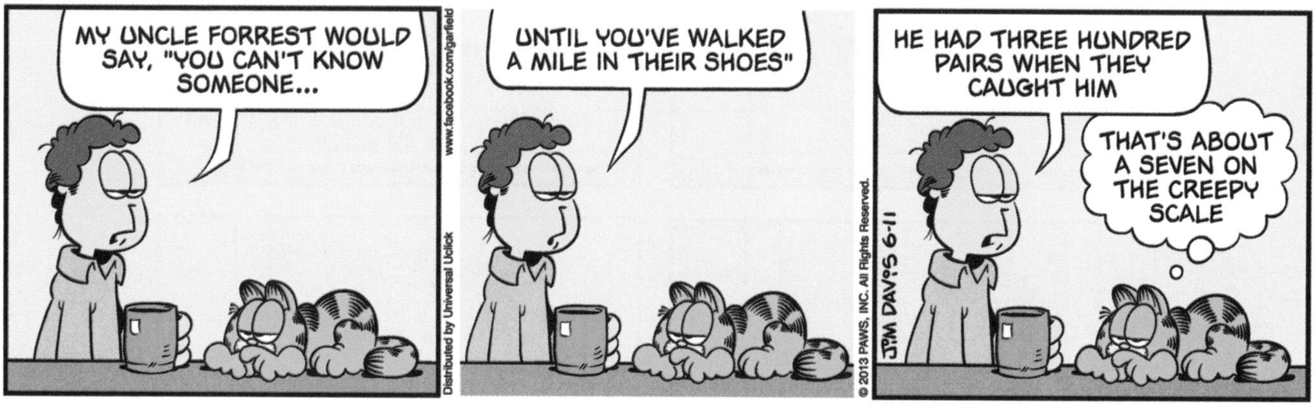
MY UNCLE FORREST WOULD SAY, "YOU CAN'T KNOW SOMEONE...
UNTIL YOU'VE WALKED A MILE IN THEIR SHOES"
HE HAD THREE HUNDRED PAIRS WHEN THEY CAUGHT HIM
THAT'S ABOUT A SEVEN ON THE CREEPY SCALE
JIM DAVIS 6-11
Distributed by Universal Uclick
www.facebook.com/garfield
© 2013 PAWS, INC. All Rights Reserved.

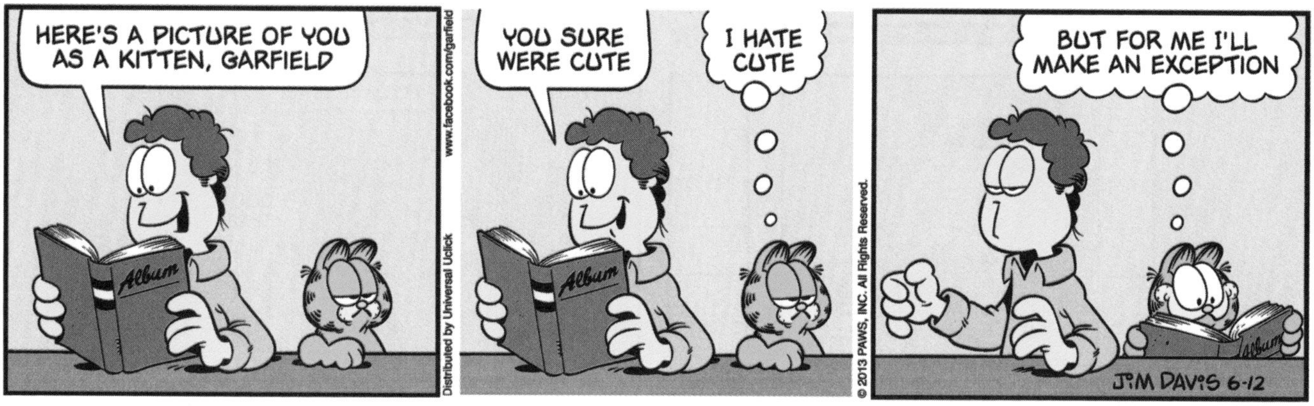
HERE'S A PICTURE OF YOU AS A KITTEN, GARFIELD
Album
YOU SURE WERE CUTE
I HATE CUTE
BUT FOR ME I'LL MAKE AN EXCEPTION
JIM DAVIS 6-12
Distributed by Universal Uclick
www.facebook.com/garfield
© 2013 PAWS, INC. All Rights Reserved.

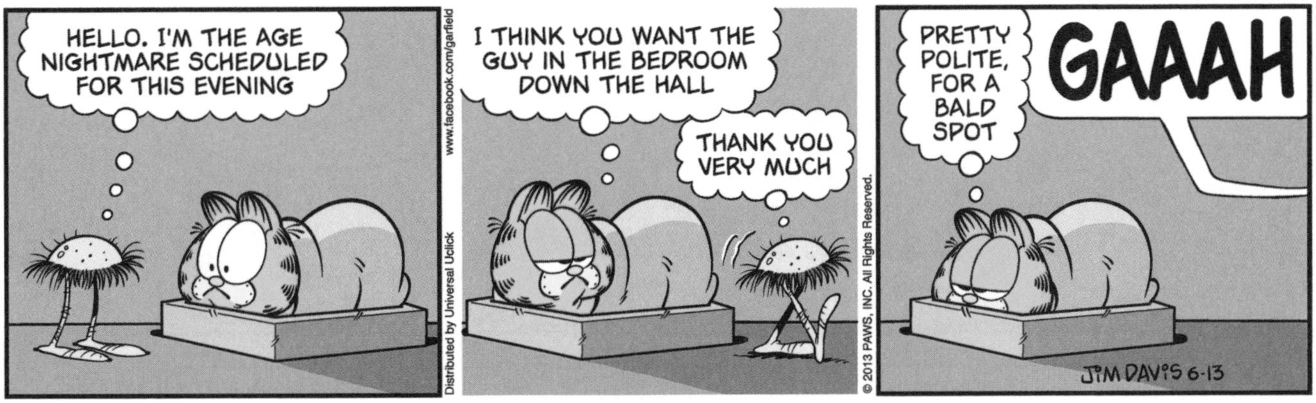
HELLO. I'M THE AGE NIGHTMARE SCHEDULED FOR THIS EVENING
Distributed by Universal Uclick www.facebook.com/garfield
I THINK YOU WANT THE GUY IN THE BEDROOM DOWN THE HALL
THANK YOU VERY MUCH
© 2013 PAWS, INC. All Rights Reserved.
PRETTY POLITE, FOR A BALD SPOT
GAAAH
JIM DAVIS 6-13

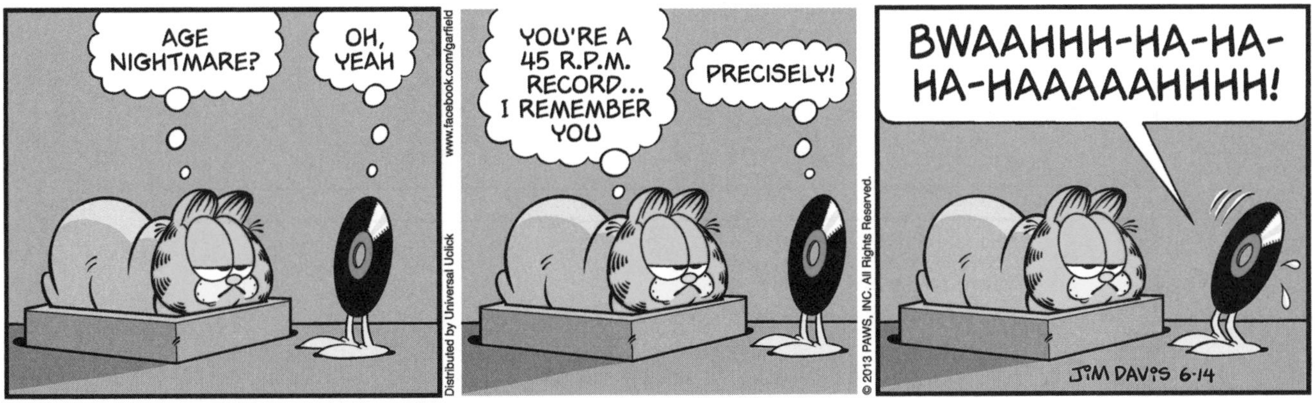
AGE NIGHTMARE?
OH, YEAH
Distributed by Universal Uclick www.facebook.com/garfield
YOU'RE A 45 R.P.M. RECORD... I REMEMBER YOU
PRECISELY!
© 2013 PAWS, INC. All Rights Reserved.
BWAAHHH-HA-HA-HA-HAAAAAHHHH!
JIM DAVIS 6-14

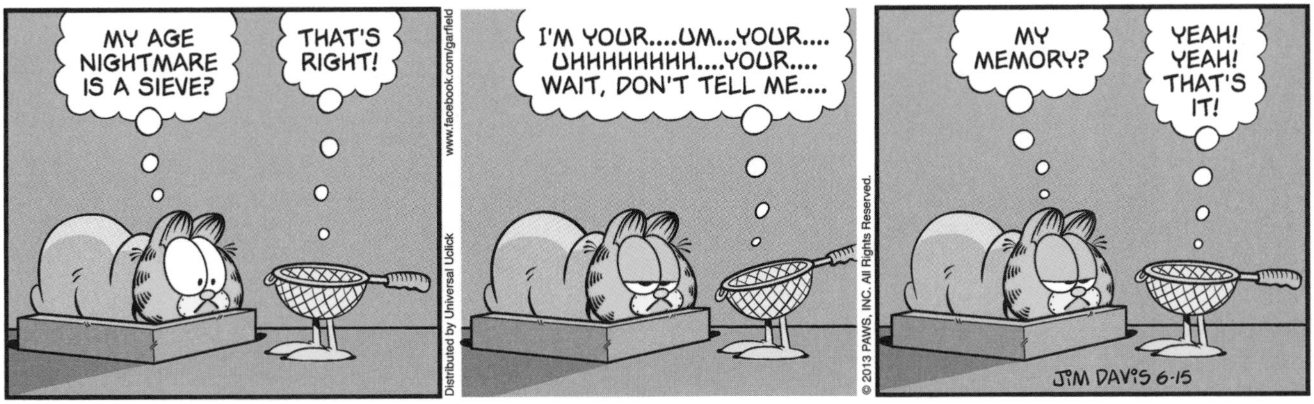
MY AGE NIGHTMARE IS A SIEVE?
THAT'S RIGHT!
Distributed by Universal Uclick www.facebook.com/garfield
I'M YOUR....UM...YOUR.... UHHHHHHHH....YOUR.... WAIT, DON'T TELL ME....
© 2013 PAWS, INC. All Rights Reserved.
MY MEMORY?
YEAH! YEAH! THAT'S IT!
JIM DAVIS 6-15

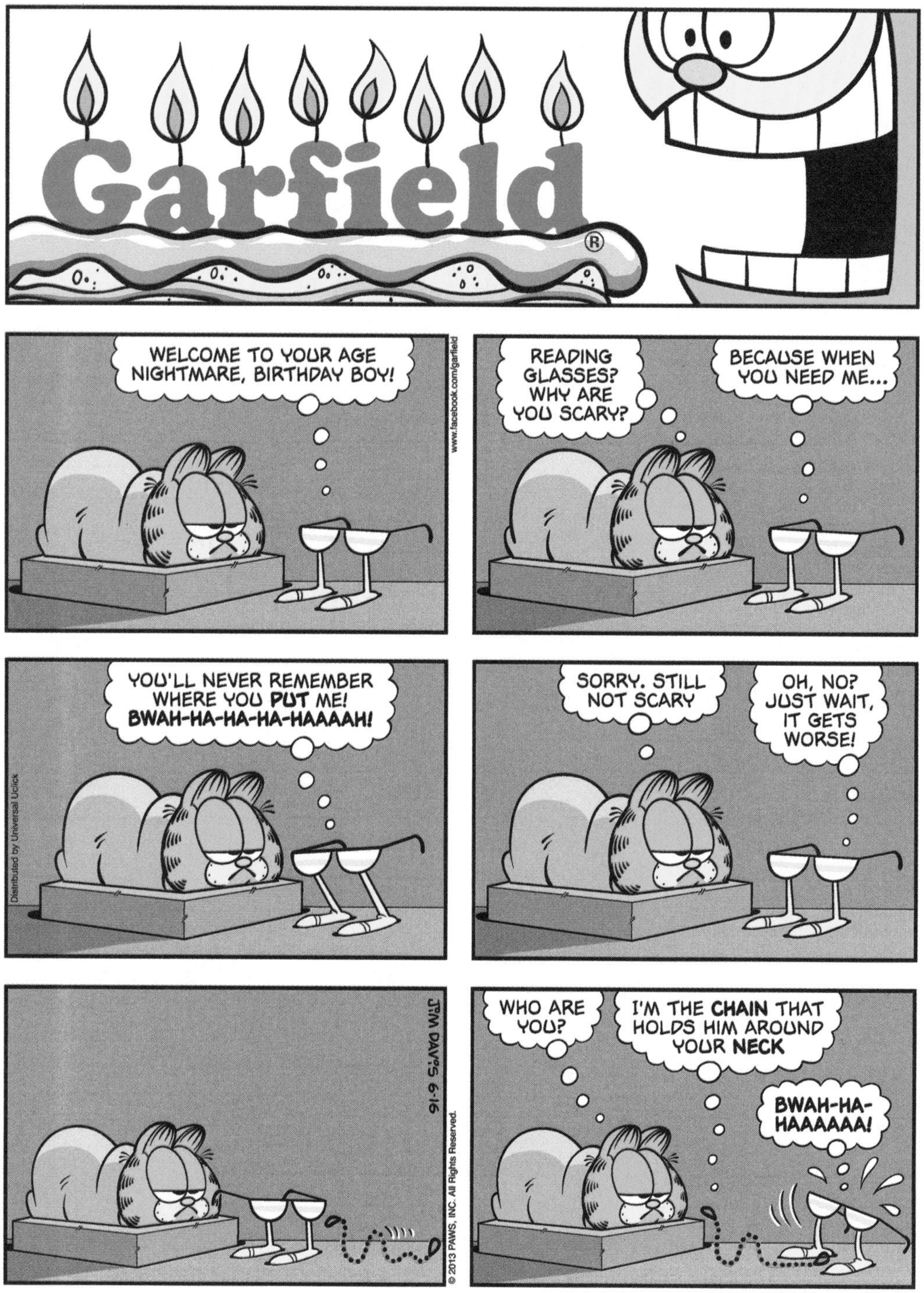
Garfield®
WELCOME TO YOUR AGE NIGHTMARE, BIRTHDAY BOY!
www.facebook.com/garfield
READING GLASSES? WHY ARE YOU SCARY?
BECAUSE WHEN YOU NEED ME...
YOU'LL NEVER REMEMBER WHERE YOU **PUT** ME! **BWAH-HA-HA-HA-HAAAAH!**
Distributed by Universal Uclick
SORRY. STILL NOT SCARY
OH, NO? JUST WAIT, IT GETS WORSE!
JPM DAVPS 6-16
© 2013 PAWS, INC. All Rights Reserved.
WHO ARE YOU?
I'M THE **CHAIN** THAT HOLDS HIM AROUND YOUR **NECK**
BWAH-HA-HAAAAAA!

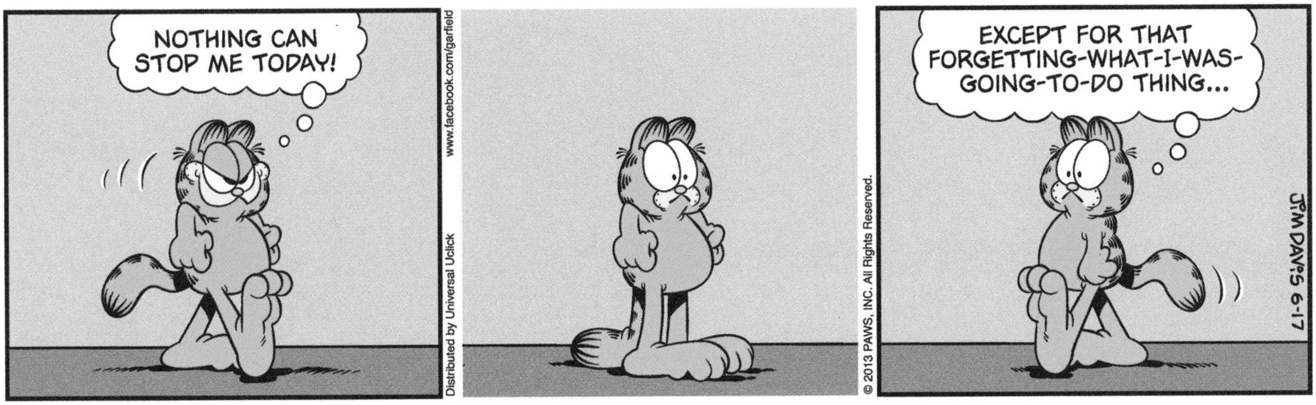
NOTHING CAN STOP ME TODAY!
EXCEPT FOR THAT FORGETTING-WHAT-I-WAS-GOING-TO-DO THING...
JIM DAVIS 6-17
Distributed by Universal Uclick www.facebook.com/garfield
© 2013 PAWS, INC. All Rights Reserved.

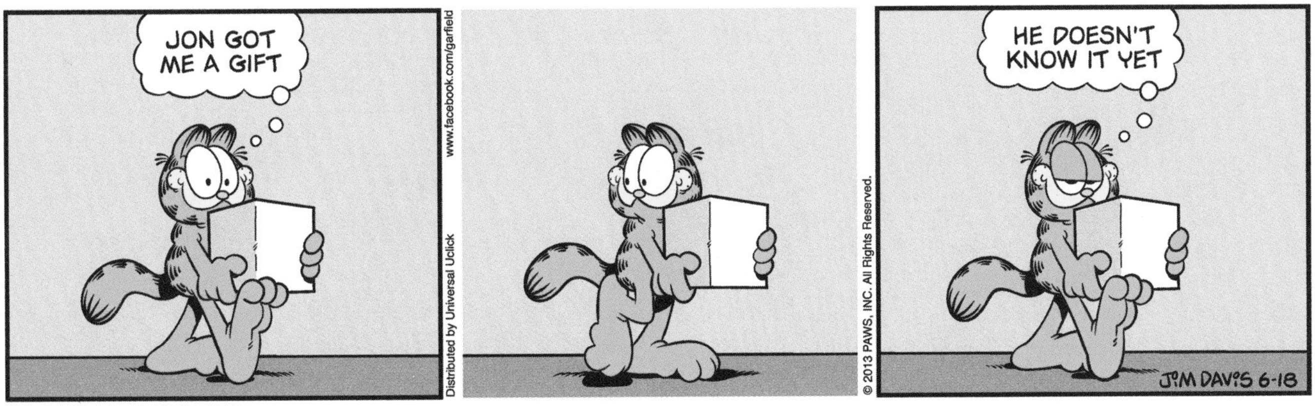
JON GOT ME A GIFT
HE DOESN'T KNOW IT YET
JIM DAVIS 6-18
Distributed by Universal Uclick www.facebook.com/garfield
© 2013 PAWS, INC. All Rights Reserved.

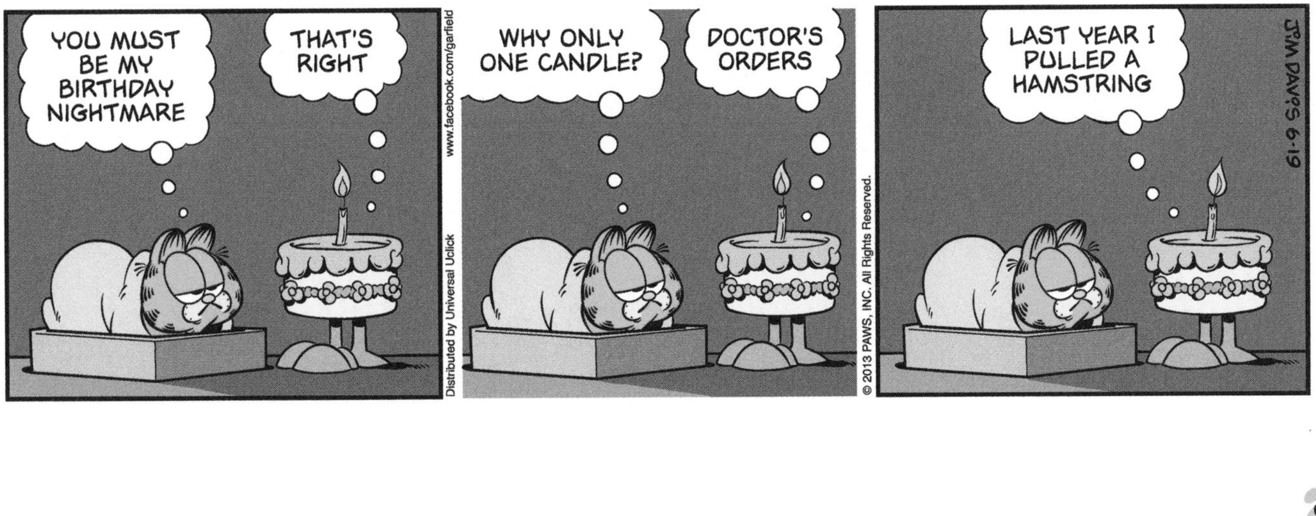
YOU MUST BE MY BIRTHDAY NIGHTMARE
THAT'S RIGHT
WHY ONLY ONE CANDLE?
DOCTOR'S ORDERS
LAST YEAR I PULLED A HAMSTRING
JIM DAVIS 6-19
Distributed by Universal Uclick www.facebook.com/garfield
© 2013 PAWS, INC. All Rights Reserved.

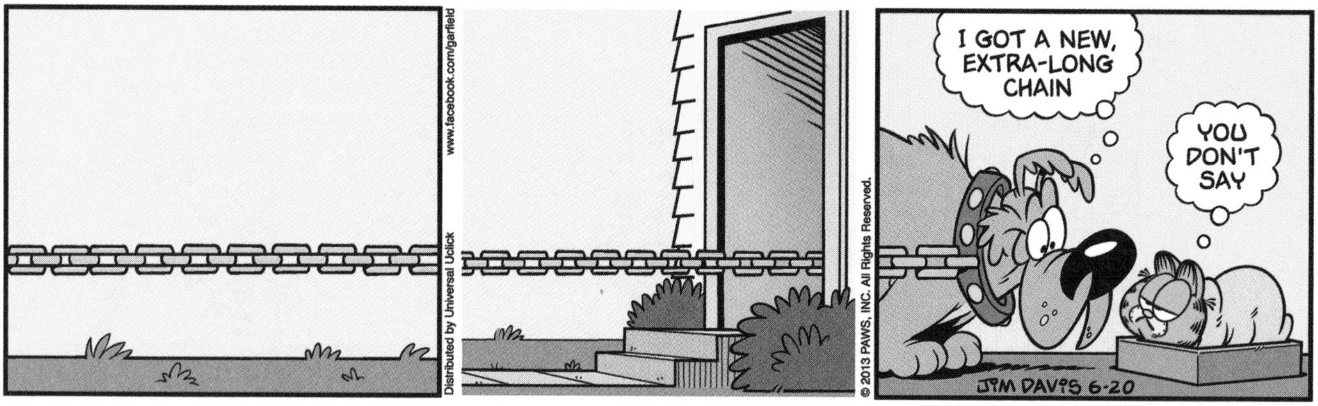
Distributed by Universal Uclick www.facebook.com/garfield
© 2013 PAWS, INC. All Rights Reserved.
I GOT A NEW, EXTRA-LONG CHAIN
YOU DON'T SAY
JIM DAVIS 6-20

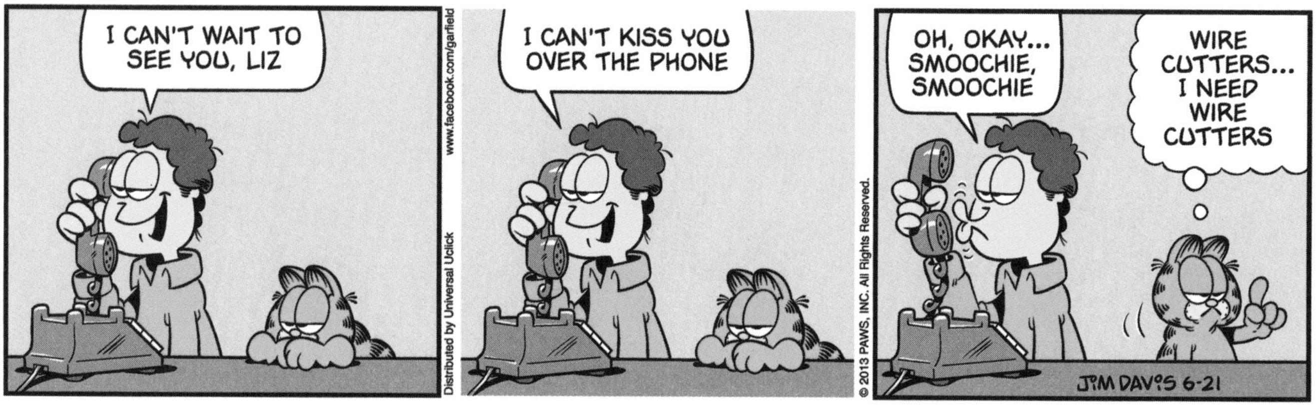
I CAN'T WAIT TO SEE YOU, LIZ
Distributed by Universal Uclick www.facebook.com/garfield
I CAN'T KISS YOU OVER THE PHONE
© 2013 PAWS, INC. All Rights Reserved.
OH, OKAY... SMOOCHIE, SMOOCHIE
WIRE CUTTERS... I NEED WIRE CUTTERS
JIM DAVIS 6-21

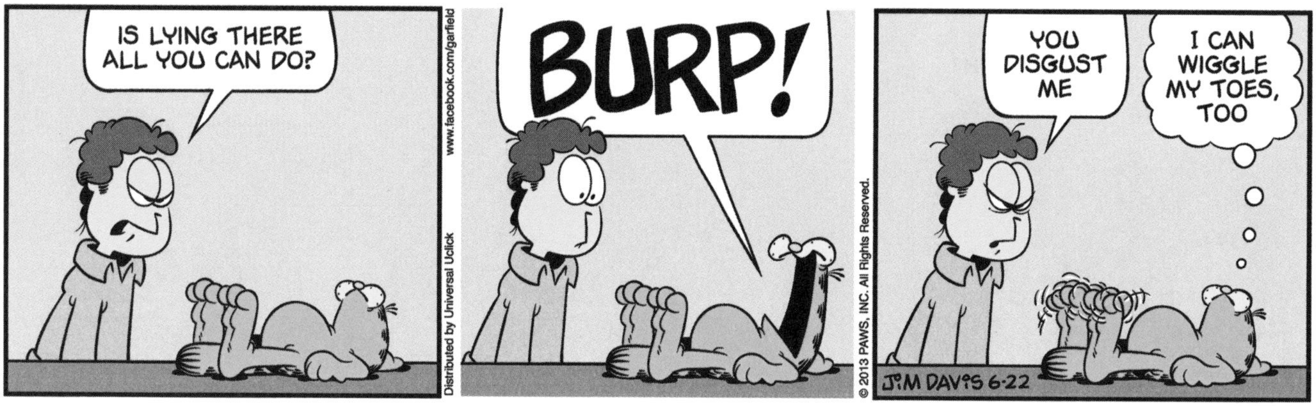
IS LYING THERE ALL YOU CAN DO?
Distributed by Universal Uclick www.facebook.com/garfield
BURP!
© 2013 PAWS, INC. All Rights Reserved.
YOU DISGUST ME
I CAN WIGGLE MY TOES, TOO
JIM DAVIS 6-22

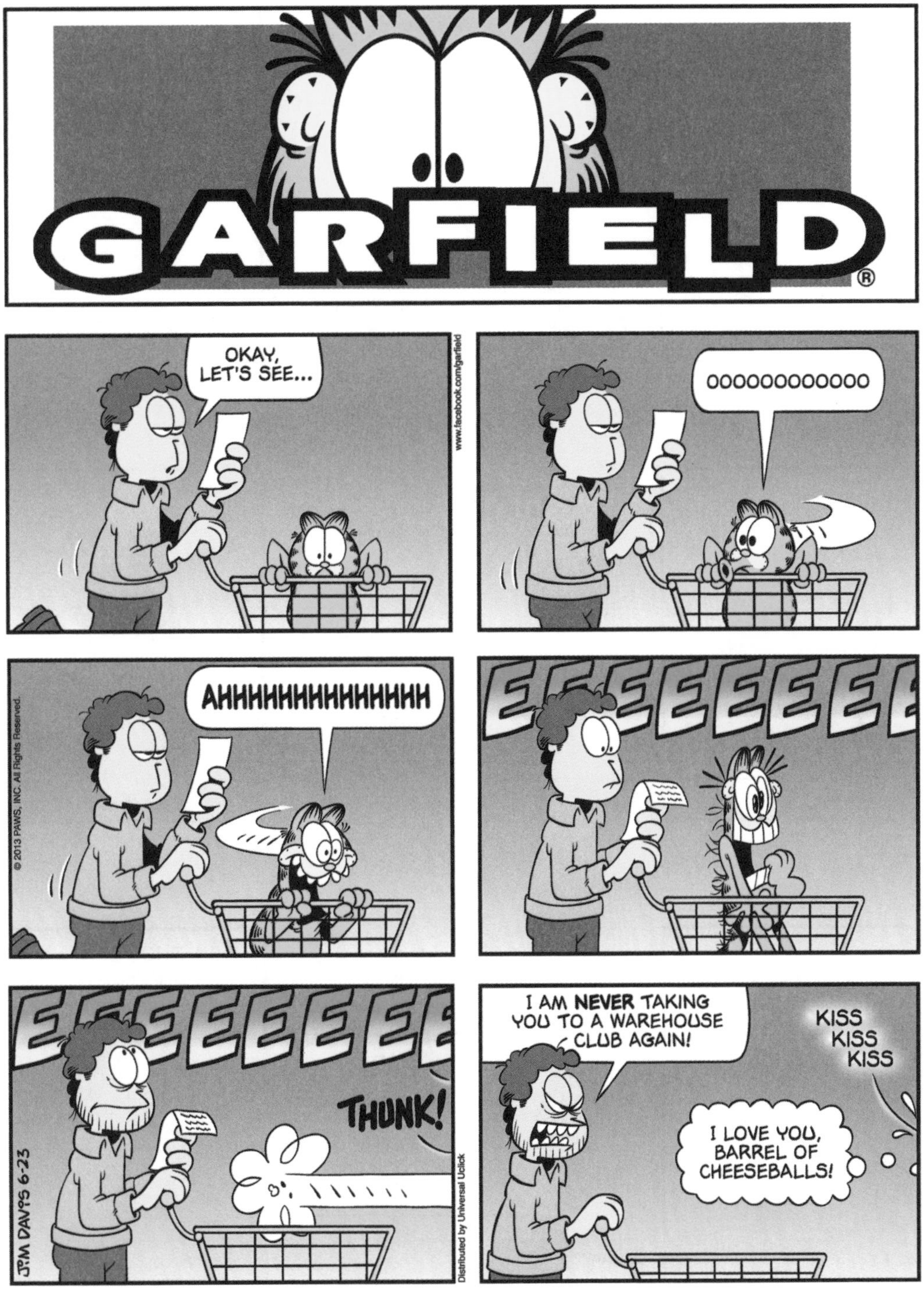
GARFIELD®
OKAY, LET'S SEE...
www.facebook.com/garfield
OOOOOOOOOOOO
© 2013 PAWS, INC. All Rights Reserved.
AHHHHHHHHHHHHHH
EEEEEEEEE
EEEEEEEEE
THUNK!
JPM DAVPS 6-23
Distributed by Universal Uclick
I AM **NEVER** TAKING YOU TO A WAREHOUSE CLUB AGAIN!
KISS KISS KISS
I LOVE YOU, BARREL OF CHEESEBALLS!

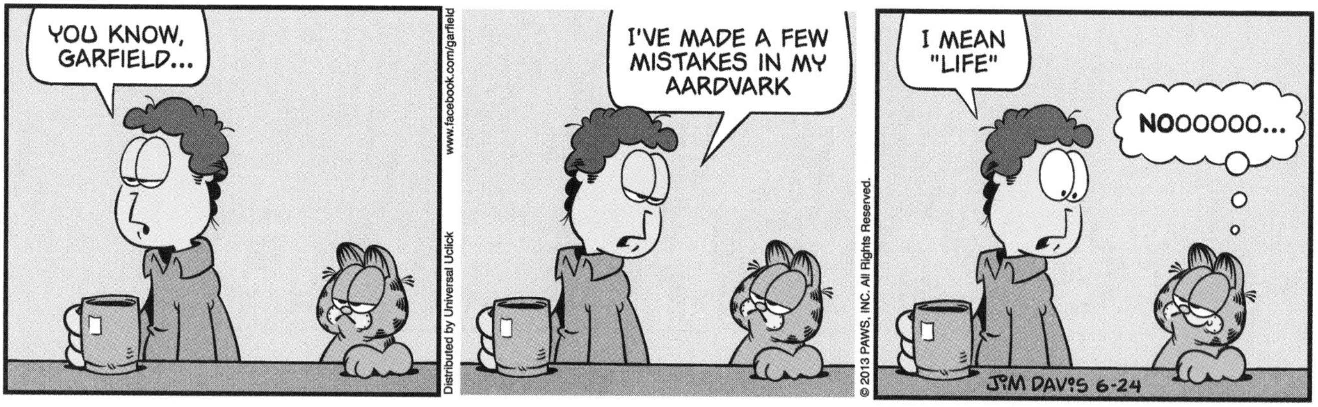
YOU KNOW, GARFIELD...
I'VE MADE A FEW MISTAKES IN MY AARDVARK
I MEAN "LIFE"
NOOOOOO...
JIM DAVIS 6-24
Distributed by Universal Uclick
www.facebook.com/garfield
© 2013 PAWS, INC. All Rights Reserved.

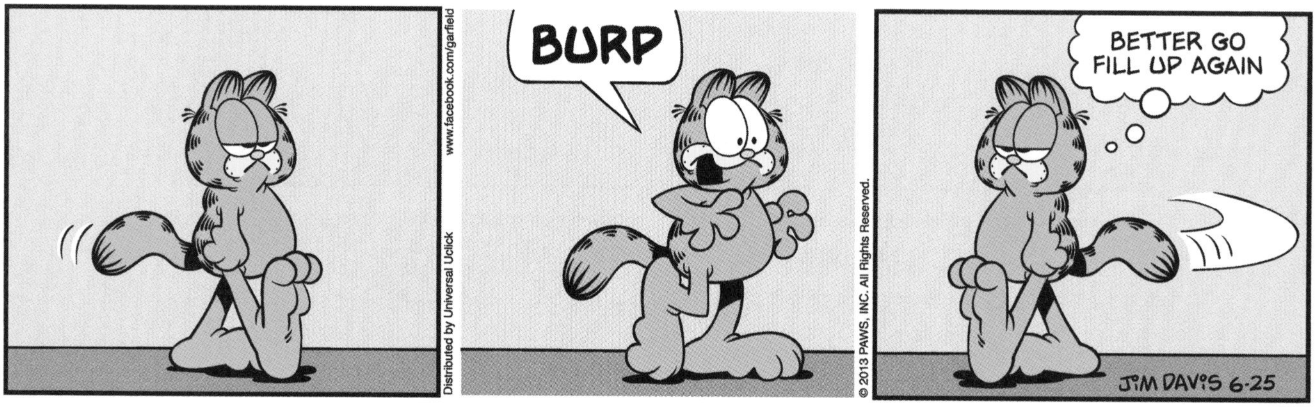
BURP
BETTER GO FILL UP AGAIN
JIM DAVIS 6-25
Distributed by Universal Uclick
www.facebook.com/garfield
© 2013 PAWS, INC. All Rights Reserved.

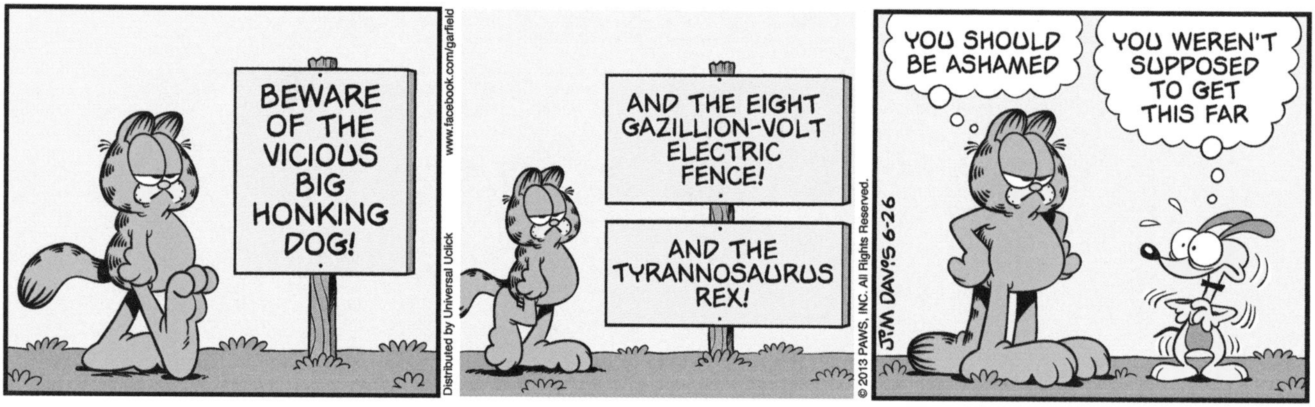
BEWARE OF THE VICIOUS BIG HONKING DOG!
AND THE EIGHT GAZILLION-VOLT ELECTRIC FENCE!
AND THE TYRANNOSAURUS REX!
YOU SHOULD BE ASHAMED
YOU WEREN'T SUPPOSED TO GET THIS FAR
JIM DAVIS 6-26
Distributed by Universal Uclick
www.facebook.com/garfield
© 2013 PAWS, INC. All Rights Reserved.

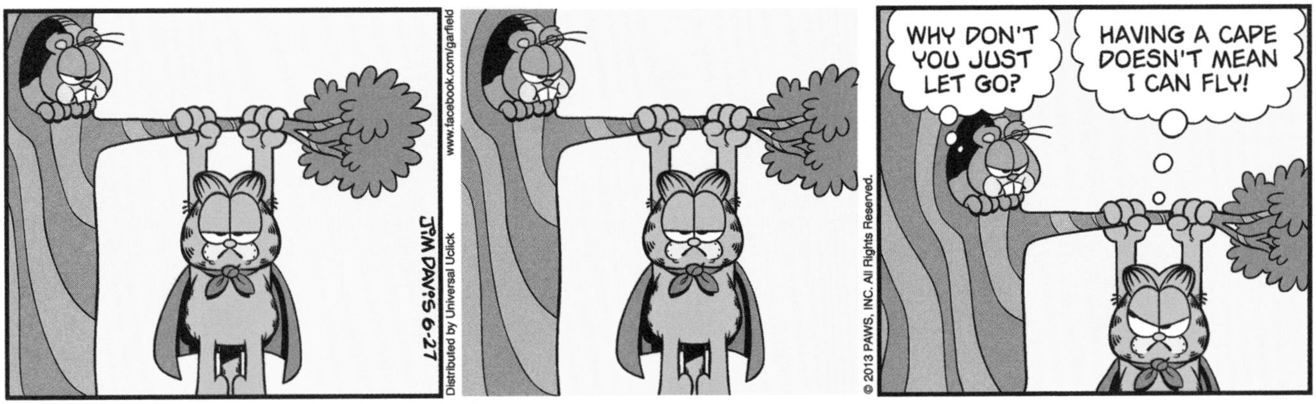
JIM DAVIS 6-27
Distributed by Universal Uclick www.facebook.com/garfield
© 2013 PAWS, INC. All Rights Reserved.
WHY DON'T YOU JUST LET GO?
HAVING A CAPE DOESN'T MEAN I CAN FLY!

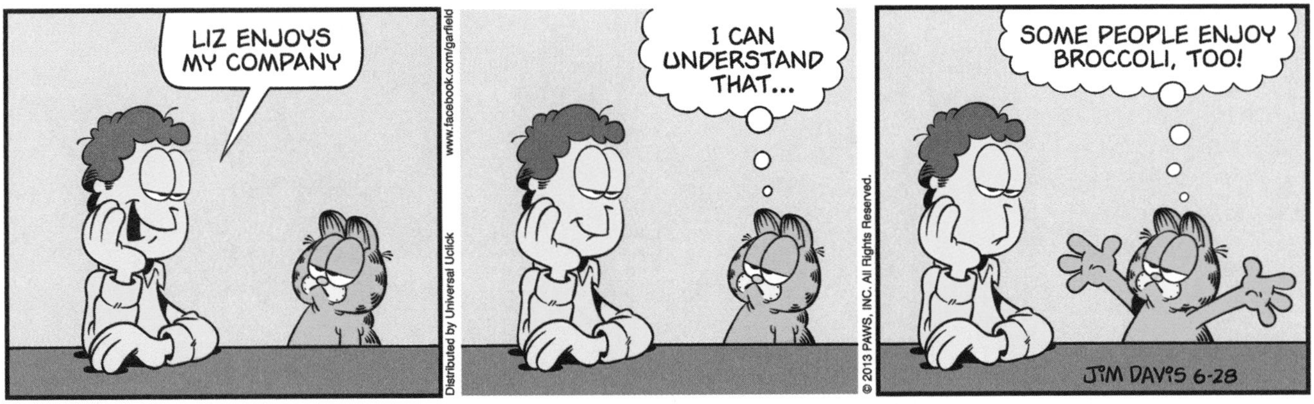
LIZ ENJOYS MY COMPANY
Distributed by Universal Uclick www.facebook.com/garfield
I CAN UNDERSTAND THAT...
© 2013 PAWS, INC. All Rights Reserved.
SOME PEOPLE ENJOY BROCCOLI, TOO!
JIM DAVIS 6-28

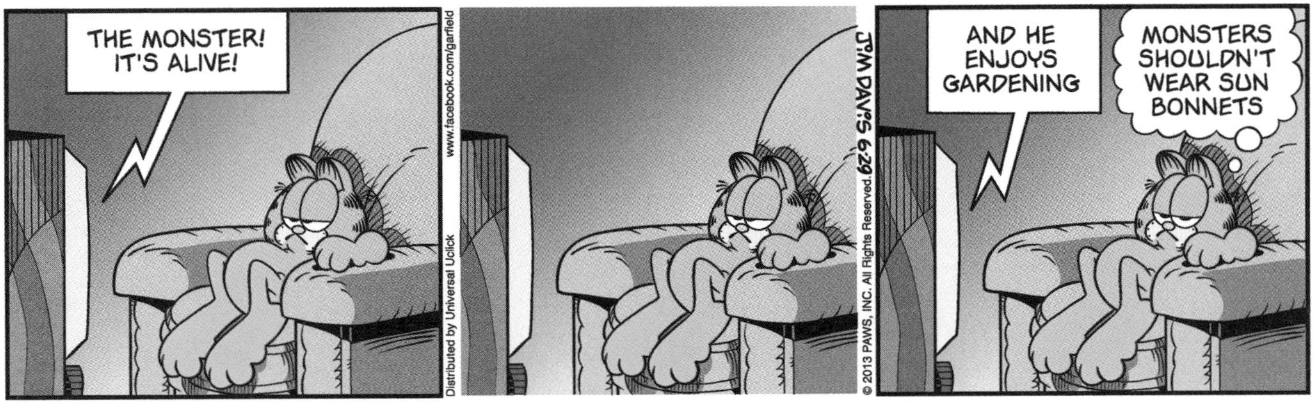
THE MONSTER! IT'S ALIVE!
Distributed by Universal Uclick www.facebook.com/garfield
JIM DAVIS 6-29
© 2013 PAWS, INC. All Rights Reserved.
AND HE ENJOYS GARDENING
MONSTERS SHOULDN'T WEAR SUN BONNETS

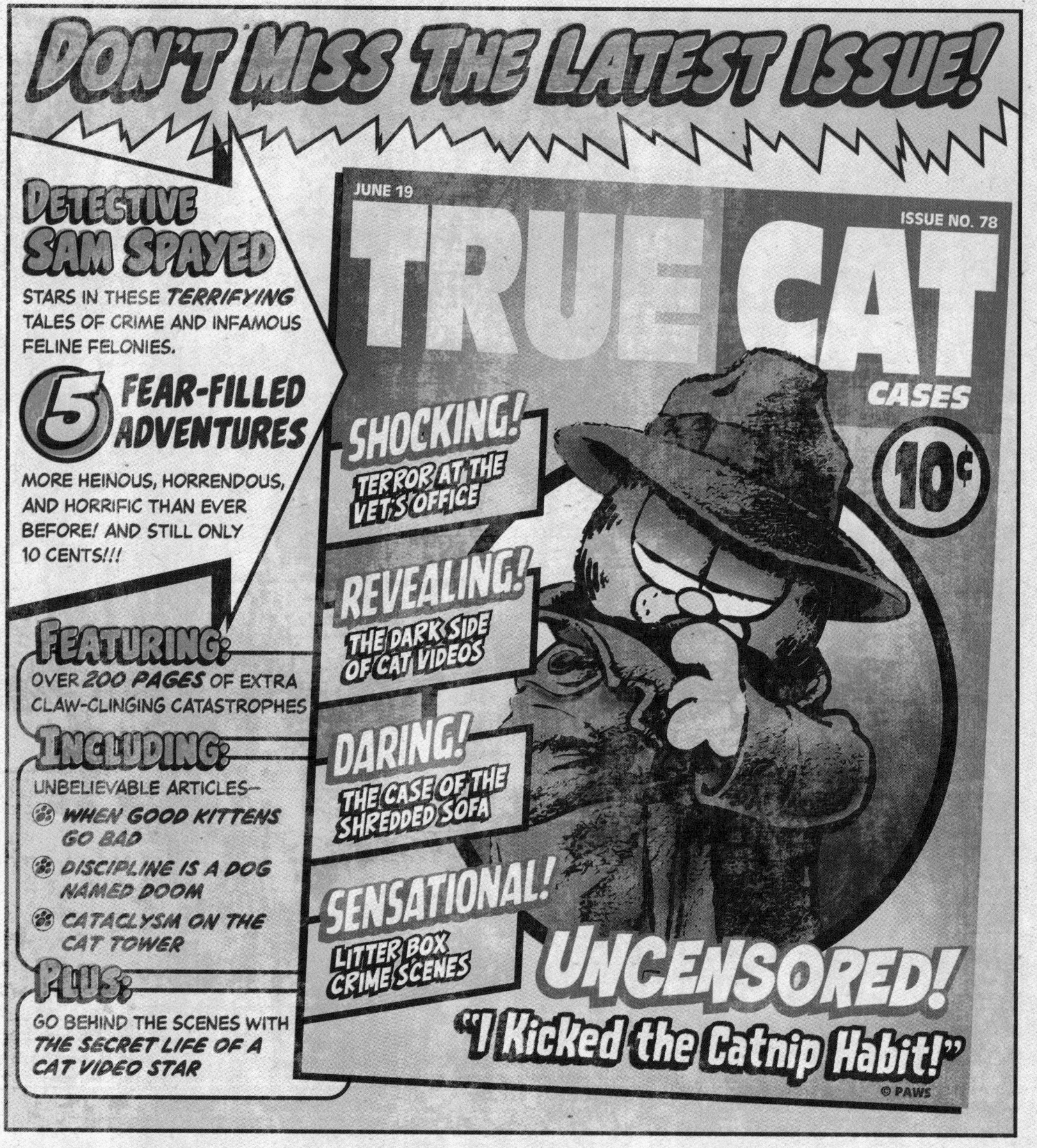
DON'T MISS THE LATEST ISSUE!
DETECTIVE SAM SPAYED
STARS IN THESE TERRIFYING TALES OF CRIME AND INFAMOUS FELINE FELONIES.
5 FEAR-FILLED ADVENTURES
MORE HEINOUS, HORRENDOUS, AND HORRIFIC THAN EVER BEFORE! AND STILL ONLY 10 CENTS!!!
FEATURING:
OVER 200 PAGES OF EXTRA CLAW-CLINGING CATASTROPHES
INCLUDING:
UNBELIEVABLE ARTICLES—
WHEN GOOD KITTENS GO BAD
DISCIPLINE IS A DOG NAMED DOOM
CATACLYSM ON THE CAT TOWER
PLUS:
GO BEHIND THE SCENES WITH THE SECRET LIFE OF A CAT VIDEO STAR
JUNE 19
ISSUE NO. 78
TRUE CAT CASES
10¢
SHOCKING! TERROR AT THE VET'S OFFICE
REVEALING! THE DARK SIDE OF CAT VIDEOS
DARING! THE CASE OF THE SHREDDED SOFA
SENSATIONAL! LITTER BOX CRIME SCENES
UNCENSORED!
"I Kicked the Catnip Habit!"
© PAWS

Watch. Read. Shop. Play.

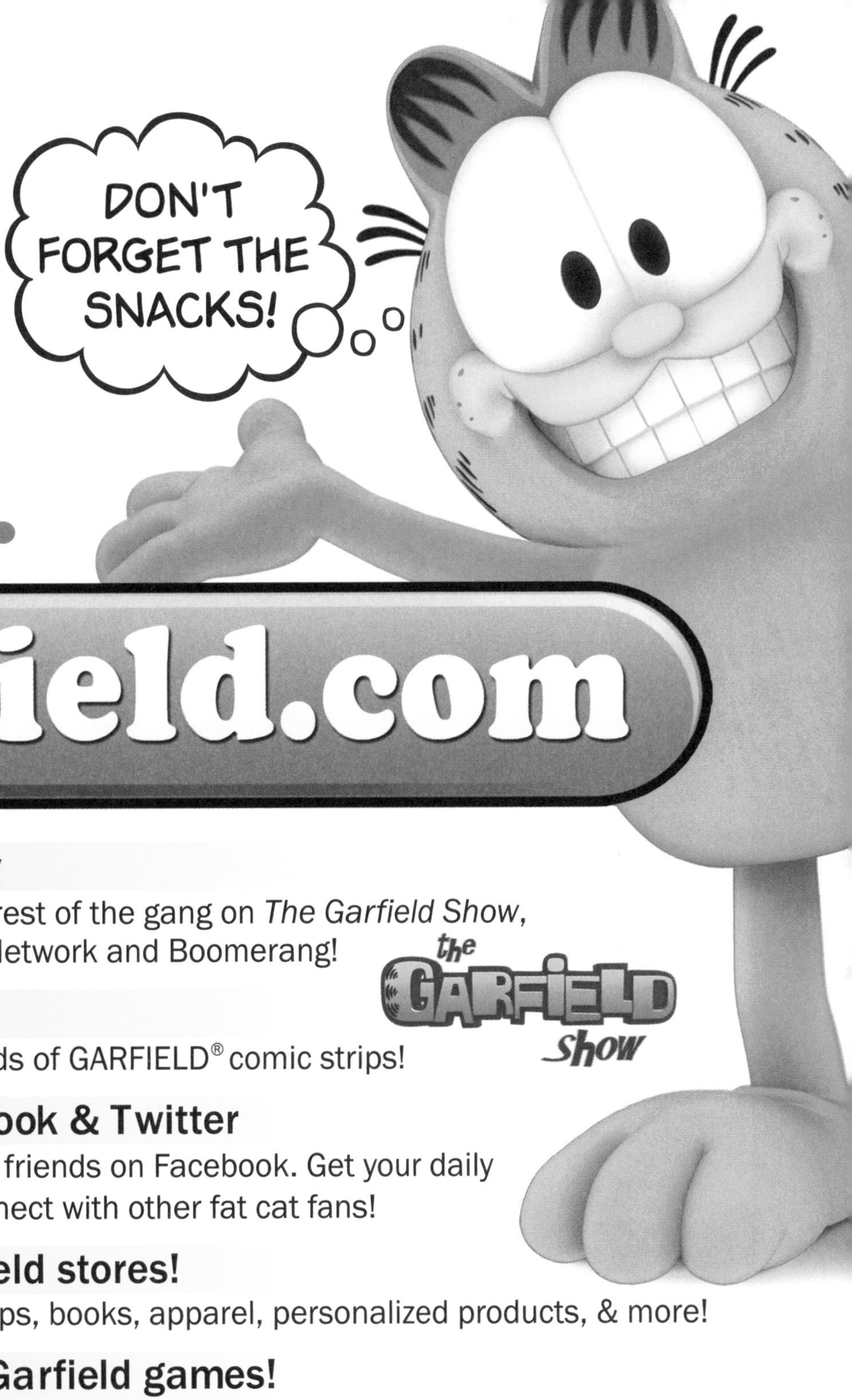
DON'T FORGET THE SNACKS!

garfield.com

The Garfield Show

Catch Garfield and the rest of the gang on *The Garfield Show*, now airing on Cartoon Network and Boomerang!

The Comic Strip

Search & read thousands of GARFIELD® comic strips!

Garfield on Facebook & Twitter

Join millions of Garfield friends on Facebook. Get your daily dose of humor and connect with other fat cat fans!

Shop all the Garfield stores!

Original art & comic strips, books, apparel, personalized products, & more!

Play FREE online Garfield games!

Plus, check out all of the FREE Garfield apps available for your smartphone, tablet, and other mobile devices.

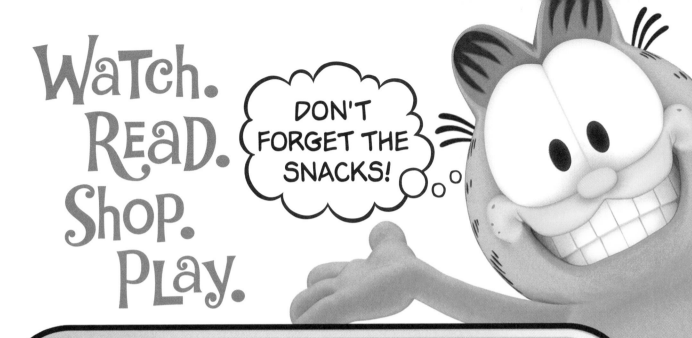

STRIPS, SPECIALS, OR BESTSELLING BOOKS . . .
GARFIELD'S ON EVERYONE'S MENU.

Don't miss even one episode in the Tubby Tabby's hilarious series!

GARFIELD AT LARGE . . . .(#1) 978-0-345-44382-3
GARFIELD GAINS WEIGHT . . . .(#2) 978-0-345-44975-7
GARFIELD BIGGER THAN LIFE . . . .(#3) 978-0-345-45027-2
GARFIELD WEIGHS IN . . . .(#4) 978-0-345-45205-4
GARFIELD TAKES THE CAKE . . . .(#5) 978-0-345-44978-8
GARFIELD EATS HIS HEART OUT . . . .(#6) 978-0-345-46459-0
GARFIELD SITS AROUND THE HOUSE . . . .(#7) 978-0-345-46463-7
GARFIELD TIPS THE SCALES . . . .(#8) 978-0-345-46909-0
GARFIELD LOSES HIS FEET . . . .(#9) 978-0-345-46467-5
GARFIELD MAKES IT BIG . . . .(#10) 978-0-345-46468-2
GARFIELD ROLLS ON . . . .(#11) 978-0-345-47561-9
GARFIELD OUT TO LUNCH . . . .(#12) 978-0-345-47562-6
GARFIELD FOOD FOR THOUGHT . . . .(#13) 978-0-345-47563-3
GARFIELD SWALLOWS HIS PRIDE . . . .(#14) 978-0-345-91386-9
GARFIELD WORLDWIDE . . . .(#15) 978-0-345-91754-6
GARFIELD ROUNDS OUT . . . .(#16) 978-0-345-49169-5
GARFIELD CHEWS THE FAT . . . .(#17) 978-0-345-49170-1
GARFIELD GOES TO WAIST . . . .(#18) 978-0-345-49173-2
GARFIELD HANGS OUT . . . .(#19) 978-0-345-49174-9
GARFIELD TAKES UP SPACE . . . .(#20) 978-0-345-49178-7
GARFIELD SAYS A MOUTHFUL . . . .(#21) 978-0-345-49179-4
GARFIELD BY THE POUND . . . .(#22) 978-0-345-52558-1
GARFIELD KEEPS HIS CHINS UP . . . .(#23) 978-0-345-52559-8
GARFIELD TAKES HIS LICKS . . . .(#24) 978-0-345-52587-1
GARFIELD HITS THE BIG TIME . . . .(#25) 978-0-345-52589-5
GARFIELD PULLS HIS WEIGHT . . . .(#26) 978-0-345-52594-9
GARFIELD DISHES IT OUT . . . .(#27) 978-0-345-52595-6
GARFIELD LIFE IN THE FAT LANE . . . .(#28) 978-0-345-52600-7
GARFIELD TONS OF FUN . . . .(#29) 978-0-345-52601-4
GARFIELD BIGGER AND BETTER . . . .(#30) 978-0-345-52605-2
GARFIELD HAMS IT UP . . . .(#31) 978-0-345-41241-6
GARFIELD THINKS BIG . . . .(#32) 978-0-345-41671-1
GARFIELD THROWS HIS WEIGHT AROUND . . . .(#33) 978-0-345-42749-6
GARFIELD LIFE TO THE FULLEST . . . .(#34) 978-0-345-43239-1
GARFIELD FEEDS THE KITTY . . . .(#35) 978-0-345-43673-3
GARFIELD HOGS THE SPOTLIGHT . . . .(#36) 978-0-345-43922-2
GARFIELD BEEFS UP . . . .(#37) 978-0-345-44109-6
GARFIELD GETS COOKIN' . . . .(#38) 978-0-345-44582-7
GARFIELD EATS CROW . . . .(#39) 978-0-345-45201-6
GARFIELD SURVIVAL OF THE FATTEST . . . .(#40) 978-0-345-46458-3
GARFIELD OLDER AND WIDER . . . .(#41) 978-0-345-46462-0
GARFIELD PIGS OUT . . . .(#42) 978-0-345-46466-8
GARFIELD BLOTS OUT THE SUN . . . .(#43) 978-0-345-46615-0
GARFIELD GOES BANANAS . . . .(#44) 978-0-345-91346-3
GARFIELD LARGE & IN CHARGE . . . .(#45) 978-0-345-49172-5
GARFIELD SPILLS THE BEANS . . . .(#46) 978-0-345-49177-0
GARFIELD GETS HIS JUST DESSERTS . . . .(#47) 978-0-345-91387-6

GARFIELD WILL EAT FOR FOOD . . . .(#48) 978-0-345-49176-3
GARFIELD WEIGHS HIS OPTIONS . . . .(#49) 978-0-345-49181-7
GARFIELD POTBELLY OF GOLD . . . .(#50) 978-0-345-52244-3
GARFIELD SHOVELS IT IN . . . .(#51) 978-0-345-52419-5
GARFIELD LARD OF THE JUNGLE . . . .(#52) 978-0-345-52584-0
GARFIELD BRINGS HOME THE BACON . . . .(#53) 978-0-345-52586-4
GARFIELD GETS IN A PICKLE . . . .(#54) 978-0-345-52590-1
GARFIELD SINGS FOR HIS SUPPER . . . .(#55) 978-0-345-52593-2
GARFIELD CAUTION: WIDE LOAD . . . .(#56) 978-0-345-52596-3
GARFIELD SOUPED UP . . . .(#57) 978-0-345-52598-7
GARFIELD GOES TO HIS HAPPY PLACE . . . .(#58) 978-0-345-52602-1
GARFIELD THE BIG CHEESE . . . .(#59) 978-0-345-52604-5

DVD TIE-INS

GARFIELD AS HIMSELF 978-0-345-47805-4
GARFIELD HOLIDAY CELEBRATIONS 978-0-345-47930-3
GARFIELD TRAVEL ADVENTURES 978-0-345-48087-3

AND DON'T MISS . . .

GARFIELD AT 25: IN DOG YEARS I'D BE DEAD 978-0-345-45204-7
GARFIELD'S JOKE ZONE/INSULTS 978-0-345-46263-3
GARFIELD FAT CAT 3-PACK/ VOL. 1 978-0-345-46455-2
GARFIELD FAT CAT 3-PACK/ VOL. 2 978-0-345-46465-1
GARFIELD FAT CAT 3-PACK/ VOL. 3 978-0-345-48088-0
GARFIELD FAT CAT 3-PACK/ VOL. 4 978-0-345-49171-8
GARFIELD FAT CAT 3-PACK/ VOL. 5 978-0-345-49180-8
GARFIELD FAT CAT 3-PACK/ VOL. 6 978-0-345-52420-1
GARFIELD FAT CAT 3-PACK/ VOL. 7 978-0-345-52588-8
GARFIELD FAT CAT 3-PACK/ VOL. 8 978-0-345-52599-4
GARFIELD FAT CAT 3-PACK/ VOL. 9 978-0-345-52607-6
GARFIELD FAT CAT 3-PACK/ VOL. 13 978-0-345-46460-6
GARFIELD FAT CAT 3-PACK/ VOL. 14 978-0-345-49175-6
GARFIELD FAT CAT 3-PACK/ VOL. 15 978-0-345-52585-7
GARFIELD FAT CAT 3-PACK/ VOL. 16 978-0-345-52592-5
GARFIELD FAT CAT 3-PACK/ VOL. 17 978-0-345-52603-8
SEASON'S EATINGS: A VERY MERRY
  GARFIELD CHRISTMAS 978-0-345-47560-2
GARFIELD'S GUIDE TO EVERYTHING 978-0-345-46461-3
ODIE UNLEASHED! 978-0-345-46464-4
GARFIELD'S BOOK OF CAT NAMES 978-0-345-48516-8
THE GARFIELD JOURNAL 978-0-345-46469-9
LIGHTS, CAMERA, HAIRBALLS!:
  GARFIELD AT THE MOVIES 978-0-345-49134-3
30 YEARS OF LAUGHS AND LASAGNA 978-0-345-50379-4
GARFIELD MINUS GARFIELD 978-0-345-51387-8
GARFIELD FROM THE TRASH BIN 978-0-345-51881-1
GARFIELD LEFT SPEECHLESS 978-0-345-53058-5
MY LAUGHABLE LIFE WITH GARFIELD 978-0-345-52591-8
GARFIELD'S SUNDAY FINEST .978-0-345-52597-0

New larger, full-color format!